Advertising
and the
Transformation of
American Society,
1865–1920

Advertising
and the
Transformation of
American Society,
1865–1920

James D. Norris

CONTRIBUTIONS IN ECONOMICS AND
ECONOMIC HISTORY,
NUMBER 110

Greenwood Press
New York • Westport, Connecticut • London

Library of Congress Cataloging-in-Publication Data

Norris, James D.
    Advertising and the transformation of American society, 1865–1920
/ James D. Norris.
        p. cm.—(Contributions in economics and economic history,
ISSN 0084-9235 ; no. 110)
    Includes bibliographical references (p.   )
    ISBN 0–313–26801–0 (lib. bdg. : alk. paper)
        1. Advertising—United States—History—19th century.
    2. Advertising—United States—History—20th century. I. Title.
II. Series.
    HF5813.U6N67   1990
    659.1'042'097309034--dc20   90–2760

British Library Cataloguing in Publication Data is available.

Library of Congress Catalog Card Number: 90–2760
ISBN: 0-313-26801-0
ISSN: 0084-9235

First published in 1990

Greenwood Press, 88 Post Road West, Westport, CT 06881
An imprint of Greenwood Publishing Group, Inc.

Printed in the United States of America

∞™

The paper used in this book complies with the
Permanent Paper Standard issued by the National
Information Standards Organization (Z39.48–1984).

10 9 8 7 6 5 4 3 2

Copyright Acknowledgments

Excerpts from *The History and Development of Advertising* by Frank Presbrey,
copyright 1929 by Frank Presbrey. Used by permission of Doubleday, a
division of Bantam, Doubleday, Dell Publishing Group, Inc.

Excerpts from Ruth S. Cowan, "The 'Industrial Revolution' in the Home:
Household Technology and Social Change in the 20th Century," *Technology
and Culture* 17: 1–23 (January 1976), reprinted with permission of The
University of Chicago Press and Ruth S. Cowan.

Excerpts from Andrew B. Jack, "The Channels of Distribution for an Innovation:
The Sewing Machine Industry in America, 1860–1865," *Explorations in Entrepreneurial
History*, 9 (February 1957), 117–118, 134.

In Memory of
Lewis E. Atherton

As a society becomes increasingly affluent, wants are increasingly created by the process by which they are satisfied. This may operate passively. Increases in consumption, the counterpart of increases in production, act by suggestion or emulation to create wants. Or producers may proceed actively to create wants through advertising and salesmanship. Wants thus come to depend on output. In technical terms, it can no longer be assumed that welfare is greater at an all-round higher level of production than at a lower one. It may be the same. The higher level of production has, merely, a higher level of want creation necessitating a higher level of want satisfaction.

—John Kenneth Galbraith,
The Affluent Society

CONTENTS

FIGURES

PREFACE

Advertisements, Marshall McLuhan argued, are "the richest and most faithful daily reflections that any society ever made of its entire range of activities."[1] This book, an historical analysis of advertisements, is based in large measure on the premise that McLuhan enunciated and is the result of examining over the past three decades literally thousands of ads. Although I have looked in a rather systematic fashion at advertisements in newspapers, ranging from large urban papers to small-town weekly papers, because of the questions I am interested in answering I have concentrated my efforts on more popular journals and magazines with national circulations. I have been interested in how we developed truly national markets in this country, in how consumers were convinced to buy and consume items made by distant and unknown producers, in how manufacturers used advertising to persuade people to buy products they had never used or seen before, much less purchased. What appeal did manufacturers use to build markets for products, many of which had previously been produced locally or in the home, among customers used to regional differences in consumption? And what did the advertisements, as mirrors of society, reflect about the values of that society?

In the period between 1865 and 1920, as the nation shifted from a rural-farming economy to an urban-manufacturing one, a major transformation also occurred in the behavior of American consumers. Nowhere is this transformation better illustrated than in the advertisements that appeared in popular magazines. In 1970, in a report to the American Philosophical Society, I argued that advertising played a major role in breaking down much of the localism that permeated the American antebellum economy. I also suggested that "By the 1920's we were a society of abundance in which consumption and spending became increasingly more important than the old virtues."[2] Since that time this theme has been vigorously pursued by an increasing number of authors, among the more successful of whom are Stuart Ewen, Daniel Horowitz, Richard Fox, Roland Marchand, and Jackson Lears.[3] Certainly the transformation to a consumer society is reflected in the advertising in popular magazines during the period.

Historians in general have ascribed a great deal of manipulative and persuasive power to advertising. Indeed, one suspects that much of the distrust and criticism of advertising from historians and social critics is rooted in a fundamental belief in and fear of its power. This distrust is different from those critics of deceptive and false advertising and from the criticism of those who bring to their study of advertising a set of values or an ideology which finds consumerism repugnant. Even those who accept what Roland Marchand has labelled the modernity of a consumer society, almost without exception, reject the notion that advertising adds any value to the product. In addition to creating artificial wants, advertising is viewed as a needless expense which adds to the cost of the product. Furthermore, critics argue that by creating false (as opposed to what they consider real) product differentiation, advertising erects barriers to entry by competing firms—allowing the larger firms that can carry the high costs of advertising to monopolize the market and charge higher prices.

Traditionally, economic historians have looked at advertising for information on prices, availability, production, and distribution of commodities. A great deal of attention has also been devoted to false and misleading advertising and to the "truth-in-advertising" movement. Many of these efforts, perhaps conditioned by personal experiences, have been very critical of advertising's role in selling often useless and sometimes harmful products to an unaware public. In truth, the advertising industry has failed far too often to exercise ethical restraint in the pursuit of sales and profits. By and large, however, economic historians have been unwilling or unable to deal with the role that advertising performed in the development of the modern American economy. They have tended to reject the concept that advertising played a vital role in the development of a national market for consumer goods, in creating demand for mass-produced items, and in shifting the consumption habits of Americans. At the same time, economic and social historians have ascribed to advertising great power to influence consumers to make unneeded and even unwanted purchases.

However scornful historians have been about the notion that advertising may indeed add to the value of a product for individual consumers, most modern economists accept the concept. Advertising may indeed add to the value of a product—value being determined subjectively by each individual. Value in these terms is measured by what an individual will give up to obtain the item and reflects the consumer's estimate of its utility as related to the utility of alternative goods—its marginal utility. In neoclassical economic theory, the marginal utility or value of a good is measured by the price a consumer is willing to pay for the marginal unit of the good purchased. At least one defender of modern advertising argued that "the fact that the value is fictitious as *perceived* by the consumer does not mean that it is unreal as *enjoyed* by the consumer."[4] There has, however, been less agreement about the macroeconomic effects of advertising.

There is little doubt that advertising played a major role in the concentration of some industries, if for no other reason than by hastening the introduction of mass production by creating demand. The extensive use of advertising created market power for firms that advertised and encouraged concentration by means of artificial product differentiation. As a recent study observed, this type of advertising is likely to be more effective when products can be "significantly differentiated," as in the case of cigarettes, cosmetics, soft drinks, soaps, dentifrice, electric refrigerators, and automobiles as compared to products that are "homogeneous like salt, sugar, canned fruit, and sheeting." The same study suggested that advertising raised costs, thereby requiring a larger output to maintain prices.[5] Hence, advertising expenditures tended to increase the minimum optimum size of the firms in an industry and thereby impeded entry. In addition, advertising may have sustained barriers to entry by protecting established differentiated products from competition.

The development of cheap and dependable overland transportation during the last quarter of the nineteenth century opened local markets to much wider competition. The existing technology supported the expansion of optimum plant size, allowing entrepreneurs to enjoy significant economies of scale. Expansion of plant size meant higher fixed costs but significantly lower variable costs by lowering the dependence on highly skilled labor, by increasing output per unit of labor, and by allowing increasing specialization of labor. The result was a shift in the total cost curves. The unit cost curves resulting from larger demand, increased plant size and economies of scale probably more closely resemble a reclining "L" as opposed to the previous "U."

Historians, perhaps overimpressed with Say's Law, which insists that supply creates its own demand, have tended to concentrate on production and supply. While we are all familiar with Adam Smith's dictum that specialization, and therefore economies of scale, is limited by the extent of the market, we have seldom taken serious account of the demand side of the equilibrium equation. Merchants have always taken demand as the critical factor, and by the last half of the nineteenth century so did manufacturers. Faced with the prospect of increased fixed costs and production for more future markets, many manufacturers sought both to expand markets and to protect the existing markets for their products. Advertising, brand names, and product differentiation through advertising offered a powerful tool to accomplish their task.

Between the end of the Civil War and the turn of the century, conditions in the American economy and in society merged to satisfy the necessary pre-conditions for advertising to play a very powerful role in creating national markets for consumer goods. Among these pre-conditions were a breakdown of localism, a collected audience and a concentrated market, an educated citizenry, an industrial structure characterized by oligopoly, the potential for mass production, a growth in per capita income, and a culture that valued consumption. By the time the United States entered World War I, the transformation was complete and the stage set for the triumph of a culture of consumerism.

Because I am convinced that advertisements did and still do reflect or mirror the society that produces them, I have attempted whenever possible to allow the ads to speak for themselves. I am also convinced that advertising copywriters, as even their critics are forced to admit, have often had a very clear view of the American Dream, of our collective notion of the good life. More than a decade ago, Richard Christiansen, in a syndicated column for the *Chicago Daily News*, arrived at the same conclusion. Christiansen, although talking about a different time and a different media, made the point with rare insight and clarity: "If you want to find a consistent and convincing picture of America in these confusing times," Christiansen noted, "look to your television screen," specifically the commercials:

Watching these familiar commercials, one sees that, though they have all been produced by vast and complex organizations, they all extoll the virtues of a simple and uncomplicated land. Here there is no maze of roadside stands offering processed foods, but a little tyke and her grandpa ordering a good old American dish. Here there are no crowded airports and polluted skies, but a walk under the clear heavens in the great outdoors. Here there is no mass consumption of endless bottles and cans of soda pop; instead, Coke has become an adjunct of Grandma's home cooking. . . .

If you accept that most advertising is indeed wish fulfillment, that it offers enticements of what its buyers would really like to see, instead of what really is, then these images in the television commercials are fascinating bits of Americana. . . .

These commercials tell us that we still long for the time and place of a happy, united and serene America. . . .

It is interesting to note that we haven't much changed our ideals of America.

The American dream has not vanished. It flourishes on the television commercial.[6]

Readers of newspapers, journals and magazines during the first two or three decades following the Civil War would have found no such image or view of the good society in the advertisements. As late as the 1880s most advertising performed the traditional function of informing consumers about the availability, the costs and the characteristics of products. True, patent medicines promised restored health through the consumption of their individual nostrum, but were not yet promising that social acceptance and status accompanied the consumption of the wares. By 1920 the image projected by advertisements in popular magazines already defined the American dream in terms of a consumption ethic. The copywriters' view of the good society was overwhelmingly upper-middle class and achieved largely through consumption of whatever product was being advertised. It is this transformation that I wish to explore.

This project has been on my agenda for a very long time, and any acknowledgements should start with my colleagues and students, first at Hiram College, then at the University of Wisconsin-Madison, and finally at the University of Missouri at St. Louis, who have endured my digressions about advertising and advertisements with such good humor. Members of the library staffs at these institutions, and at Northern Illinois University, have been more than helpful in meeting my requests for magazines and periodicals, have shared my disappointment upon discovering that the advertising had been removed prior to binding or microfilming, and have then quietly reordered the same items from other sources hoping to find them with the advertising intact. I thank them all.

I am grateful to Northern Illinois University for a sabbatical leave in Spring 1988, which freed me from my duties as dean and allowed me to finish this manuscript. A grant from the American Philosophical Society allowed me to spend Summer 1969 at the Wisconsin State Historical Society. At the end of that summer my colleague, the late Gilman Ostrander, urged me to "write it." Had I followed Gilman's advice, which was usually very sound, this would have been a very different and, in my view, a less satisfactory book. The reason, which will be immediately apparent to readers of this book, is that I owe a major debt to those scholars whose work in the intervening years has contributed so much to our understanding of advertising and the consumption ethic in American society. I gladly acknowledge that debt.

I am grateful to my staff, Charles Trott, Sue Doederlein, and Judy Hacker, all of whom took on an additional burden during my leave. A very special thanks is due my friend, colleague, and associate dean, Peter Nicholls, who assumed all my duties during my sabbatical leave and allowed me to devote all my time and efforts to this manuscript. I owe a special thanks to Paul Kleppner, the Director, and all the other folks at the Institute for Social Science Research at Northern Illinois University for the support and hospitality I received as a member of the Institute during my leave. Helen Satterlee and Cheryl Fuller, members of the college manuscript service, processed several versions of this manuscript with good humor as well as great expertise. My secretary, Janet Freeman, cheerfully rearranged my schedule to allow me blocks of time to finish the manuscript. Karen Grubb did all the photography, and I am grateful for her careful and professional eye in preparing the illustrations.

A very special thanks is due to my colleague Professor W. Bruce Lincoln who encouraged me in my attempt to address a much broader audience in my writing and most of all to "write it." Tom Mertes, my research assistant, hunted down sources, checked footnotes, double-checked direct quotes, read several versions of the manuscript, and has generally done all those things a really good research assistant does and has done them well. I owe a very special and personal debt to my assistant, Jamie Rothstein, who not only read and edited the manuscript through every version, but also provided support and encouragement in many ways that only I can appreciate. My deep and lasting gratitude to the late Lewis E. Atherton, teacher, mentor, scholar, colleague, and friend is only inadequately expressed by the dedication.

Advertising and the Transformation of American Society, 1865–1920

1

THE AMERICAN ECONOMY
IN TRANSITION

When my pop he said, "Let a hog in the house and he'll crawl on yer table," he wasn't agin' hogs . . . Pop was jest statin' a plain fact about hogs. All I aim to do tonight is state plain facts. . . . They is some wild-eyed folks likes to hollar, "Abolish advertisin'." Shucks, tryin' to stop advertisin' in this land is like tryin to stop freckles with a rubber eraser . . . . Only thing is, I look around our land and right now I say . . . we got a hog in the house.
—Father Calvin Stanfield's sermon
in Herman Wouk's *Aurora Dawn,*
or The True Story of Andrew Reale, 196–197

The golden spike driven on May 10, 1869, at Promontory Point, Utah, connecting the Central Pacific and the Union Pacific to form the nation's first transcontinental railroad, marked an epoch in the history of the United States. The celebration that followed carried with it symbolic significance even beyond that which the participants realized. Most suggested that it marked the unification of the country from East to West, and no doubt a few ventured to suggest that it foreshadowed the end of the frontier; a very few—politicians no doubt—suggested that the first transcontinental railway signalled the unification of the nation in a much broader and even spiritual sense. The Civil War was over. The North and South and the East and West were now united and the nation could "get on" with its destiny—which all were sure was glorious. For the merchants and the manufacturers, present and prospective, many of whom had lobbied for the railroad, it no doubt symbolized great economic opportunity—a chance to exploit the abundant natural resources and the potential to build a truly national market.

Before the potential could become the reality of a national market, several interrelated developments needed to take place. The construction of a single transcontinental railroad, however significant symbolically, fell far short of providing the inexpensive and dependable transportation network needed to tie the vast interior of the nation into a unified market. Clearly, additional major capital investment in transportation was necessary. Major portions of the Trans-Mississippi West could claim only a population of less than two inhabitants per square mile. The westward movement and the process of exploitation of the natural resources of this vast area would continue to occupy much of the next generation of Americans. It was not simply that to achieve a national market a high population density was required; it was also that the almost subsistence farming economy that had characterized so much of the frontier movement in the United States had to give way to a much more market-oriented agriculture and a reasonable balance between the rural and urban population achieved. It would have been foolish for businessmen to think that the regionalism, sectionalism, and localism that characterized antebellum America disappeared with the end of the Civil War. What markets that did exist were divided by the local patterns of taste and consumption that had been cultivated by locally produced goods. To tap these markets, manufacturers would have to find ways to homogenize tastes and to convince these consumers to purchase items produced by faraway manufacturers. For markets to expand, it would not be sufficient for the population to increase; per capita income must be capable of transforming the needs and wants of the population into effective demand. Only when these preconditions were satisfied could manufacturers and merchants be free to go about the relatively simple tasks of satisfying, and in some cases creating, the demands generated by the new national market. Viewed in retrospect, these tasks appear staggering and the accomplishments of the American economy over the following three decades spectacular.

Railway construction, which had declined to less than 1,000 miles a year during the war, quickly resumed, and the 46,800 miles of track owned by railroads in 1869 was nearly doubled in each of the succeeding decades to 86,556 and 161,272 in 1879 and 1889, respectively.[1] Construction activity generally followed the level of economic activity, peaking in 1872 with nearly 7,500 miles of new track and in 1881 with nearly 10,000 miles. In view of the duration of the contraction phases of the domestic long-swings in economic activity during the period between the Civil War and the turn of the century, the total construction represented an amazing capital investment. The periods of rapid railroad expansion occurred during the upswing of the cycles of economic activity—the late 1860s and early 1870s, and the late 1890s and early 1900s. By the turn of the century, nearly 200,000 miles of track networked the nation and during the next twenty years a high of over a quarter million miles was reached.[2]

As might be expected, the expansion of the railroad network in the late nineteenth century heavily favored geographic areas outside the already developed New England States. As Figure 1.1 illustrates, mileage in the Middle States and South tripled, while that in the Western States and

Figure 1.1
Railroad Mileage Increase, 1860–1890

	1860	1870	1880	1890
New England	3,660	4,494	5,982	6,831
Middle States	6,705	10,964	15,872	21,536
Southern States	8,838	11,192	14,778	29,209
Western States and Territories	11,400	24,587	52,589	62,394
Pacific States and Territories	23	1,677	4,080	9,804

Source: Chauncey M. Depew, ed., *One Hundred Years of American Commerce,
1795–1895* (New York, 1895), Volume I, 111.

territories increased sixfold. Before the turn of the century, four transcontinental railroad lines bound the East and the West economically. During the same period, the construction of a network of feeder lines provided cheap and dependable transportation for most of the nation. Certainly by no later than the beginning of the twentieth century, most small cities, villages, and even hamlets in the nation east of the Great Plains were capable of being served by the network, which not only hauled the efforts of their labors to a wider market but also opened their heretofore protected local markets to competition.

While a few might, with some reason, grumble that the government had been too generous in its support, most Westerners realized that without the railroads the area could not have entered the national market. Transportation costs declined, and even Robert Fogel, who argued that railroads were not indispensable for economic growth, has estimated that without the railroads the costs of shipping agricultural products in 1890 would have been double. Government generosity may have provided the railroads with an additional one per cent return on their investments, but the "social return" on the federal support amounted to more than 24 per cent, as measured in economic growth and output per manpower unit.[3] Between 1870 and 1900, over a million new farms were established, many in the Upper Midwest and the Great Plains States, greatly contributing to the agricultural production of the country. Harold Vatter has claimed that although the terms of domestic agricultural trade (the ratio of prices received to prices paid) changed very little or even improved, the expansion of frontier farming made it easier and cheaper to feed the growing urban non-farming population, thereby encouraging the more rapid development of the industrial sector.[4]

The growth in total miles constructed, owned, and operated, dramatic

Figure 1.2
Rectified Series for Steam-Railroad Tons and Passengers by Fiscal Years,
1870–1914

Year	Tons (unit: one million tons)	Passengers (unit: one million passengers)	Year	Tons (unit: one million tons)	Passengers (unit: one million passengers)
1870	147.6	150.4	1895	756	530
1875	204	190.1	1900	1,081	576
1880	338	222	1905	1,427	738
1885	451	364	1910	1,849	971
1890	691	520	1914	2,002	1,063

Tons and passengers hauled by steam-railroads, 1869–1914. Frickey based his calculations on steam-railroads in order to eliminate the short-line, mostly interurban electric lines.

Source: Adapted from Edwin Frickey, Production in the United States, 1860–1914 (Cambridge, Mass.: Harvard University Press, 1947), 100. Reprinted by permission.

as it was, failed to provide an accurate insight into the significant role railroads performed in building a national market. As Figure 1.2 indicates, the real significance lay in the people and goods moved by the increased rail network. In 1869, railroads moved nearly 130 million tons of freight and slightly more than 135 million passengers; thirty years later, this had increased to nearly a billion tons of freight and 538 million passengers. In 1914, the amount of freight hauled passed 2 billion tons and more than a billion passengers were served.

Vital as the development of the inexpensive and dependable overland transportation system was to economic growth in the United States and especially to the Midwest and the Great Plains, population growth was equally necessary. During the half-century following 1870, two almost disparate population movements occurred simultaneously. First, there was a continuing migration from more settled areas in the East into the unsettled and more lightly populated sections of the West (Figure 1.3). At the same time, the historic movement from rural into urban areas continued unabated. With the closing of the frontier, the rate of population redistribution between geographic regions slowed, but the shift from rural to urban accelerated. Recent studies of the settlement process which was so fundamental to the development of the American resource base suggest that it is also one of the distinctive features of the American experience. Unlike European countries where modern economic development took place after settlement, "In the

Figure 1.3
Regional Distribution of Population, by Percentage

Year	New England	Middle Atlantic	East North Central	West North Central	South Atlantic	East South Central	West South Central	Mountain	Pacific
1870	9	25	24	10	12	11	5	1	2
1880	8	23	22	12	13	11	7	1	2
1890	8	22	22	14	12	10	8	2	3
1900	7	22	21	14	12	10	9	2	3
1910	7	23	20	13	11	9	10	3	5

Source: Richard A. Easterlin, "Interregional Difference in Per Capita Income, Population and Total Income, 1840–1950," in National Bureau of Economic Research, Conference on Research in Income and Wealth, *Trends in the American Economy in the Nineteenth Century* (Princeton, N.J.: Princeton University Press, 1960), 136. Reprinted by permission. Percentages may not sum to 100 because of rounding. Regions are defined as follows. *New England:* Maine, Vermont, New Hampshire, Massachusetts, Connecticut, and Rhode Island. *Middle Atlantic:* New York, New Jersey, Pennsylvania, Delaware, and Maryland. *East North Central:* Ohio, Indiana, Illinois, Michigan, and Wisconsin. *West North Central:* Minnesota, Iowa, Missouri, North Dakota, South Dakota, Nebraska, and Kansas. *South Atlantic:* Virginia, West Virginia, North Carolina, South Carolina, Georgia, and Florida. *East South Central:* Kentucky, Tennessee, Alabama, and Mississippi. *West South Central:* Arkansas, Louisiana, Oklahoma, and Texas. *Mountain:* Montana, Idaho, Wyoming, Colorado, New Mexico, Arizona, Utah, and Nevada. *Pacific:* Washington, Oregon, and California.

United States settlement and modern economic growth for the most part took place concurrently."[5]

To populate (however sparsely in comparison with the older sections) and develop the great landed area opened by the railroad network in the Trans-Mississippi West, while at the same time providing the urban labor force demanded by industrialization, required a massive increase in the population. Maps of the density of population by decades (Figures 1.4, 1.5, and 1.6) illustrate both the size of the task and the scope of accomplishment in population growth. This should not be surprising, however, since the United States had historically enjoyed a rapidly growing population. From the time of the first census in 1790 until the Civil War, the rate of growth hovered around 35 per cent per decade. Following the war the *rate* of increase began a secular decline. Although the declining *rate* of increase is significant, it should not obscure the actual increases which were, as Figure 1.7 indicates, massive.

Figure 1.4
Spatial Distribution of Population, 1870

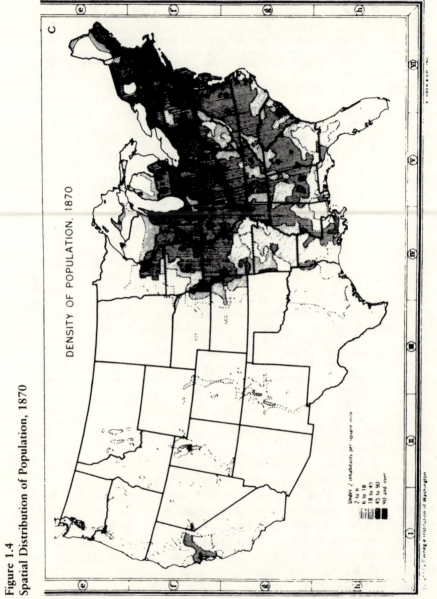

Source: C. O. Paulin, *Atlas of the Historical Geography of the United States* (Washington, D.C.: Carnegie Institution, 1932), plate 77c. Reprinted courtesy of the Carnegie Institution.

Figure 1.5
Spatial Distribution of Population, 1880

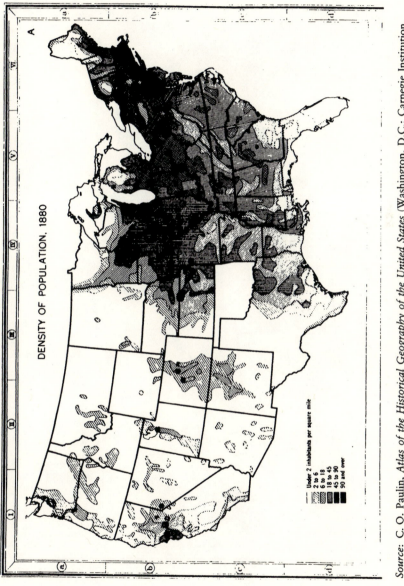

DENSITY OF POPULATION. 1880

Under 2 inhabitants per square mile
2 to 6
6 to 18
18 to 45
45 to 90
90 and over

Source: C. O. Paulin, *Atlas of the Historical Geography of the United States* (Washington, D.C.: Carnegie Institution, 1932), plate 78a. Reprinted courtesy of the Carnegie Institution.

Figure 1.6
Spatial Distribution of Population, 1890

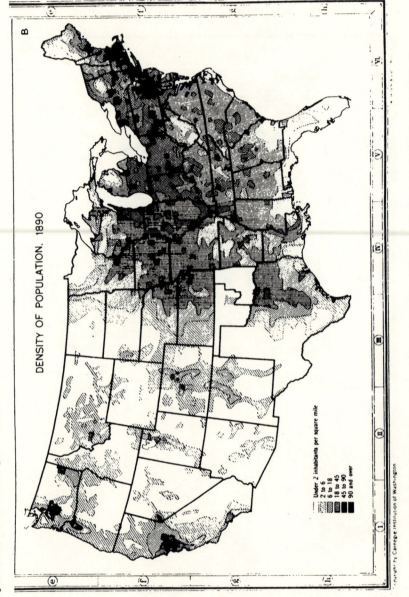

DENSITY OF POPULATION. 1890

Under 2 inhabitants per square mile
2 to 6
6 to 18
18 to 45
45 to 90
90 and over

Source: C. O. Paulin, *Atlas of the Historical Geography of the United States* (Washington, D.C.: Carnegie Institution, 1932), plate 78b. Reprinted courtesy of the Carnegie Institution.

Figure 1.7
Population, 1870–1920

Year	Population (thousands)	Increase in Decade (thousands)	Percentage Increase
1870	39,905	8,392	26.6%
1880	50,262	10,357	25.9
1890	63,056	12,794	25.0
1900	76,094	13,038	20.6
1910	92,407	15,953	20.9
1920	106,461	14,054	15.2

Source: U.S. Department of Commerce, Bureau of the Census, *Historical Statistics of the United States: Colonial Times to 1970*, Part I (Washington, D.C., 1976).

Each decade from 1870 to 1920, the population increased by more than 10 million. The *growth* during the last thirty years of the nineteenth century exceeded that from the founding of the English colonies to the Civil War. In the half-century following the end of the war, the actual population more than tripled. The greatest immigration in American history bolstered the rapid natural increase. After the Civil War, the rate of arrivals quickly exceeded pre-war levels, and the upward trend continued until World War I. Annual immigration reached peaks of approximately 800,000 in the early 1880s and in 1910 and seldom fell below 200,000, with an average of about 400,000 during the period between 1870 and the onslaught of war in Europe in 1914. Generally, as Robert Higgs has pointed out, immigration displayed a "rough correspondence with the fluctuations of prosperity and depression in the United States, [with] all the great surges of immigration occurring during periods of American prosperity."[6] Higgs calculated that immigration during these peak years "accounted for about a fifth of the increase in population," the other four-fifths resulting from the high birth rate and a declining death rate. In the half-century following 1870, the total population increased from slightly less than 40 million to more than 100 million. In the same period, the average age in the United States rose from 20 to 25, while the average age of foreign-born increased by about five years, from 35 to 40. Literacy, which had always been high by comparison with Europe, increased from 80 per cent in 1870 to 94 per cent by 1920. Most striking were the gains in literacy of the Black population, from close to 80 per cent illiteracy to nearly 80 per cent literacy in the same period. For the entire period, the United States enjoyed a rapidly growing population at the height of its producing and consuming age, with the education necessary for an industrializing economy. None of this necessarily suggested that the

Figure 1.8
Residence and Occupation, 1870–1920

Year	Percentage of total population Urban	Number of cities over 2,500	over 50,000	Percentage of work force engaged in agriculture
1870	26	663	28	53%
1880	28	939	35	51
1890	35	1348	57	43
1900	40	1737	78	40
1910	46	2262	109	31
1920	51	2722	144	26

Source: Stanley Lebergott, *Manpower in Economic Growth: The American Record Since 1800* (New York: McGraw-Hill, 1946), 510; and U.S. Department of Commerce, Bureau of the Census, *Historical Statistics of U.S.*, 10–12. By 1980 three cities had a population of 3 million, but no others reached that size until 1930. Reprinted courtesy of McGraw-Hill, Inc.

rate of growth, especially as measured by per capita income, was causally related to either the rapid population increase or the massive immigration. However, a different case could be made for the size (extent) of the market. Finally, the American population displayed an increasing proclivity for urban living.[7]

As the percentage of the labor force engaged in agriculture declined, the percentage of population living in urban areas increased. As Figure 1.8 illustrates, in the fifty years following 1870 the swing in each category amounted to about 25 per cent, so that by 1920 only 26 per cent of the work force made their living by farming and over half the population lived in communities of 2,500 or more, which the census bureau defined as urban. Not only did farming decline in comparison with other sectors of the economy, but farm employment, which had grown very little since the closing of the frontier, peaked in 1910 and began a slow but steady secular decline. While the census definition of "places" of 2,500 or more as urban suggested a movement from farms into villages, actually, as Figure 1.8 indicates, urbanization occurred across a broad spectrum.

Entrepreneurs contemplating long-term investments during the last decades of the nineteenth century could find a great deal of reassurance in the growing size of the population, in its increasingly urban character, in the greatly enhanced ability to reach the market by railroads, and in the rising per capita incomes. Per capita income in the United States, measured either in current or constant dollars, continued its antebellum secular rise. Indeed, much of the public outcry against the rising cost of living in the period immediately prior to America's entry into World War I was conditioned by the experience of over two generations with a rising standard of living. Moreover, recent evidence suggests that income inequality, while it remained great, did not increase with the rise in per capita income. Indeed, some authors have suggested that in the late nineteenth century "personal income distribution was decreasing in inequality."[8] The combination of factors discussed above produced "the Nineteenth Century's highest level of per capita income and rate of increase in per capita income" in the period 1869-1913. Indeed one study has suggested that in the three decades prior to World War I, the levels of income for the various sectors of the work force "did not deviate greatly from those to which they aspired."[9]

Aspiring entrepreneurs looking at the national scene in 1869 would have had to have been gifted with unusual powers of foresight and have been great optimists to discern the shift in market conditions during the next thirty years. True, the trends were there, and Americans had always been great optimists. Still, the decade of the 1870s opened with major portions of the interior overwhelmingly rural, isolated by inadequate transportation, with the majority of the population engaged in farming, often at almost subsistence level, and with only a very modest disposable cash income. Lance Davis has argued that the large rural population, combined with a growing urban working class with limited income to spend on items other than food and shelter, helped to create the market for lower-cost mass-produced goods.

Households with limited resources are usually willing to accept uniformity in the design of the articles they buy. Though rural communities were scattered, the flow of goods designed and manufactured in other places worked against the development of local tastes and preferences fixed by tradition. . . . In their adaption, blending, and borrowing, the forms of things, like the people [immigrants], became Americanized. The functional designs in furniture, tableware, clocks, family wagons, and stoves which were spreading through the rural communities . . . prepared the way for industrialization in the manufacture of consumer durable goods.[10]

While rural households would continue to dominate the market into the twentieth century, they would enjoy a rising per capita income. In the same period that the population trebled, agricultural production increased more than 400 per cent and, although consumer preference displayed some shift among items, the demand for foodstuffs exhibited income inelasticity. As Figure 1.9 illustrates, per capita income increased, hence the share of income remaining after food purchases tended also to increase.

In the decade of the 1880s the secular decline in the consumption-income ratio kinked and was replaced by an upward trend. The consumption function is culturally derived and is considered by economists to remain remarkably stable over long periods of time. Simon Kuznets suggested that

Figure 1.9
Per Capita Income, 1850–1920

Year	Total Income (Billions)	Per Capita	Constant Prices Per Capita (1926)
1850	2.2	$ 95	152
1860	3.6	115	189
1870	6.7	174	201
1880	7.4	147	226
1890	12.1	192	341
1900	18.0	236	420
1910	30.7	333	473
1915	37.1	373	536
1920	68.1	639	413

Source: Neil Borden, *The Economic Effects of Advertising* (Chicago: Richard D. Irwin, 1942), 683. (From *Verbatim Record of the Proceedings of the Temporary National Economic Committee* (Washington, D.C., January 11, 1939), Vol. 1, Reference Data Section III, p. 41. The table contains the following statement of sources: U.S. Department of Commerce, for 1929–38; Kuznets in *National Income and Capital Formation*, 1919–1935, the National Bureau of Economic Research, on 1919–1928; and W. I. King, in *Wealth and Income of the People of the United States* for 1850–1918; spliced into a single reasonably comparable series by the Department of Commerce. Reduced to a per capita basis by use of population estimates for the continental United States prepared by the Census Bureau. *Statistical Abstract of the United States, 1940.*) Reprinted by permission.

the important factors in producing the "kink" included shifts in population from rural to urban living, a change from individual entrepreneur to employee status, "the impact of new consumer goods, and . . . changes in the distribution of income by size." Recent studies argue that expansion of advertising concomitant with the factors suggested by Kuznets could well have had "a causative factor."[11]

A booming economy with an expanding population and rising real per capita income was enough to encourage merchants and manufacturers to expand their production and stocks with the expectation of increased demand. To serve these new markets two new institutions developed: the mail order houses to serve the expanding rural population and department stores to serve the burgeoning urban centers. Both depended on advertising to attract customers. But then, merchants had always depended on advertising.

Advertisements in local newspapers in the period immediately following the Civil War closely resembled their antebellum counterparts. Although enterprising store owners used any and every available means to hawk their goods—signs, handbills, and occasionally street criers—the most common vehicle was the local newspaper. Typically, newspapers in the period grouped advertisements on the first page of each edition of the paper and tended to restrict ads to rather modest size and character. Illustrations seldom accompanied the conventional column form ads. A few highly stylized woodcuts occasionally were included in ads. Most consisted of no more than crude line drawings of the product or of the brand name. Local store keepers almost never featured illustrations of brand names in their ads. For the most part, small-town advertising by local merchants served the intended purpose of providing information about the variety of selection, low prices, and availability of goods. In advertising, local merchants seldom mentioned specific prices, but assured prospective customers of their overall low prices and the quality and freshness of the merchants' large stock of goods.[12]

While the format, content, and even appeal of local advertisements in the decade which followed the Civil War retained an essential antebellum appearance, Lewis Atherton has suggested several new roles for small-town advertising. Commercial travelers, drummers, wholesalers, and on occasion representatives of manufacturers advertised new products in the local papers. Often the local editors were given samples and urged to "pump" the qualities of the product. For example, in 1865, J. L. Mohler's store in Lacon, Illinois, advertised a new stock of canned goods and fruit. In the same paper the local editor, who had obviously received free samples, lamented the fact that canned goods were not generally accepted in Lacon and suggested that only old-fashioned folks distrusted the quality of these new products. He praised the taste, freshness, purity, and convenience of the canned goods and predicted that they represented the future. In addition to helping to introduce new products, Atherton also maintained that the significant addition in post-Civil War small-town advertising was the appearance of ads promoting neighboring small-town merchants and even stores in relatively distant large cities. Besides eliminating local monopolies (which because of the profusion of local stores Atherton doubted ever really existed), advertisements for new products, from neighboring and sometimes rather distant stores, combined with the availability of railway travel to enlarge the market for goods and services.[13]

The local storekeeper advertising in the country newspapers sought not so much to shift the demand curve for general classes of merchandise or to introduce new products into the local market, but rather to ensure and even increase their respective shares of the demand that existed. Yet by informing their customers about the availability of products, including new items in the market, the effect was to shift the total demand curve. Country newspaper editors took their advertisements, like their news stories, wherever they could find them. Along with the ads from prominent mercantile establishments in larger cities, a consumer could find ads for canned goods, ready-made clothing, baking powder, patent medicines, soap, cleaning powders, candy, soft drinks, gum, watches, musical instruments, pens, stationery, as well as seeds, farm equipment, paint, building materials, furniture, firearms, and sewing machines. Sales for land received as grants by railroads were advertised as were fares and excursions. Increasingly, manufacturers or producers included brand names in their advertisements along with specific qualities peculiar to their individual brands.

Atherton concluded that national advertising "revolutionized merchandising procedures." After the Civil War, merchants who had always secured their goods from whatever source they wanted found themselves forced to stock specific items. "Any item whose quality and price had been widely praised in advertising literature," he noted, "had to appear in local stores. . . . In this way," Atherton argued, "manufacturers and wholesalers influenced selection of goods, prices, and even methods of salesmanship in retail stores."[14] While retail advertising retained both a local character and the direct action purpose of attracting customers to shop at individual stores, nevertheless local merchants, willingly or unwillingly, found themselves increasingly integrated into the national market.[15]

Most small-town merchants first experienced the power of national advertising when their customers began demanding that they stock one or more of the highly advertised patent medicines. Even before the Civil War, patent medicine makers invested heavily in advertising. In his excellent study of the patent medicine industry, James Harvey Young argued that the patent medicine entrepreneur "blazed a merchandising trail," being the first "to seek out a national market . . . [and] to help merchants who retailed his wares by going directly to consumers with a message about the product."[16] The patent medicine promoter was, as Young pointed out, the first "to test out a multitude of psychological lures by which people might be enticed to buy his wares. While other advertising in the press was dull, his was vivid; while other appeals were straight forward, his were devilishly clever."[17] In addition to the local newspapers, patent medicine promoters utilized the growing volume of popular national magazines to hawk their wares. For the most part, the advertisers used the same approach and appeal; often even the same ads were placed in the local and national media.

Mail order and direct order sales had existed prior to the Civil War. Agricultural periodicals often carried ads inviting prospective customers to "correspond" or to "write for price lists" for a wide variety of products. For example, in 1860 readers of the *Southern Planter* were encouraged to purchase the "celebrated premium iron cylinder GRAIN DRILL" from C. F. Corser, in Baltimore, who represented himself as the exclusive agent for the manufacturers Bickford and Huffman. In the same issue, testimonials from four tobacco growers encouraged customers to purchase American guano, imported under the "protection of the U.S. Government," from Felix H. Cave in Richmond, Virginia.[18] Seven years later, the list of direct mail sales opportunities had expanded to include ready-made clothes, carriages, watches, plows and agricultural implements, seeds, and jewelry.[19] Advertisements for direct mail order sales appeared not only in agricultural journals, such as the *Southern Planter, American Agriculturist,* and *Country Gentleman*; readers of such popular national journals as *Peterson's Magazine, Godey's Lady's Book and Magazine,* and *Harper's Weekly* found the same inducements and many more. For the most part, each firm sold only one line of goods, and a few sold only by mail.

The early mail order houses depended completely upon advertising; indeed, some of them established periodicals primarily to serve as a vehicle for advertisements. In 1869, E. C. Allan, an Augusta, Maine, direct order businessman who had started in business by selling recipes for washing compounds, established the *Peoples' Literary Companion*, which contained a few pages of literature of doubtful value and a great many advertisements for mail order products. Allan's innovation was easily imitated, and the combined circulation of these "mail order" periodicals quickly ran into the millions.[20]

In 1872, the year of its founding, Montgomery Ward & Co. issued its first catalogue. The publication, reportedly the first of its kind in this country, was a hundred pages long and listed several hundred articles along with descriptions and prices. Aaron Montgomery Ward opened his firm with the intention of catering to discontented farmers and planned to sell through the Granges. His business was an immediate success. Montgomery Ward & Co. quickly found itself competing with firms such as Spiegel, May, Stern, and National Bellus Hess, and in 1893 Sears, Roebuck and Company joined the large mail order houses. The publication of catalogues quickly became an art. A mail order firm's very existence depended on the effectiveness of its advertising.[21]

Successful mail order houses utilized all the media available to supplement their catalogues. Advertisements for both Montgomery Ward & Co. and Sears, Roebuck and Company appeared in mail order magazines, farm periodicals, newspapers, and national journals. Richard Sears, in an effort to overcome the bitter opposition of retail merchants, ran institutional ads which stressed the stability and size of the company, the absolute "money back" guarantee on all Sears products, and the quality of the merchandise. Both Montgomery Ward and Sears equipped special trains that toured the countryside with their merchandise in an effort to offset the determined opposition of local merchants. Local storekeepers countered the competition by spreading rumors that the products advertised in mail order catalogues were of shoddy quality. The trains provided an opportunity for rural customers to satisfy their apprehension about the quality of the product before ordering. Mail order houses slanted the appeal of their ads to a rural consumer, and for many an isolated farm wife, the large, lavishly illustrated catalogue became an important cultural document. Boris Emmett and John

Jeuck's comments in their study of Sears, Roebuck and Company applied to successful mail order houses in general:

Sears, Roebuck and Company grew to young corporate manhood in an era when America was still to a very considerable extent a pioneer country. And Sears customers were, for many years, drawn almost entirely from farmers and residents of small rural communities. "Quality" was a word and a concept with connotation peculiar to rural residents. Quality meant serviceability and value; a piece of merchandise had to be good enough to perform the function the catalogue said it would perform, and the price had to be low enough for them to afford it. . . . It apparently meant little or nothing to the farmer that the ghastly, standardized furniture sold by Sears, Roebuck was almost utterly devoid of aesthetic quality.[22]

No doubt the large and richly illustrated catalogues of the mail order houses, as was also true of their ads in journals and newspapers, were intended to capture consumer demand for the individual firm. Nevertheless, the overall effect on the American economy was to introduce new goods and to shift the total demand curve for many of the items being advertised.[23] The distribution function performed so well for rural communities by mail order houses found a counterpart in the department stores.

Even before the Civil War, retail stores in the larger urban areas, both in terms of stock and in terms of sales, had reached such a size and handled such a wide variety of goods that it was probably incorrect to think of them as "large general stores." A. T. Stewart, who had attracted widespread attention by advertising a "one-price policy," claimed to have often exceeded ten thousand dollars a day in sales, and Oak Hall in Boston claimed annual sales of half-million dollars. Although A. T. Stewart advertised widely, his ads invariably played on his "one-price policy" with such claims as "No haggling, one price for all and always worth the price." Stewart's was a dry-goods specialty house and Oak Hall, at the time, the largest clothing store in the country. Regardless of John Wanamaker's insistence that a department store was nothing but an overgrown general store, neither Stewart's nor Oak Hall fit the classification of department stores. On the other hand, by the end of the war, firms like Lord and Taylor and R. C. Macy in New York, John Wanamaker in Philadelphia, Marshall Field in Chicago, F. and R. Lazarus in Columbus, and Gimbel Brothers in Milwaukee were buying directly from the producer and at least beginning to organize their merchandise and management along departmental lines—both distinguishing characteristics of department stores.[24]

In 1861, John Wanamaker, who started his business career as a tailor, and his partner, Nathan Brown, purchased the entire stock of a clothing manufacturer and immediately launched a major advertising campaign. By 1869, Wanamaker and Brown claimed to be the largest men's ready-made clothing retail dealer in the United States. Stewart advertised extensively, but reportedly Wanamaker advertised more in a week than Stewart had in a year. Wanamaker's innovations were not confined to the volume of advertising. His ads more often featured quality and size of stock handled rather than price. In addition, Wanamaker often repeated his advertisement over and over again in the same media and often on the same page. In 1879, he placed what was reported to be the first whole-page newspaper advertisement by an American department store.[25]

Following the American Centennial, Wanamaker purchased the huge depot that the Pennsylvania Railroad had constructed to handle the huge crowds attending that event. With a great deal of fanfare and advertisement, Wanamaker opened his "new kind of store" with its more than two miles of aisles and showcases. His ads claimed that the new store had been stocked with a wide variety of goods worth more than a half million dollars. In newspapers and periodicals throughout the nation, Wanamaker advertised his "GRAND EVENT," the "BRILLIANT OPENING" of the "GRAND DEPOT." The advance publicity drew what Wanamaker claimed to be a crowd of 70,000 for the grand opening of the new "DRY GOODS EMPORIUM."[26]

In full-page ads announcing the opening and later boasting about the opening itself, Wanamaker emphasized the two acres of "choicest dry goods." In a transparent attempt to appeal to women customers, Wanamaker called special attention to his new policies regarding returned merchandise which he referred to as "new business for ladies." The return policy simply guaranteed each purchase, at a "price fixed for all," with assurances of a return of the purchase price or an exchange of any good that the customer was not completely satisfied with. "This radical plan," he assured the public, had "never been applied to dry goods, but we adopt it in EVERY DEPARTMENT."[27] In an era when the success of businessmen was widely admired and publicized, Wanamaker's success was often attributed to his innovations in advertising. In fact, until 1880 when he hired John E. Powers, Wanamaker's innovation was largely confined to the scale of his campaigns or to easily imitated slogans. It was Powers, often referred to as "the father of modern advertising," who transformed Wanamaker's advertising copy with an honest, direct, and fresh appeal. Style, elegance, comfort, and even luxury, not price and durability, characterized Powers' advertising appeal.

John Powers' rather straightforward and descriptive advertising copy seemed specifically designed to appeal to a rising urban middle class. Other merchants often imitated Powers' style in an effort to attract potential customers to shop at their department stores. The ads were designed to lure urban middle-class women to the store. When they arrived at the new department stores, shoppers found, in Susan Benson's words, "an unprecedented level of beauty and comfort":

Windows were dressed with an artistic eye, as managers renounced the traditional practice of cramming windows with vast quantities of unrelated merchandise and instead presented smaller lots of related items in a pleasing and esthetic way.... [W]indow shopping became a welcome diversion. Parading up and down the streets, women examined the goods displayed.... They stopped to discuss the merchandise and the quality of the displays with their friends, their loitering in public space legitimated by its association with consumption.[28]

One expert estimated that by 1900, only newspaper and magazine advertising outdistanced window displays as a means to promote department store buying. Perhaps the growth of window-dressers as a specialized occupation illustrated as well as any other measurement the rapid acceptance of advertising as the means to encourage consumption. By the opening of the twentieth century, in addition to the regular clerks utilized on a part-time basis, over 1,500 persons made their living as full-time window decorators. In August 1898, the National Association of Window Trimmers met in Chicago for their first annual meeting.[29]

It is difficult to overestimate the role of these large and luxurious department stores in the cultivation of a consumer culture in the United States. The attractively trimmed windows and the beautifully appointed interiors exerted a powerful persuasion on the urban middle class—to shop, to buy, to consume. The culture represented by the large department stores proved prevalent and most small towns soon had at least pale imitations of Macy's or Marshall Field's. More importantly, advertising placed by the department stores in newspapers and popular magazines circulated to a much wider audience than customers in the immediate urban community. As the department stores became larger, more numerous, and more elaborate, so did their advertisements. The railroads, which networked the nation and reached into rural villages and small towns, brought into those communities newspapers, magazines, and catalogues, all of which lessened the isolation, physical and mental, of rural living. The ease of travel, the relatively low cost of passenger rates, and the excursions promoted by railroads encouraged more frequent trips to larger cities and brought the rural population in closer contact with urban life and tastes. After all, window-shopping was free, and if a farm woman could not afford the item she saw in Macy's window or in their advertisement, perhaps she could find a less expensive imitation in the Sears, Roebuck catalogue.

Macy's, Marshall Field's, and other department stores' intensive advertising campaigns, while intended primarily to attract customers to purchase from their individual firms, also worked to shift the total demand curve. In the same way, manufacturers, even patent medicine promoters, advertising primarily to create demand for their products, regardless of the retail outlet, also increased total demand at the same time they sought to differentiate their product from similar competing products. Not surprising, department stores tended to emphasize their store names and manufacturers stressed brand names and trademarks in their advertising.

Names like Fairbanks Scale, Singer Sewing Machines, and Remington Firearms, familiar names even to modern readers, appeared in newspapers and magazine advertisements even before the Civil War. As early as 1866, the Magic Ruffle Company advised customers in a *Harper's* advertisement that unless their trademark appeared on each box and piece of material it was not a genuine Magic Ruffle and was not only "worthless"; it also was an "infringement of the patents of the Magic Ruffle Company."[30] During the decade of the 1870s, the United States Patent Office registered brand names and trademarks at an accelerating pace. From only a few in 1870, the registered names and brands increased to 121 the following year and to 1,138 in 1875. Indeed, by the end of the century many of the names familiar to modern shoppers appeared in newspapers and magazines with increasing frequency as manufacturers, eager to protect their names and to differentiate their products from competitors, hastened to register their individual trademarks and brand names. By 1906, the Patent Office had recorded over 10,500 brands and marks, and before the decade of the 1920s this figure reached 50,000.[31]

For illustrative purposes, any number of examples of advertising tactics could be drawn from among those manufacturers who registered their brand names and trademarks during the decade after the U.S. Patent Office began accepting registrations. Among the early industries whose firms rushed to register trademarks and brand names and which quickly turned to advertising to reach existing markets and differentiate similar products satisfying the same wants were soap, sewing machine, and farm equipment manufacturers. While these three industries represent widely divergent products, and firms within these industries all faced different marketing problems, all advertised extensively in an effort to create product differentiation.

Patent medicine promoters, while among the first to engage in large-scale advertising campaigns to differentiate one remedy from the others, never really had the field to themselves. Indeed, in a nation that supposedly valued cleanliness next to godliness it was somewhat surprising that soap manufacturers entered the fray as late as they did. Not until 1869 did Enoch Morgan's Sons, a soap manufacturing firm that had been in business for sixty years, launch a campaign for a scouring cleanser, "Sapolio." The ads for Sapolio, a mixture of ground silex and vegetable oil soap sold in cake form, featured an illustration of a young man staring at his reflection in the bottom of a shiny pan. The illustration became Sapolio's trademark. Ads appeared with great frequency in most of the popular national magazines, such as *Harper's Weekly* and *Frank Leslie's Illustrated Weekly Newspaper*.[32] The early copy for Sapolio ads stressed its usefulness with statements like "better and cheaper than soap" and "the best thing known for polishing metal and brass signs." Within a year after launching the campaign, Sapolio claimed that "Five hundred thousand persons have it in daily use in house and shop."[33]

Advertising expenditures for the first year of the campaign are not known, but in 1871 Enoch Morgan's Sons spent $15,000 promoting their cleanser. During the depression of 1873 the firm experienced some difficult financial years and reduced expenditures on advertising. In 1877, the firm spent only $3,000 on advertising. In 1884, the same year that George F. Morgan, then president of the company, hired the flamboyant Artemus Ward as advertising manager, Sapolio spent $28,000 for advertisements. Under Ward's direction, the budget for his department multiplied from $69,000 in 1885 to $400,000 in 1896. Sales seemed to follow the advertising budget; by 1905 over 16.5 million cakes were sold—roughly one for every family in the nation. The lesson for advertising and soap firms seemed obvious—advertise and the demand for your product multiplies.[34] Few innovations proved easier to imitate than launching an advertising campaign, and Ivory Soap, Pears' Soap, and a host of others soon joined the campaign to keep Americans clean.

In spite of the success of Sapolio's advertising campaign and the very large share of the market for cleansers that it captured, the firm never felt secure enough to increase prices in an attempt to exploit its position in the market. Even more important, the large expenditures for advertising and the success of Enoch Morgan's Sons in differentiating its product never represented a sufficient barrier to prevent other cleansers from entering the market. Bon Ami, Sapolio's major competitor, entered the market in 1886, and by 1904 both Armour and Swift had cleansers in the market. In 1905, Old Dutch Cleanser, produced by Cudahy Packing Company, joined the competition. Old Dutch launched a major advertising and promotional campaign which attempted to differentiate the product by featuring the innovation of a powdered cleanser packaged in a sifter-top can. The Old Dutch innovation proved very popular, and in spite of a major advertising campaign, Sapolio, like other products that failed to keep up with consumer preference, lost its position in the market.[35]

No industry depended more on keeping abreast of competitor's innovations more than sewing machines. Indeed, in the bewildering maze of conflicting patent claims which characterized the early sewing machine industry, much of the advertising centered around intimidation by threatening potential customers of rival products with law suits involving patent infringement. I. M. Singer & Co. and the two major rival companies originally sold the right to sell and use their patented machines in specific territories in an effort to reassure agents. After 1853, when a Boston court ruled that Singer had infringed on Elias B. Howe's 1846 patent, a sewing machine patent pool was established which lasted from 1856 to 1876. To Howe's patent, which he contributed for a fixed fee per machine, Wheeler and Wilson Manufacturing Company, Singer, and the Grover and Baker Sewing Machine Company added their respective patents.[36] After 1856, three major sewing machine firms, no longer hampered by fear of possible patent infringement, concentrated on production and marketing.

Andrew Jack suggested that sewing machines presented marketing problems peculiar to consumer innovations where competition may be based on continuous product improvement. Because the sewing machine represented the first major consumer appliance, Jack argued that the industry needed to develop "an entirely new structure of marketing institutions" to meet these problems. He observed that the Singer Company inevitably marketed their machines through local sales offices, a strategy rapidly adopted by the other sewing machine firms, because "the sewing machine was sold in a consumer market and particularly a consumer market which demanded demonstration, instruction and supplies and accessories."[37]

While the need for an inexpensive, practical family sewing machine had existed for years, the antebellum sewing machine manufacturers faced the need to market a very new innovation. The problem was simply that the machines in the early years failed the test of practical, workable versatility. As Jack pointed out, they might sew, "but in a very limited sense."[38] By the Civil War, most of the practical problems with the early machines had been worked out. After a period of experimenting with franchised dealers, the disruption caused by the war convinced Singer to drop the agency system and establish its own sales offices:

The company's experience with franchised agencies had been that they represented a drain of operating capital which was not compensated by the services they performed. While many of them had done a valuable pioneering work in introducing the new product, they had not been amenable to introducing the new models, or of adopting the lower prices which the maturing market demanded. In comparison with the sales offices, they had proved to be less effective and more expensive. The smaller agencies which were supplied and serviced by the nearest sales office continued to exist for some time. But . . . the company inevitably expanded the number of local sales offices.[39]

Perhaps because of the general disapprobation of advertising by many businessmen at the time, but more than likely because of the Singer Company's conviction that new and mechanically complex consumer products like the sewing machine needed to be demonstrated, the company's early advertising efforts were relatively modest. In the period immediately after the Civil War, Singer's campaign in newspapers and magazines featured invitations for demonstrations and advised prospective purchasers of the location of the nearest company sales office. Interestingly Singer's ads, unlike its rivals, seldom mentioned the possibility of direct sales of its machine. Beginning in the years immediately prior to the Civil War, Singer placed a few tasteful advertisements in prominent magazines, such as

Harper's Weekly, which discussed in an informative fashion the features of their machines and invited potential agents to contact the company. Unlike many of its competitors, Singer's promotional literature tended to emphasize features of its machine. In 1856, the company founded *The Singer Gazette*, which they supplied in small numbers to agents without charge.[40] In addition, agents could place individual ads in the *Gazette*. The company printed attractive catalogues of its machines, provided "handsome lithographs" of the various models for window display, and provided inexpensive examples of work performed by the machines. Singer's rivals had no such disapprobation about extensive newspaper and magazine advertising.[41]

Even after the establishment of the patent pool, a few of the advertisements for sewing machines continued to contain references to "patented" and veiled warnings that customers purchasing other machines risked prosecution for infringement. For example, as late as 1870, the Buckeye $20 Shuttle Sewing Machine advertised for agents and claimed that the Buckeye was the only "LICENSED SHUTTLE MACHINE sold in the United States for less than $40." All others were "infringements, and the seller and *user* are liable to prosecution and *imprisonment*."[42] In context, the real implication these companies were attempting to convey by the warnings was that the advertised machine was so desirable and so superior that it was apt to be copied. Hence, the message was "buy the genuine" product.[43] Not to be outdone by the patent medicine promoters, sewing machine firms advertised their machines as "celebrated," "perfected," and the "newest and best." The Weed Company promised "unusual adaption, unequalled beauty and simplicity, perfection of material and finish." The Domestic Company, advertising for agents, modestly concluded that it was "the best and the easiest to sell." The Blees ads emphasized that their machine used a lock-stitch (by that time all the major machines used a lock-stitch), was noiseless, and "challenged the world in perfection of work, strength and beauty of stitch, durability of construction and rapidity of motion." The "improved Wilson Shuttle Sewing Machine," which like the Blees included a simple illustration of its machine in their advertising, listed the functions performed by their product, claiming that for "stitching, hemming, tucking, felling, quilting, cording, binding, braiding, gathering, gathering [sic] and sewing on gathers, it is unexcelled." Perhaps the Wilson ad stressed the machine's practical use since it was addressed exclusively to prospective agents.[44]

No doubt a great deal of the motivation behind the early advertisements were the efforts of manufacturers of essentially standardized products to secure some product differentiation. If patent medicine promoters provided the model, one needs to keep in mind that no practical differences existed between the functional appeals presented, since they all claimed to cure most of mankind's ailments.

Figure 1.10
Sewing Machine Production, 1865–1875

Year	Wheeler & Wilson	Willcox & Gibbs	Singer
1865	39,157	NA	26,340
1868	NA	14,150	59,629
1870	83,208	28,890	127,833
1871	128,526	30,127	181,260
1872	174,088	33,639	219,758
1873	119,190	15,881	232,444
1874	92,827	13,710	241,679
1875	103,740	14,502	249,852

Source: David Hounshell, *From the American System to Mass Production, 1800–1932* (Baltimore: The Johns Hopkins University Press, 1984), 70, 89. Reprinted with permission.

Although the advertising campaigns of American sewing machine firms followed similar patterns, one is struck with the great differences in advertising for sewing machines between the United States and Great Britain. For the most part, companies in the United States confined their efforts to securing a share of the demand which they simply assumed existed. At the same time, in June 1869, John Powers took a full-page back-cover-position advertisement for the American-manufactured Willcox and Gibbs sewing machine in the popular English family magazine, the *Golden Hours*. Powers realized that even in the nation that led the world in clothing-production, there was a huge potential market for family sewing machines. Potential customers in England, like their American counterparts, were assured that the Willcox and Gibbs machine did the "finest, strongest, most beautiful, most durable" work. More importantly, Powers offered a month's free trial, with instructions and "easy terms of payment, without extra charge, for those who cannot pay the full price at once."[45] While agents often granted credit in the United States, no manufacturer had offered a free trial or had openly advertised credit in an effort to expand the demand. In addition, Powers reassured his customers that the Willcox and Gibbs machine was easy to learn, reliable, and a perfect family machine that could be used by anyone. The success of Powers' approach is illustrated by Figures 1.10 and 1.11. Not until 1874 did the volume of sales in the United States equal the volume exported to Great Britain alone. Indeed, the demand in Great Britain, created at least in part by Powers' creative advertising, exceeded the ability of Willcox and Gibbs to meet it. As Figures 1.10 and 1.11 illustrate,

Figure 1.11
Value of Sewing Machines Sold, 1865–1875

Year	Domestic	Exported To All Countries	Exported To Great Britain Only
1865	$ 94,923	$ 1,999,274	$ 753,792
1868	243,129	1,650,340	723,003
1870	334,484	2,233,326	926,896
1871	706,094	1,898,864	986,553
1872	851,226	2,436,085	898,405
1873	658,506	2,150,720	768,903
1874	527,918	1,594,296	512,323
1875	1,056,703	1,797,929	567,764

Source: Andrew B. Jack, "The Channels of Distribution for an Innovation: The Sewing Machine Industry in America, 1860–1865," Explorations in Entrepreneurial History, 9 (February 1957), 113. Reprinted by permission. One needs to keep in mind that the price of sewing machines declined sharply during the period 1865–1875.

the demand in England grew faster than did the United States domestic market.

Figure 1.10 illustrates the growth in manufacturing output in the sewing machine industry. The patent pool fairly well assured that the industry would be dominated by a few large firms, and by the end of the pool in 1876, the Singer Company clearly dominated the other firms. As David Hounshell has demonstrated, even though the Singer Company never achieved perfectly interchangeable parts and mass production, with the exception of the production of wooden cabinets, the firm did enjoy significant economies of scale and lower unit costs of production. Singer certainly possessed the power to exert price leadership in an oligopolistic market; nevertheless, the Singer Company failed to use its power to either raise or maintain prices. Indeed, during the first twenty years of its existence, Singer consistently passed on to the consumer most of the economies of scale it enjoyed and led the industry in reducing prices.

Like sewing machines, the demand for affordable, practical, and labor-saving farm equipment needed little advertising to sustain it. Even ante-bellum farm implement manufacturers and their agents sought to convince farmers and planters that their particular implement would best satisfy the existing need as opposed to creating new demands. As early as 1855, in an advertisement in the Southern Planter, an agent for the M. D. Wells Improved Patent Seed Sower assured farmers that the Wells seeder, which had won the first premium at the Virginia State Fair, would save time and money. Five years later, a Richmond, Virginia, agent for Bickford and

Huffman, manufacturers of farm implements, utilized the same appeal in regular ads in the *Southern Planter*. The celebrated, premium, and patented grain drill was pronounced the "best ever offered to the public" by the farmers who used it "South, North and West."[46]

Rural journals like the *Southern Planter*, the *Country Gentleman*, and the *American Farmer* carried an increasing number of farm implement advertisements, along with ads for seeds, plants, building materials, tools, improved breeding livestock, fencing materials, fertilizers, patent medicines, dry goods, and an assortment of goods found in most popular magazine ads. While manufacturers occasionally advertised a specific implement or even a line of implements, these ads were usually in conjunction with advertisements for agents to handle the products. Much more common were advertisements from implement agents, such as the January 1868 ad of Norris & Pusey, a Baltimore, Maryland, firm which carried Wood's self-rake reapers and mowers and "Agricultural implements and machinery of every description," including plows, cultivators, harrows, grain drills, threshers, and corn shellers "of all kinds."[47] While testimonials became increasingly popular during the 1870s, for the most part these simply assured prospective customers that the implement being advertised performed its function in an excellent fashion. For example, Frank G. Ruffin, vice-president of the Virginia State Agricultural Society, offered a testimonial for the Johnston "Sweepstakes" self-raking reaper which stated simply "the reaper has proved itself good." The remainder of Ruffin's testimonial simply explained the way he operated the reaper in terms a farmer would understand.[48] Ruffin clearly felt that he did not need to convince farmers of the value of reapers in general, only of the merits of the "Sweepstakes."

Most implement agents sought to carry a complete line of farm equipment that they simply could not obtain from one manufacturer. As a result, any number of brands or manufacturers might appear in an agent's advertisement. As late as the summer of 1881, Griffith and Turner, agricultural merchants in Baltimore, featured McCormick harvesting machinery in their advertisement, along with a variety of other firms' equipment. Ballard's hay tedder, Hagerstown's horse rake, Foust's hay loader, Fitzhugh's hay unloader, Empire's thrasher, Oliver's chilled plow, and Malta's steam plow were offered for sale in the same ad as McCormick's self-raking reapers, droppers, and new iron mowers.[49] In simple fact, Griffith and Turner sought not to create demand through their advertising, but to capture as large a share as possible. As far as manufacturers were concerned, as Hounshell concluded, McCormick's problem was not in selling his product, but in producing enough to meet the demand.[50]

The same appeal in advertising copy used by soap, sewing machine, and agricultural equipment manufacturers in the period up to the Panic of 1873 was evident in the advertisements of other products. Most businessmen wrote their own ad copy. Moreover, since few had learnéd to actually differentiate their products by building differences into items capable of satisfying the same needs, the advertisements relied on superlatives. Even ads for products as generic as lamp oil (kerosene) displayed a great similarity of appeal; for example, both Wicks' Eclectic Oil and Denslow and Bucks' Premium Safety Oil made substantially the same claims to being the "best," the "safest" illuminating oil available, and both assured the public that their product was sold "everywhere."[51]

As late as the early 1870s, journals and magazines such as *Harper's Weekly, Frank Leslie's Illustrated Weekly Newspaper,* and *Peterson's Ladies' National Magazine* carried only four to five pages of advertisements, usually separated from the news and editorial portions of the periodical and with few illustrations. The November 1871 edition of *Harper's* had only five pages with thirty different ads, eight of which were illustrated. The same pattern applied to that issue of *Peterson's.*[52] One is struck not only by the relative paucity of ads, which would quickly multiply to more than a hundred pages in *Harper's* during the next twenty years, but even more striking is the lack of variety in goods offered and in the appeals used to attract customers. Practically all the goods offered, even patent medicines, in a society as preoccupied with death and illness and characterized by inadequate and sometimes poorly trained medical services as the United States could be classified as essential goods for which a demand already existed. With the exception of one new parlor game advertised by Milton Bradley and Company, only the books, periodicals, sheet music, and musical instruments could clearly be classified as consumption identified with luxury or leisure. Even within this limited selection, the appeal of the advertisements was essentially the same as it was for the more essential items. Books were "the handsomest and most valuable book to an American ever published," or "the most comprehensive, amusing, refining and instructive book ever published." Sheet music was the latest and the cheapest, and the musical instruments, chiefly organs and pianos, the cheapest and the best, with "thoroughness of construction and finish." In particular, no attempt was made to use social status or acceptance as advertising appeal.

Even if patent medicines are included, the fact remains that advertising in the United States prior to the Panic of 1873 contained small appeal for increased consumption of consumer goods. Unlike John Powers' efforts in England, which were designed to increase the total demand for a product, manufacturers and merchants in the United States seemed contented in their advertisements to maintaining the present market or perhaps capture a little more of the existing market. American businessmen seemed unaware of the emerging power of mass production or of the potential of advertising to create national markets of unparalleled size. Clearly, the stage was set for Powers and his counterparts to revolutionize the advertising industry.

THE MEN, THE MEDIA,
AND THE MESSAGE, 1865–1900

But what does an advertising man do? He induces human beings
to want things they don't want. Now, I will be obliged if you will
tell me by what links of logic anybody can be convinced that your
activity—the creation of want where want does not exist—is a useful
one. . . . Doesn't it seem, rather, the worst sort of mischief, deserving
to be starved into extinction?

—Michael Wilde's oration
in Herman Wouk's *Aurora Dawn;*
Or The True Story of Andrew Reale, 110

Even before the Civil War, magazine and newspaper publishing was a
booming business. Frank L. Mott estimated that, excluding newspapers,
over 600 periodicals appeared on a more or less regular basis immediately
prior to the Panic of 1857. With newspapers included, the total publications
probably exceeded 4,000. The Panic and the outbreak of hostilities took
its toll on these journals, and the Census of 1860 indicated a loss of
more than a hundred periodicals during the three years. The high failure
rate for magazines is not surprising; it was true of business ventures in
general, and even in the best of times many of the periodicals enjoyed
only marginal financial security. Mott estimated that as many as 2,500
different magazines had been published in the decade of the 1850s, with
an average life-span of less than four years and some making only a single
appearance. The Eighth Census, in 1860, placed the average circulation
for quarterlies at 3,700; monthlies at 12,000; and weeklies, including
newspapers, at 2,400. Nevertheless, Mott concluded that the trend, both
in the number of magazines and in circulation, "was up." Even during
the Civil War, magazine readership continued to increase, and at least a
dozen periodicals reached or exceeded a circulation of 100,000 during the
war years.[1]

Figure 2.1
Estimates of Advertising Volume, 1880–1920

Year	(1) Census of Manufacturing Publications' Ad Receipts (Millions)	(2) Pope's Advertising Estimate (Millions)	(3) GNP (Billions)	Column 2 or per cent of GNP
1880	39.1	104	11.2[a]	0.9%
1890	71.2	190	13.1	1.5
1900	95.9	256	18.7	1.4
1904	145.5	388	22.9	1.7
1909	202.5	540	32.2	1.7
1914	255.6	682	36.4	1.9
1919	528.3	1409	78.9	1.8

[a]1879–1888 decade average.

Source: Adapted from *The Making of Modern Advertising*, by Daniel Pope, pp. 23, 26. Copyright © 1983 by Basic Books, Inc. Reprinted by permission of Basic Books, Inc., Publishers, New York. I have accepted Pope's revised and more modest estimate of advertising's place in distribution.

Mott's figures correspond closely with other experts in the field. Frank Presbrey, for example, divided the 3,000 publications enumerated in 1850 into 2,300 weekly newspapers, 200 daily papers, and 500 literary, religious, and agricultural and scientific periodicals. New York alone boasted 15 daily papers, Boston 12, Philadelphia and New Orleans 10, and Baltimore, Chicago, Pittsburgh, Buffalo, and several other large cities had 2 or more. The estimated combined circulation of the dailies exceeded a million copies a day.[2] The increase in newspaper and magazine circulation reflected the growing population, an increasingly literate public, and the rapid economic development of the United States. The increasing revenue available from advertising undoubtedly fueled the growth in media (see Figure 2.1). An 1848 estimate placed the number of newspaper ads of the previous year at approximately 11 million; 50 years later the number was estimated to exceed 350 million a year. This occurred in spite of the fact that in the intervening years magazines had become major rivals to newspapers for national advertising dollars.[3]

George P. Rowell, a pioneering advertising agent who entered the business by selling potential advertisers space in newspapers, suggested to his clients that the magazines then in circulation were not worth consideration in planning an advertising campaign. However, Rowell hardly qualified as a disinterested expert. In truth, even ante-bellum periodicals often carried advertisements. The nation's two most respected business journals, *Hunts' Merchants Magazine* and *DeBow's Review*, averaged more than ten pages of ads per issue even before the war. Respected agricultural journals, such as the *Southern Planter*, the *American Farmer*, and the *Country Gentleman*, included advertising "sheets" in their publication. Most of the numerous religious periodicals, such as the *Christian Parlor* and the *National Baptist* magazines, counted on the revenue from discreet advertising to help sustain their publication.

Even as late as 1870, more than 400 journals could be classified as being in the religious category, with a combined circulation of nearly 5 million.[4] So popular were such religious magazines as *Episcopalian, Lutheran Observer, Presbyterian, Methodist Home Journal*, and *Christian Recorder* that as early as 1867 the New York advertising agency of Carlton and Smith specialized in that media. The preaching of Henry Ward Beecher and Phillips Brooks, the evangelical movement in the late nineteenth century, the controversy between fundamentalism and the Social Gospel movement, and the national publicity accompanying the arguments over Darwin's *On the Origin of Species* stimulated the demand for religious publications. As the circulation of religious journals increased, Carlton and Smith found a ready market for the space they controlled in these journals.[5] In particular, patent medicine proprietors found the religious media attractive, and Presbrey went so far as to suggest that some of the journals owed their continued existence to the desire of patent medicine manufacturers to spread their "message of good cheer" among the religious folks. He noted with some humor that "temperate readers of the religious weeklies, who abhorred the saloon and its wares, may not have been aware of the high alcoholic content of bitters." He added, "goodly numbers found in the bitters something that their 'stomach trouble' required with regularity. . . . In the country drug store it was not unusual for the purchaser of bitters to open the bottle and take a deep draft at the counter."[6] A few of the religious papers did censor advertising, and an even fewer refused much of the offered patent medicine advertisement; most, however, sought and accepted it as a major source of income.

In analyzing advertising in a typical issue of a leading religious journal, a reader would have noted ads for Lyon's Tooth Powder, Babbitt's Soap, Tiffany & Co., Gorham Manufacturing Company, Great American Tea Company, Elgin Watches, and a variety of ads for musical instruments, mowing machines, books, magazines, department stores, schools, bankers and brokers, and more than a dozen insurance companies, which were often the leading advertisers in the religious media.[7] Circulation of religious journals, and probably their influence on manners and style as well, peaked in the decade of the 1870s, as did advertisers' special interest in them as an advertising medium. Within a few years, agencies would no longer issue special lists of religious periodicals, and even in the heyday of the religious magazines, secular newspapers and magazines had a far greater circulation. For example, in 1870 issues of dailies exceeded 2.5 million and the weeklies over 10 million copies.[8]

Like religious periodicals, farm magazines and even the budding business and trade journals and magazines sought to increase their income with advertising revenue. Long-established journals like the *American Farmer* and the *Southern Planter* were joined by an increasing number of specialized and local journals, such as the *American Stock Journal* and the *Prairie Farmer*, and in 1870 the total publication of the ninety-three "agricultural" journals was estimated at over three quarters of a million. In 1874, N. W. Ayer & Son issued a list of fifty-seven popular farm magazines, led by the *American Agriculturalist* with a circulation of over 100,000.[9] As one might suspect, farm implements, tools, seeds, plants, land, and livestock ads were prominent in such journals, along with sewing machines, watches, books, magazines, and the ubiquitous patent medicines. Mail-order houses advertised extensively in agricultural papers, usually using the small column ads to announce the availability of a product and occasionally to solicit agents. For the most part, advertising copy in farm journals throughout the nineteenth century retained a simple and direct appeal, assuming that the demand existed and seeking to increase the share of each advertiser.[10]

Although, as Mott has pointed out, it is difficult to define exactly which magazines were designed specifically for women, certainly the farm journals and religious periodicals all carried items of interest to women readers. Nevertheless, the increasing emphasis on women's issues and home departments in many magazines is clear, as is the growing attention national advertisers paid to directing advertisements to potential women consumers. Certainly, the number of magazines which joined *Peterson's* and *Godey's* as primarily directed to female readers increased.[11] Even antebellum advertisers were much too shrewd to pass up a homogeneous reader group, and Rowell's self-serving advice not to advertise in magazines was continually ignored. Along with fiction, serials, articles on fashion, fancywork, and recipes, women readers found in the advertising sections ads for musical instruments, home furnishings, sewing machines, silverware, watches, and the ever-present patent medicines.

Some of the older and more conservative literary magazines, such as the *North American Review*, the *Southern Literary Messenger*, and even the popular *Youth's Companion*, capitulated to commercialism slowly and reluctantly. But capitulate they did. In the July 1844 issue, the *Southern Literary Messenger*, a distinguished and conservative literary journal that Edgar Allan Poe had edited only seven years earlier, carried a single dignified and clearly labeled "advertisement" for "Lieut. Maury's Paper on the Gulf Stream and currents of the Sea."[12] In 1857, *Youth's Companion*, which

had been founded thirty years earlier and would include among its authors
Harriet Beecher Stowe, John Denison Champlin, Hamlin Garland, Lyman
Abbott, Francis Parkman, and Woodrow Wilson, accepted advertising. The
fall from grace hardly hurt *Youth's Companion*'s popularity. Circulation,
which had been about 5,000 when the editors first accepted advertisement,
exceeded 50,000 in 1868. Before the end of the nineteenth century, circulation of the magazine would exceed a half million.[13]

Not all the old literary journals, however, abandoned their position
quickly or easily. *Vanity Fair*, in poking fun at advertising in the New
York *Herald*, "waxed satirical over the new art, as," to quote Mott, "was
its wont."

A model advertisement-writer in the *Herald* calls the Sewing machine "a swift-fin-
gered sister of love and charity." Let us hereafter speak of the Cooking-Range as the
warm-hearted minister to appetite and contentment, of the Daguerrotype-apparatus
as the bright-faced reflector of beauty and worth; and among other ingenious
contrivances, of the model advertisement-writer as the soft-headed distributor of
mellifluous soap.[14]

Even the old and conservative *North American Review* converted and
by September 1893 carried over forty pages of advertisements. Indeed, the
venerable old *Review* quartered its back cover for Royal Baking Powder
("Absolutely Pure"); W. & J. Sloane ("Axministers, Wiltons, Velvets,
Moquettes, Brussels"); W. Baker & Co. Breakfast Cocoa, which had won a
Gold Medal at Paris in 1878; and Waterbury Watches, whose advertisement
savored of the stud farm and the track ("Well-bred watches *result from noble
ancestry*, early association, discipline, and natural selection").[15]

While a close correlation existed between the dramatic increase in circulation of popular magazines and the rise of national advertising, that
correlation should not be construed as causative. The rapid growth of
population, which even by modern standards was very literate, with a
rising per capita income created an expanding demand for popular low-cost
magazines. The development of faster and lower-cost printing, reduced
paper prices, and favorable postage rates all combined with the revenue
available from advertising to encourage a wider and larger distribution of
low-cost popular newspapers, magazines, and journals.

Harper's Magazine, *Atlantic Monthly*, and *Scribner's Monthly* (later the
Century), certainly three of the more prestigious literary monthlies, provide
excellent examples of the transformation that occurred in journals and
advertising aimed at upper-class and aspiring middle-class consumers. All
three were edited and addressed to educated readers who could easily afford
the journals and the products advertised in them. All three also enjoyed
respectable circulations for the period. For example, in 1870, *Harper's*
claimed 130,000 subscribers.[16] *Harper's*, which had been founded in 1850,

refused advertising until the July 1864 issue. *Atlantic*, on the other hand, accepted its first ads in 1860, only three years after it started publication, and was first among the truly excellent literary magazines to use advertising income to bid aggressively for prominent authors' work.[17] *Scribner's*, which started publishing in 1870, accepted, indeed solicited, advertising from the beginning. Roswell Smith, one of the owners and the business manager, made the following announcement to advertisers in a very early issue:

The Publishers of *Scribner's Monthly* will insert in each number of the magazine certain pages devoted to advertisements of a character likely to interest magazine readers. . . . They will add to the ability of the publishers to render their magazine readable and attractive. . . . Our edition will be very large and it will have a national circulation. It is now well understood that a first-class popular magazine furnishes to all men who seek a national market the very best medium for advertising that exists. It is both widely distributed to the prosperous and intelligent classes of society, and carefully read and preserved.[18]

Scribner's solicited advertising more aggressively than its two major rivals, and was quite serious about using the revenue to enhance the literary and artistic quality of its issues. In truth, *Scribner's* was more richly illustrated than the other two and the editor, Dr. J. G. Holland, spent a good deal of money on editorial material. For example, he convinced General Grant to write his memoirs and to allow *Scribner's* to publish them. Holland also commissioned, for a reported $50,000, Nicolay and Hay to write their famous "Life of Lincoln." While perhaps the most prominent, Grant, Nicolay, and Hay were certainly not the most famous or talented writers to grace the pages of these three journals. Prominent among the list of authors and editors publishing in the three magazines were Dickens, Thackeray, Mark Twain, Emerson, Lowell, Longfellow, Whittier, Julia Ward Howe, Oliver Wendell Holmes, and Henry James.

For the most part, the publishers of the literary magazines viewed advertising as a necessary evil, to be tolerated but kept in place. Ads remained confined to a special section usually at the rear of the journal, or otherwise carefully segregated from the literary content. Most editors screened the copy and format of ads to conform to very conservative guidelines of size and style. As the volume of ads increased, however, many individual advertisers worried that their message was being lost among the sea of ads in the advertisement section and hence was failing to attract the desired attention. Faced with continual pressure, national advertisers turned to magazines such as *Godey's*, *Peterson's*, and the *Saturday Evening Post*, whose large pages and absence of restrictions allowed them to experiment with art and copy to achieve the best presentation for their messages. Perhaps because of Roswell Smith's influence and the fact that *Scribner's* solicited, as opposed to accepted, advertising, it also allowed advertisers

greater freedom as to the size and format of their copy. As a result, it
rapidly outdistanced its major rivals, *Harper's* and *Atlantic*, in volume of
advertising.[19]

For manufacturers and merchants seeking to create demand, especially
for new products, for non-essentials, and even for luxury items, *Atlantic*,
Scribner's, and *Harper's* all offered an ideal medium to reach a large
homogeneous group of readers. After a slow and even hesitant start,
Harper's became much more aggressive in the 1880s in courting advertising,
progressing from 6 to 7 pages of 20 to 30 ads in the early 1870s to 113 pages
with 409 ads, of which 250 were illustrated in 1891.[20]

In his analysis of *Harper's* advertisements Sidney Sherman divided the
ads into twenty-nine categories, ranging from agents, architects, art goods,
and silverware, etc., to sporting goods, typewriters, vehicles, and writing
materials. His analysis indicated that the November 1891 issue of *Harper's*
contained ads in every category except hotels and resorts, livestock, and real
estate. However, within the year these gaps would be filled. *Harper's* had,
as one expert put it, "a select and moneyed clientele" which was regularly
offered excursions to California, to Denver, to the Mediterranean, and
to Jamaica. From the same issues, readers could secure the services of a
banker or a broker and purchase bills of exchange or traveler's checks,
as well as buy bird cages, mineral water, or architectural plans simply by
consulting the advertising section. Arnold Constable & Co., Broadway and
19th Street, New York, offered fancy silks, gowns, coats, hats, and bonnets,
as well as parasols and umbrellas in the latest Paris and London styles, as
did R. C. Macy & Co. of the same city. Readers could order wines, liquor,
bonbons, bicycles, and lawn tennis and croquet sets with the same ease
as they could purchase refrigerators, carriages, fine furniture, and musical
instruments.[21]

Still, readers of less prestigious mediums would have recognized a good
many of the advertisements. Pears' Soap, Colgate's Cashmere Bouquet
Perfume, Cherry Blossom Toilet Powder and Soap, Rowland's Odonto
Tooth Powder, and Williams Barber's Soap or Traveler's Shaving Stick
promised to satisfy most of the ordinary toilet needs. Batchelor's Hair
Dye, Ayer's Hair Vigor, Glenn's Sulphur Soap, and Cuticura, on the other
hand, provided relief for any known skin or hair problem. Patent medicines
were exceeded only by books and general household furnishings in volume
of advertising, and the more gullible could find cures for every ailment from
cholera morbus and consumption to a sluggish liver and opium addiction, or
they could purchase a building lot in Florida for fifteen dollars. Royal Baking
Powder still promised to be "absolutely pure," and with the Kodak Camera
"you press the button, . . . we do the rest."[22] The transition in advertising
reflected in *Harper's* in the 1880s involved not only the growing volume
of non-essential or luxury items; even more telling was the shift in the copy
used to sell these new goods.

True Pears' Soap, soapmaker to His Royal Highness the Prince of Wales, was still the purest and the most economical, and Professor H. A. Mott, a government scientist, still testified to Royal Baking Powder as being absolutely pure and the most reliable; the other products in these categories remained the cleanest, the purest, the patented, the certified, the best, the celebrated, useful, dependable, and economical—utilizing the same appeal as in antebellum advertising. However, the luxury items, while still relatively few in number, and the copy, still relatively primitive, nevertheless exhibited a shift in the appeal toward more emphasis on flair, status, fashion, design, elegance, and convenience. Still, modern advertising, designed to create demand and meaningful product differentiation, remained rare. Among the major advertisers only Murphy Varnishes, under the leadership of John Powers, and Eastman Kodak Cameras utilized a modern, simple, and direct copy that Powers made famous.[23]

In spite of the growth in numbers and in circulation of magazines and advertising revenues (see Figure 2.1), the "average citizen was not a magazine reader," as a leading student of magazines noted.[24] Most popular magazines were either cheap weeklies, with poor-quality reporting and either melodramatic or sensationalistic literary material, or magazines like *Harper's*, *Scribner's*, or *Century*, which were priced beyond the average person's income and edited beyond their interest. As one critic pointed out, the reader of these three journals could settle down for an evening, reading on such topics as "Street scenes of India," "The social side of yachting," or "The young Whist player's novitiate," hardly reading material directed to the average citizen.[25] Still, the subscriber could rest assured that the journals were well edited, that they printed the best and most popular authors of the day, and that the illustrations and make-up of the magazines earned them a place on the most discriminating coffee tables in the country. Regardless of the quality of the writing, one could hardly argue that the content was attuned to the major issues of the period. Since the subscribers of these magazines also regularly received several daily newspapers that they could count on for the more immediate local, national, and international news, perhaps they felt no need for the journals to keep them abreast of the times.

Unserved by either end of the scale of magazines was a large and growing audience for a lower-priced popular journal edited for the more general reader. Moreover, the time was ripe for some enterprising publisher to tap this market.

The Postal Act of 1879 granted very favorable mailing rates and privileges to journals and magazines primarily as recognition of their educational value. In 1886, R. Hoe and Company built a rotary press to replace the older and slower flat-bed press then used to print *Century*. The newly developed rotary press was not only faster, but even more important, it was much less expensive to operate and did ten times the work of the old flat-bed press. Four years later, C. B. Cotrell and Sons Company produced a rotary web perfecting press and it was quickly adopted by *Youth's Companion, Harper's, McCall's,* and other magazines.[26] In the same period, the mid-1880s, Frederick Ives developed the modern half-tone process for printing illustrations and photographs. Prior to Ives' invention, attractive illustrations and art work represented one of the larger expenses for publishers. Engravings alone cost *Century* magazine $5,000 a month, and *Godey's* reportedly hired 150 women to tint its illustrations. In 1890, the Hoe rotary art press, built for *Century*, incorporated the Ives' process and the press produced fine half-tone illustrations from curved plates for a fraction of the previous cost. Three years later, Hoe constructed the first multicolored rotary press. To these technical developments, publishers could look to the price of paper, which had been falling, to enable magazines to be published even more cheaply.[27]

The technological advances in printing favored the publisher who was enterprising enough to try for the large circulation that developments in marketing and expansion in transportation had made possible. They enabled him to compete on fairly equal terms with the established publisher with large working capital. . . . Setting copy into type and getting the printing forms ready for printing represented fixed costs, the same regardless of circulation. Presses were efficient enough to turn out attractive magazines at a low unit cost; and the public, accustomed to price reductions on other commodities, was in a mood to welcome price cuts in its reading fare.[28]

In short, the publishers, like many of the manufacturers who sought their pages in which to advertise, enjoyed unit least-cost curves, which now resembled a reclining "L" as opposed to a "U," making it attractive to print larger issues than heretofore—if they could be marketed. Not surprisingly, many publishers turned to large-scale advertising campaigns to increase their circulation.

For the most part, these new magazines originated not as vehicles to disseminate a point of view on current issues or as an outlet for a group of authors. Rather, the publishers seized an opportunity to make money. *Ladies' Home Journal* (1883), *Cosmopolitan* (1886), *Munsey's* (1889), and *McClure's* (1893), while certainly not typical of the new popular magazines, were representative. From the very beginning, they were intended to make money primarily from advertising, and the editorial content deliberately was directed toward the increasingly numerous and prosperous urban middle classes, who, while literate, had been "untouched by, untroubled by, and uninterested in the literary monthlies."[29]

The publishers of these four popular magazines, Cyrus H. K. Curtis, John B. Walker, Frank A. Munsey, and Samuel S. McClure, all launched their respective ventures with the expectation of securing as much profit as possible from advertising. Curtis, after brief careers as a dry goods clerk, newspaper advertising solicitor, and publisher, moved to Philadelphia and with a partner edited and published the *Tribune and Farmer*; the paper enjoyed only indifferent success. However, the women's department, edited by his wife, Louisa Knapp Curtis, proved very popular, and Curtis decided to publish it as a separate monthly supplement. The first issue, which appeared in December 1883 as the *Ladies' Home Journal*, enjoyed immediate popularity. The original issue contained only eight pages of fashion notes, child-care hints, serialized fiction, recipes, and advertising. Curtis split with his former partner over philosophical issues and left the *Tribune and Farmer* to concentrate on promoting the new *Ladies' Home Journal*. In late 1889, Curtis hired Edward W. Bok to take over the editorship of the *Journal*, and traditionally Bok's name has been associated with its huge success. Bok was an excellent editor, but in truth he took over a thriving journal. Under Louisa Curtis's direction, the circulation had already reached nearly half a million, and Curtis, confident of his readership, doubled the price of a year's subscription to the *Journal* from fifty cents to one dollar in the same year that he hired Bok. Louisa Curtis, however, deserved the credit for having already established the editorial policy of offering women readers timely advice on issues of particular concern to them and serious fiction from the best available writers.

Bok built well on the foundation that Louisa Curtis had established, and by the turn of the century circulation exceeded 1 million.[30] He published Kipling, Howells, Arthur Conan Doyle, Sarah Orne Jewett, Kate Douglas Wiggins, Joel Chandler Harris, Eugene Fields, James Whitcomb Riley, and of course Mark Twain. Each issue of the *Journal* carried features and articles of particular interest to middle-class women, offering advice on how to dress, cook, feed their families, decorate their homes, care for their health, and raise their children. Bok sought to bring his readers the best possible fiction, attractive illustrations, practical advice, and real-life stories whenever possible. Little wonder that the *Journal* became known as "the monthly Bible of the American home," a title which Mark Sullivan, in *Our Times*, suggested contained "a measure of allegorical truth."[31] While Bok sought to build reader loyalty by providing the best possible magazine, he well understood the importance of advertising in this process. "The fact must never be forgotten," Bok told his readers in urging them to buy from *Journal* advertisers, "that no magazine published in the United States could give what it is giving to the reader each month if it were not for the revenue which the advertiser brings to the magazine."[32]

Of course, Bok was not lecturing to his publisher. Curtis understood better than most that profits did not come from the sale of magazines, but rather from the advertisers. Early in his career, Curtis asked an audience of manufacturers, "Do you know why we publish the *Ladies' Home Journal*?" He went on to explain, "The editor thinks it is for the benefit of American women. That is an illusion, but a very proper one for him to have. But I will tell you; the real reason, the publisher's reason, is to give you people who manufacture things that American women want and buy a chance to tell them about your products."[33] Curtis's only mistake was that even he underestimated the ability of advertising to create demands, and therefore he failed to charge high enough advertising rates to support the explosive increase in circulation.

Still, Curtis knew that he had found a formula for success. A mass-circulated journal, taking advantage of low unit costs of production, aimed and edited for the growing middle class, proved extremely attractive to advertisers. The purchase of the almost defunct *Saturday Evening Post* in 1897 offered Curtis another chance to prove his formula and exploit the power of advertising. After a year of allowing the *Post* to limp along with its tired editorial style and only about two thousand subscribers, Curtis decided to shift the content to appeal to men readers, as a counterpart to the *Ladies' Home Journal*. Perhaps as important, he decided to create demand for advertising in the *Post*. In 1899, Curtis chose George H. Lorimer, who had experience in business and professional training as a journalist, as editor. He instructed Lorimer to aim his editorial content to capture the public's growing fascination with big business. While circulation of the five-cent *Post* increased from 2,231 in 1897 to 97,000 in 1899, and doubled that during the next year, the revenue, including that from advertising, failed to meet Curtis's expenses. The deficit, paid from the profits realized by the *Ladies' Home Journal*, reached $1.25 million. Through it all, Curtis retained faith in his formula. Advertising revenue, spurred by a large promotional campaign, stood at $159,300 in 1900, but five years later it exceeded a million dollars. In 1917, on the eve of World War I, the *Post's* circulation exceeded 1.8 million and its advertising revenues $16 million.[34] Curtis's large expenditures on advertising in the *Post* paid handsome dividends; he took full advantage of the available economies of scale, and as one author noted, "From slim beginnings, the *Post* waxed fat and conservative."[35]

At the age of seventeen, eight years after he arrived in the United States from Ireland, Samuel S. McClure enrolled in Knox College in Galesburg, Illinois. Lacking the money to remain in college, McClure drifted into journalism. While working for the Century Company, he began reading the back files of the *St. Nicholas* and decided to syndicate some of the old fiction published by that journal, which he was sure only a few had read, and market the stories to weekly magazines which were starved for decent fiction and whose readers had probably never heard of the Century Company's *St. Nicholas*. His syndicated material found a ready market. McClure realized that his early venture succeeded because he aimed his stories at precisely the reading public that the old literary magazines ignored. In 1893, just as the panic of that year hit, he released the first issue of *McClure's Magazine*. At the time, the more established monthly magazines were selling for twenty-five to thirty-five cents, but McClure priced his at fifteen cents. McClure's price reduction fueled immediate competition. John B. Walker promptly dropped the price of *Cosmopolitan* to twelve-and-a-half cents an issue. Immediately upon the heels of McClure's and Walker's price reductions, Frank Munsey announced that he had cut the price of *Munsey's Magazine*, which he had recently converted from a weekly to a monthly magazine, to ten cents an issue and the yearly subscription from three dollars to one dollar.[36] Munsey's move had been born out of desperation; the Panic of 1893 found him with two struggling magazines and deeply in debt. In the September 1893 issue he announced:

There are times when it is well to get down to bed rock—to get away down to the very substratum of things. At ten cents per copy and a dollar a year for subscriptions in advance, *Munsey's* will have reached that point, a point below which no good magazine will ever go, but to which all magazines of large circulation in America must eventually come. The present low price of paper and the perfecting of printing machinery make it possible to sell at a profit a magazine at these prices—as good a magazine as has ever been issued, provided it is not too heavily freighted with advertisements.[37]

Few publishers would ever more heavily freight advertising. The price reductions enhanced the circulation of all of the competing journals. *Mc-Clure's* circulation jumped from less than 10,000 for the first issue to over a quarter of a million in two years. *Cosmopolitan* increased from 16,000 to more than 400,000 in five years, and *Munsey's* went from 40,000 for the first ten-cent issue to more than 500,000 in less than two years. Munsey, McClure, and Curtis demonstrated a very fundamental principle: if demand increased it was possible to increase your business without necessarily hurting your competitors. By the turn of the century, each of the new magazines, *Ladies' Home Journal, McClure's, Munsey's,* and *Cosmopolitan,* enjoyed a circulation that exceeded the combined total of *Harper's, Atlantic,* and *Century,* the three old literary journals. The *Saturday Evening Post* would soon eclipse them all.[38]

Actually, the new popular magazines captured neither the advertising nor the readers of the older journals. The demand for advertising space seemed to increase faster than the supply, and the new magazines were directed at a different class of readers. Frank Munsey argued that during the last decade of the nineteenth century the ten-cent magazines tripled the buying public, from 250,000 to 750,000. For once, the flamboyant Munsey's estimates were conservative; by the turn of the century, over fifty popular magazines could claim more than a hundred thousand regular readers and *Ladies' Home Journal* more than a million.[39]

Not everyone welcomed the new enterprising publishers. Munsey frankly admitted that he was in business to make money, and professional journalists tended to hold him in contempt. Many journalists undoubtedly would have agreed with William Allen White's obituary when White concluded that "Frank Munsey contributed to the journalism of his day the talent of a meat packer, the morals of a money changer and the manners of an undertaker. He and his kind have about succeeded in transforming a once-noble profession into an 8 per cent security. May he rest in trust."[40]

Munsey tied his advertising rates to circulation—charging a dollar a page for each one thousand copies distributed; by 1895 this amounted to more than $500 a page, and *Munsey's Magazine* often carried a hundred pages of ads. Munsey's decision was simply sound business practice. S. S. McClure's failure to do the same demonstrated that when circulation outdistances advertising rates, the number of copies per issue and hence publishing costs to meet the public demand tend to escalate faster than revenue, endangering the entire operation.[41] By the turn of the century, Munsey's innovation had become standard practice.

Munsey knew that to attract a loyal reading public, which his advertisers demanded, he would have to wrap the advertisements in an attractive package. Munsey, McClure, Curtis, indeed most of the publishers of the new popular magazines, provided their readers excellent fare. Wrapped around some twenty-eight pages of advertisements for soap, hams, bacon, bicycles, chewing gum, soft-drinks, tonics, life insurance, patent medicines, typewriters, and scientific suspenders in its July 1894 issue, for example, *McClure's* would offer its readers fiction by Bret Harte and Robert Louis Stevenson, and an article by Ida Tarbell on the municipal laboratory in Paris which she labelled a "Chemical Detective Bureau." The same issue contained a piece on Alphonse Daudet and an excellent photographic section entitled "Human Documents."[42] The better-quality popular magazine attempted to maintain a ratio of two pages of editorial content for each page of advertising. At times, however, the demand for advertising space made it difficult to sustain this standard.

By the turn of the century, advertising in popular magazines often exceeded a hundred pages an issue, and they were helping to make such products as Sapolio, Ivory Soap, Welch's Grape Juice, Knox Gelatin, VanCamp Soup, Hires Root Beer, Lea & Perrin's Sauce, Woodbury's Soap, Johnson's Wax, National Biscuit Company, Hart, Schaffner & Marx, Elgin Watches, Kodak, and a host of other products and brand names household words. *Cosmopolitan*, which numbered among its contributors Mark Twain, Henry James, Arthur Conan Doyle, Rudyard Kipling, H. G. Wells, Booth Tarkington, and Ambrose Bierce, sometimes carried as much advertising as it did editorial material. In an early effort to assure advertisers of the value of their magazine, *Cosmopolitan* inserted a notice at the bottom of each page of advertisements asking readers "when you write please mention the *Cosmopolitan*."[43] In the expanding market for popular low-priced magazines, even the *Literary Digest*, founded in 1890, became successful. As one observer noted, "Never literary and scarcely a digest," the magazine was strictly a scissors and paste production. The editors simply clipped and pasted together from newspapers and magazines items on current issues; "they did not digest, rewrite, or interpret." By the end of World War I the *Literary Digest* enjoyed a circulation of nearly two million.[44]

The last decade of the nineteenth century "was a happy time for magazines." Publishers made fortunes, large masses of heretofore ignored readers purchased ever larger numbers of magazines, and the new journals served "a large and untapped class of advertisers, advertisers as eager for inexpensive space rates as readers were for inexpensive magazines."[45] In March 1910, in a speech to the Sphinx Club in New York, Colonel George Harvey, then president of Harper & Brothers and later Ambassador to Great Britain, summed up the significance of the new popular low-cost magazines:

The alert new periodicals have been called national newspapers, and to this extent the term is warranted: They do deal largely with vital topics of immediate interest, they do take sides, they do aim to guide as well as to interpret public opinion, and their field is the whole country. They are public journals.[46]

In any analysis of the social cost of advertising, the social benefit of the new popular low-cost magazines must also be weighed.

Advertising in the new inexpensive magazines supplemented, not replaced, the advertising in the older literary journals. *Atlantic*, *Century* (which replaced *Scribner's*), and *Harper's* continued to provide an attractive media for many manufacturers. Indeed, at the turn of the century *Harper's* regularly carried over a hundred pages of advertising, containing about three hundred ads, half of which were illustrated. In contrast to the new popular magazines, *Harper's Bazar* (1867), *Vanity Fair* (1868), and *Vogue* (1892) attracted advertising for gowns, cosmetics, lingerie, jewelry, yarns, patterns for dresses and gowns, fashionable women's ready-wear clothing, fabrics, and household items such as carpets, silverware, and crystal, as well as ads for fashionable resorts, spas, and travel.[47] However, for the majority of advertisers, for the producers of consumer goods hoping to enjoy reduced costs from economies of scale, for the businessmen hoping to reach a growing middle class, for the manufacturer seeking a national market, the new popular magazines provided a much more appropriate media for their messages.

In 1900, the more than 3,500 magazines published in the United States enjoyed a circulation of 65 million copies per issue, to be distributed to a population of approximately 78 million. By every conceivable standard publishing and advertising had become a major industry. Receipts from newspaper and magazine advertisements leaped from less than $40 million in 1880 to nearly $100 million in 1900. Daniel Pope has estimated that the total expenditures on advertising exceeded $256 million in 1900, up from little over $100 million twenty years earlier.[48] More important, advertising was growing at a faster pace than the economy as a whole (see Figure 2.1).

As advertising became a major industry and the role of the publisher shifted, so did the functions performed by the nation's advertising agencies. The day was gone when the publisher was most often a journalist, concerned about the editorial content for his readers. He became a producer; his readers became consumers of the goods and services. Publishers provided a media for their advertisers' message, to a group of homogeneous potential customers, and hence directed the editorial content to ensure homogeneous readers. For the new popular magazines the group sought was the newly affluent middle class. As publishers sought to enjoy the economies of scale of increased production, magazine publishing became large enterprise and joined the entire system of marketing and distribution. Publishers, enjoying wider and wider markets for their magazines, were able to specialize and thereby offer advertisers access to increasingly homogeneous groups of readers. Within the publishing business other firms specializing in specific activities developed.

In 1900 there were over 13,000 individual news dealers, booksellers, and stationers in the United States and Canada who sold newspapers, magazines, and periodicals. As early as 1864, the American News Company in New York offered publishers an inexpensive means to distribute their publications to these retail outlets. By 1900, the American News Company had become a national service which purchased entire editions other than those distributed to regular subscribers, sorted them, and put in a single package the items destined for a single dealer. The distribution service provided by the News Company yielded a yearly business of about $15 million. The essential monopoly of distribution services by the American News Company caused it on occasion to become a bit arrogant. When Frank Munsey announced a ten-cent price for his magazine, the News Company, realizing that ten-cent magazines threatened their profit margin, declined Munsey's offer to handle the magazine at six-and-a-half cents and told Munsey they would only take his publication at four-and-a-half cents, as a favor. The response was short and victorious; Munsey demonstrated the power of advertising to force a virtual monopoly to terms. He wrote letters to retail dealers by the thousands, and he took out ads for his magazines in thousands of newspapers and magazines. Dealers, like all merchants, responded when customers kept asking for *Munsey's* ten-cent magazine. The American News Company quickly found itself forced to come to terms for Munsey's second issue.[49]

Munsey's advertising pricing policy, a dollar a page per thousand copies in circulation, was rapidly emulated. Not surprisingly advertisers, paying by the size of the circulation, became unwilling to take the publisher's unverified figures or the estimate of an advertising agency which made its money by selling space. Both parties had vested interest in inflating the circulation. For the most part, publishers had long regarded circulation as a trade secret, and in 1899 when the Association of American Advertisers first sought to verify circulations, they met with suspicion and refusal. Curtis, when asked to join the effort, supposedly replied, "No one doubts the circulation statements of my company."[50] Faced with hostility on the part of publishers, indifference on the part of agencies, and lack of support on the part of many advertisers, the early efforts to verify circulation figures proved inadequate. In 1913, both the Association of National Advertisers and the Association of American Advertisers launched separate circulation audit groups. A year later, the two groups merged and became the Audit Bureau of Circulations, which provided some service to advertisers.[51]

To provide advertisers and their agencies evidence that the ads they paid for had indeed appeared, clipping bureaus expanded their services to include ads. By 1900, there were at least twenty such bureaus clipping thousands of items on a daily basis. For direct-mail advertisers, "letter brokers" and owners of address lists provided addresses at so much per thousand. The advertiser could obtain lists by location, occupation, or social class. Most of the addresses came from publishers. Even further categorization was possible if the advertiser desired. Addressing companies would obtain the lists, address the envelopes, fold and enclose the materials, and mail the materials for set fees per thousand.[52]

In the heyday of specialized journals and magazines, it was only natural for advertisers, agencies, and copywriters to have a journal devoted to their interests. Indeed, several would appear before the turn of the century. *Printers' Ink*, the oldest, the most prestigious, and the largest in circulation, was founded in New York in 1888. By 1900, it enjoyed a circulation of about 20,000 per weekly issue. The typical issue carried interviews with advertisers, news about advertising, articles written by "experts" on the subject, editorials, and usually fifteen to twenty-five pages of newspaper, magazine, and agency advertisements. Before the turn of the century, *Printers' Ink*, referring to them as "*Printers' Ink* babies," noted that more than a dozen additional journals devoted to some phase of advertising had started business. Perhaps the best evidence of the growth and acceptance of advertising came when *Printers' Ink* carried announcements for two newly founded educational institutions specializing in advertising.[53]

One of the most obvious indications of the significance of advertising was the shift in the function of advertising agencies and the growing number of advertising professionals. Early advertising agents were essentially space brokers, either purchasing space from newspapers and magazines at a discount and then selling it to potential advertisers, or placing advertisements and collecting a commission from the publishers. For most early manufacturers with limited advertising budgets and little or no experience, advertising agencies performed the vital function of bringing together buyers and sellers of media space. So entrenched was the system that in 1898 when Frank Munsey denounced the practice, saying that the commissions paid to agents were nothing more than "a bribe to influence the advertisers' trusted agent to place advertising with the publisher," Munsey was unable to make good his threat to refuse to pay commissions.[54] Most medium-sized cities had at least one advertising agency, and the number tended to multiply as the cities grew larger. In New York, of course, they were the most numerous. Clustered on Park Row in lower Manhattan, usually with fewer than a half-dozen employees, the New York agents, according to one estimate, placed nine-tenths of the national advertising.

The early agencies took no responsibility for preparing copy or planning a campaign; with very few exceptions, manufacturers and merchants wrote their own advertising copy, and the agents' only function was to place it in media largely selected by the advertiser. As late as 1872, George Rowell would argue that "advertisers should write their own advertisements. The man who cannot do this is not fit to advertise."[55] Less than a quarter of a century later, *Printers' Ink* would declare that, "Generally neither the merchants nor the solicitor [for newspapers and magazines] is able to make a good advertisement."[56] As clients devoted more resources to advertising, they demanded more professional services and more demonstrated results from their investments. Well before the turn of the century, the most progressive and successful agencies developed staffs to assist clients with copy, illustration, design and lay-out, and media campaigns. A few very progressive agencies, such as N. W. Ayer & Son, had even experimented with marketing research. By the second decade of the twentieth century, advertising agencies would insist that their service was "merchandising," which, as one agency explained, included everything "involved in getting a commodity from the factory to the consumer."[57]

In 1880, when John Wanamaker hired John Powers to handle his advertising copy, he established a precedent. Powers, supposedly the first person in the United States to make a living from writing advertising, developed a unique style. The Powers ads featured detailed descriptions of the product, its uses, and its peculiar advantages. Although the "Powers style" seemed ideally tailored to department-store advertising and was indeed quickly imitated by more than fifty large department stores, it also proved very effective in introducing new consumer goods. His advertisements for Murphy Varnishes, which employed his famous plain-spoken descriptions, proved unusually successful in selling paints and varnishing products not easily differentiated in consumers' minds. Powers may have been the first professional copywriter, but he did not remain so for long. Even a few serious writers like Bret Harte, Hart Crane, Stephen Vincent Benet, John P. Marquand, and F. Scott Fitzgerald tried their hands at writing copy. Perhaps F. Scott Fitzgerald's memorable slogan for an Iowa laundry, "We keep you clean in Muscatine," explains best why few creative writers stayed long at the task. Clearly this was work better suited for other hands. Enoch Morgan's Sons hired the flamboyant Artemus Ward to sell Sapolio Cleanser; Claude Hopkins praised Bissell Carpet Sweepers; and other well-known advertising copywriters like Charles A. Bates, John E. Kennedy, and Manly Gillam made excellent livings writing copy for beer, hair restoratives, and patent medicines.[58] In 1900, Sherman noted that while the majority of the more than 2,500 national advertisers using magazines and periodicals prepared their own advertisements, during the previous fifteen years the tendency had been to employ professional copywriters and that literally hundreds of men and women earned very good livings at this fast-growing profession.[59]

Not all copywriters employed Powers' style; some, indeed a growing number of copywriters and advertisers, would resort to rhymes, jingles, and slogans. Powers' influence was quickly tempered by that of Walter Dill Scott, a Northwestern University psychologist who argued that since "man is a creature that rarely reasons at all," advertising copy should appeal to emotions—not to reason. Scott's basic position would dominate advertising from the turn of the century to the depression in the 1930s. Unfortunately, often forgotten by advertising agents was Scott's insistence that emotion and attracting attention was not enough. Good advertising, Scott preached, must be intimately connected to the product. The ad should arouse in the reader the same sensation as the product it advertised. Most important, Scott insisted that advertising which failed to create wants and a desire to buy was simply failing to do its job.[60] Whether copywriters and advertisers utilized Powers', Scott's, a combination of the two, or an altogether different appeal in their ads, they would agree with the turn of the century remarks by a Pears' Soap spokesman that "Any fool can make soap. It takes a clever man to sell it."[61]

The National Biscuit Company advertisement that appeared in the June 1901 issue of *McClure's Magazine* illustrated how far the art of advertising had progressed in the period between the Civil War and the turn of the century. The ad, a full-page inset of a beautifully reproduced lithograph in full color, showed on one side a blonde girl in a Dutch costume holding in "her chubby hands" a package of Uneeda Biscuits with the phrase "Do You Know You Needa Biscuit" lettered across the bottom of her skirt. The other side featured Ramona and Athena Sugar Wafers tumbling out of a cookie jar. This, one writer noted, was the pièce de résistance of advertising of the period.[62]

National magazine advertising made the products and the companies that advertised in the pages of widely circulated magazines household names. They convinced local consumers to purchase products manufactured by distant producers; they introduced new companies and new products; they created wants and expanded markets; they allowed manufacturers to take advantage of economies of scale and often allowed the producer to pass some of these on to consumers as lower unit prices; and in the end they would help to induce the American people to consume. By the beginning of the twentieth century the media, the means, and the technology were in place and were in the process of transforming American values from those traditionally equated with a rural, agrarian, production-oriented society to those associated with an urban, industrial, consumption-oriented society.

3

Any Fool Can Make Soap

I'll tell you a secret about the soap business, Mr. Norman. There's no damn difference between soaps. Except for perfume and color, soap is soap. Oh, maybe we got a few manufacturing tricks, but the public don't give a damn about that. But the difference you see is in the selling and advertising. We sell soap twice as fast as our nearest competitor because we outsell and out-advertise 'em.
—Evan Llewelyn Evans to Victor Norman in
Frederic Wakeman's *The Hucksters* (New York, 1946), 23

Before the last decades of the nineteenth century, the few advertisers who sought to create demand had, for the most part, directed their efforts toward middle-class consumers. Given the lack of disposable income among most of the urban working class, this represented simply a wise business decision. Why advertise luxury items to people with hardly sufficient income to purchase the necessities? However, as previously noted, during the last quarter of the nineteenth century, per capita income increased by about 50 per cent and real per capita income by approximately 100 per cent. Working-class families enjoyed at least some modest discretionary income, and middle-class status seemed within the grasp of many Americans (see Figure 1.9). Many of the new consumer industries such as soap and toilet goods, prepared foods, tobacco, and even popular magazines, enjoyed decreasing cost and low enough unit prices to be well within the means of working-class consumers. In these industries, national markets and mass consumption became obtainable goals. Advertising professionals, especially copy writers, realized that advertisements, regardless of the social status of prospective consumers, needed to appeal to the deep-seated desire of Americans for middle-class status. Little wonder that both these industries and advertising flourished.

In his analysis of the development of national advertising, Frank Presbrey noted that advertising designed to create acceptance and demand for new products was essentially a phenomenon of the last decade of the nineteenth century. Prior to then, while a significant number of American manufacturing firms already had secured surprisingly large markets for their products, most of these concerns continued to direct their advertising copy to soliciting agents, or to securing direct-mail orders, or to convincing retail dealers to stock and sell their products. Altogether, Presbrey listed only some seventy-four firms that during the decade of the 1880s advertised on a "more or less" regular basis in national media. Another four hundred or so took ads in magazines and newspapers with national circulation on what he called an "All-right-I'll-take-an-ad" response to solicitation as opposed to an organized and planned advertising campaign.[1]

Only four firms employed advertising in what Presbrey considered an organized and systematic fashion designed to create demand—Royal Baking Powder, Sapolio, Pears' Soap, and Ivory Soap. Other firms, such as Baker's Cocoa, Castoria, Pearline Washing Compound, Remington Typewriters, Douglas Shoes, Sozodont Dentrifrice, Garland Stoves, Williams' Shaving Stick, Kirk's Soap, Colgate's Perfume, and Esterbrook and Spencerian Steel Pen companies, advertised on a regular basis.[2] The distinction between the big four—Royal Baking Powder, Sapolio, Pears' Soap, and Ivory Soap—and other advertisers lay not so much in the frequency of advertising as in a planned and systematic effort to increase the demand for the total product as well as to secure as large a share of the market as possible.

A rough breakdown of the seventy-four firms that advertised on a more or less regular basis indicated that the category of soaps and toilet articles led the field with fourteen, followed by food products with ten, and home furnishings, musical instruments, department stores, ready-made clothing, railroads, ink pens, patent medicines, and bicycles trailed behind with seven, six, five, four, four, four, and three, respectively.[3] Although Presbrey included less than five proprietary or patent medicines among the seventy-four firms that advertised with "more or less regularity," this was a clear oversight on his part. Perhaps this neglect of patent medicine advertising reflected more Presbrey's disapprobation of the product rather than the reality of its prominence among nineteenth-century advertising. Any fair analysis of national magazine and newspaper advertising in the period would have to rank patent medicines as the most numerous. Even the more prestigious magazines, which were edited to appeal to upper-class readers, carried more patent medicine ads than for any other category. For twenty-five years after 1864, when they started accepting advertising, *Harper's*, for example, carried more ads for proprietary medicine than in any other category. Only in 1889 did educational and home furnishing advertisements finally surpass patent medicine ads.

Nevertheless, the announcement of the *Ladies' Home Journal* in 1892 that it would no longer accept medical advertising signalled the beginning

Figure 3.1
Advertising in Newspapers and Periodicals, 1880–1920

Year	(1) Total Revenue from Advertising (1000)	(2) Total Revenue (1000)	(3) Advertising Percentage of Total (1)/(2)	Percent Increase of (1) by Decade
1880	$ 39,136	$ 89,009	43.9%	----
1890	71,243	143,586	49.6%	82%
1900	95,861	175,789	54.5%	34%
1910	202,533	337,596	59.9%	111%
1914	255,632	419,209	60.9%	26%
1920	528,299	806,305	65.5%	260%

Source: U.S. Department of Commerce, Bureau of the Census, *Twelfth Census of the United States, 1900. Volume IX, Manufacturers* (Washington, D.C., 1902), 1056; and U.S. Department of Commerce, Bureau of the Census, *Abstract of the Fourteenth Census of the United States, 1920* (Washington, D.C., 1923), 1105.

of the decline in patent medicine advertising. It was, however, a long time in declining. Commendable as Curtis' action may have been, he took it with little fear of losing revenue, knowing full well that other aspiring entrepreneurs were clamoring for space in his magazines to create markets for their products. Regardless of Curtis' motives, the fact remained that the *Ladies' Home Journal* touched off the fight against the excesses and abuses of the patent medicine industry. Not only did Curtis refuse patent medicine advertising, the *Journal* and then *Collier's Weekly* published a series of articles exposing the frauds in that industry.

Concern that aroused public opinion might harm the entire advertising business led the more reputable advertising agencies to curtail their business with patent medicine firms. In the 1890s N. W. Ayer & Son, for example, dropped the accounts of both "Paine's Celery Compound" and "Dr. Williams' Pink Pills for Pale People" because of "outrageous claims" made by the vendors. While Ayer continued to have accounts with some medicine vendors, Ralph Hower later claimed that after 1905, the agency no longer accepted copy which contained extravagant claims like "Rapid recovery follows relief by Dr. Davis' Compound Syrup Wild Cherry and Tar in all cases of Consumption, Coughs, Asthma, Influenza, Bronchitis, Croup, Whooping Cough, Palpitation of the Heart."[4] Like Curtis, Ayer could slowly phase out his agency's dependency on patent medicine advertising, confident of even more profitable clients.

In 1877-78, patent medicines topped the list of Ayer's clients and approximately two-thirds of his income came from the combination of patent medicines (21.6%); printed matter, books, tracts, cards, newspapers, and periodicals (20.8%); jewelry and silverware (8.6%); dry goods and clothing (7.5%); and seeds and nursery stock (6.7%). By 1900-1901, patent medicines had dropped to fifth (8.39%) behind foods (17.69%), fuel and lubricants (10.14%), education (8.95%), and printed matter (8.50%), and was followed closely by both dry goods (7.54%) and tobacco (7.15%). In the same period, the agency's total expenditures for advertising space had increased nearly 1,000 per cent from $317,148 to $3,366,803. Thirty years later, about the same percentage increase (to $38,068,734) in total advertising placed automobiles, tires, and accessories at the head of the list, followed by tobacco, food and drinks, and drugs and toilet goods to make up two-thirds of the agency's business.[5] The experience of N. W. Ayer & Son, if not typical, was representative of the experience of other well-known advertising agencies. Coincidental with the attacks on patent medicines by newspapers and magazines, prior to the Pure Food and Drug Act and long before the truth-in-advertising movement during the Progressive period, patent medicines had lost their preeminent position within the advertising industry.[6]

It was not that patent medicine promoters ceased advertising; far from that. A tabulation by *Press and Printer* in 1898 of general advertisers using magazines and general weeklies indicated that one-sixth of the 2,583 advertisers were makers of proprietary medicines—almost double the number in any other classification.[7] Nevertheless, by the end of the century, patent medicine proprietors had fallen into disrepute and the producers of other classes of consumer goods were clamoring for advertising space in popular magazines to establish markets for their products. To the four large advertisers who utilized planned campaigns in the 1880s to increase demand—Royal Baking Powder, Sapolio, Ivory Soap, and Pears' Soap—Presbrey added Eastman Kodak, Sears, Roebuck & Co., Quaker Oats, Shredded Wheat, Postum Cereal, H. L. Heinz, Gold Dust, and National Biscuit Company in the 1890s.

Perhaps the most significant trend discernible during the last two decades of the nineteenth century was not the raw growth of advertising, as impressive as it was; rather, it was the utilization of advertising to introduce new products, to homogenize tastes, and to create demand. The last decade also witnessed the growth of national, as opposed to regional, advertising campaigns. By the turn of the century, advertising had assumed its modern function and patterns. Presbrey noted that a number of firms, which prior to the last decade of the century had advertised only regionally or "only in states near the plant," had by the end of the century joined the ranks of national advertisers. In addition, Presbrey's list of "more or less" regular advertisers had grown from 74 to over 150. The most notable change in the composition of the list was the large increase in firms advertising soaps and toilet articles, prepared foods (including beer and whiskey), ready-made clothing, and a surprising number (133) of bicycles.[8]

Writing in the latter part of the nineteenth century, Samuel Colgate noted that the rapid growth of the soap industry was a very recent phenomenon. Indeed, the 1890 census indicated a rather remarkable recent growth in the soap industry. During the previous ten years, while the number of establishments manufacturing soap had declined slightly, the number of employees nearly doubled and their wages more than doubled. Since the Civil War, soap production had been increasing, but until the decade of the 1890s the rate of increase was actually less than the rate of increase in population. Throughout the period, the United States had been a large net exporter of soap. The explanation for this was not just that we were a dirty people, which prior to the last quarter of the nineteenth century, we may indeed have been, but that also a great deal of soap was produced and consumed in the household. The 1880 census reported $26.5 million spent in soap production, up only $4 million from the previous census. In 1899 the value of the products reported by the industry nearly doubled and exceeded $43.6 million, and by 1909 more than doubled again, jumping to nearly $115 million.[9]

In spite of mechanization of the soap-making process, which as Colgate noted had greatly reduced labor costs and resulted in increased efficiency in the utilization of raw materials, the demand kept pace with the supply.[10] Advertising played a fundamental role in creating that demand. It tapped a deep-seated desire on the part of people to be accepted, and more than that to be accepted into middle- and upper-class America.

Personal cleanliness was an absolute essential requirement for acceptance. . . . Messages from a hundred sources left no doubt that a dirty face and a smelly body would never pass. Together, the admonitions and the scorn of the clean for the unclean induced all who could muster soap and water to adopt cleanliness rituals after the middle of the nineteenth century. . . . In the expanding world of middle-class respectability, people cleansed themselves to be assured of simple dignity and respect.[11]

Shrewd advertising campaigns made good use of the "cleanliness movement" in progress since the middle of the nineteenth century. It was a situation heaven-sent for soap and toilet article manufacturers and their advertising agents.

To be sure, soaps had long been advertised in the United States. The style used by Benjamin Franklin in 1729, when his *Pennsylvania Gazette* carried a small notice among the other column ads for "choice hard soap, very reasonable," changed little in the next 150 years.[12] Potential consumers seeking information regarding the availability of soap, either for laundry, bath, or general purpose use, could have found small column advertisements for washing compounds, formulas for making their own compounds, and soaps of various descriptions in local newspapers, magazines, and periodicals well before the major manufacturers launched their national campaigns. For example, readers of the May 16, 1868, *Harpers' Weekly* could have found, tucked away between F. Blume's ad for sheet music and George Woodward's ad for complete architectural plans for churches and country homes, an inch and a quarter single-column advertisement urging readers to "TRY" B.T. Babbitt's Toilet Soaps. Prospective customers were assured that Babbitt's soap "Cured Chapped Hands and in cleansing and healing the Flesh excels all other soaps."[13] Ten years later, Babbitt's notice had grown to a double-column six-inch illustrated advertisement which admonished readers that "cleanliness is the scale of civilization."[14] As late as 1888, John H. Woodbury advertised his practice as a dermatologist and his "Woodbury's Facial Soap" in a one-inch single-column ad in *Ladies' Home Journal*, featuring Woodbury's famous neckless head as an illustration. Four years later, while the ad had grown to eight inches double columned, the neckless head and the appeal remained the same. What few skin problems Woodbury's soap could not handle, the Doctor himself promised to cure.

Ivory Soap and Pears' Soap, which Presbrey listed as among the first companies to launch systematic advertising campaigns to achieve a national market for their products, used very different appeals in their ads. For some years, Procter & Gamble had sold a mild vegetable-oil soap primarily as an excellent laundry product, which they referred to simply as "White Soap." During the production of a batch of white soap in 1875, air bubbles formed in the vegetable oil. All of the soap in that particular batch floated and customers began to ask for more of the soap that floats. Four years later, seeking a distinctive name to launch an advertising campaign, Harley Procter renamed the product Ivory Soap, supposedly after hearing the Forty-fifth Psalm in church: "All thy garments smell of myrrh and aloes and cassia out of the ivory palaces whereby they have made thee glad." In 1880, Procter & Gamble took the leadership in national magazine advertising with a budget of less than $12,000. While this seems a very small sum, the published rate for *Harper's Monthly*, one of the most prestigious and expensive media open to advertisers, was only $75 for an inside quarter page and double that for the same space on the outside page. *Harper's Weekly* charged slightly less. Presbrey noted that with a modest, but ever increasing, advertising budget and a policy of regularly scheduled ads in the standard monthlies, in ten years Ivory built a market for 30 million cakes a year.[15]

Reprinted from *Harper's Weekly*, February 16, 1878.

Reprinted from *Harper's Weekly*, February 23, 1878.

In 1897, *Printers' Ink* claimed that "Ivory Soap has the prettiest advertisements," and Presbrey credited Ivory with leadership in the entire advertising field in the "formative days." Ivory's ads utilized Powers' style—simple, straightforward copy with a consistent theme. Early Ivory ads, in simple, direct language, described Ivory as being "especially adapted for washing laces, infant clothes, silk hose . . . and all articles of fine texture and delicate color" and appealed to the experienced homemakers to realize that such delicate items required a very mild soap and one free from harsh grit. The ads went on to note that Ivory was "the finest White Castile soap," perfect for bath, toilet, and even the nursery.[16] Whether a full page, half page, or even less and regardless of how they were illustrated, each Ivory ad contained, as Presbrey noted, "an idea" and always the two slogans "99 and 44/100 per cent pure" and "it floats."

All soap advertisements took great pains to seek customer identification by the use of brand names. Regardless of the make-up of the ad, Ivory's basic theme remained the same: the ad sought to identify "Ivory" with "99 and 44/100 per cent pure" and "it floats." In 1902, for example, a beautifully illustrated advertisement placed in a number of national magazines featured a lovely young lady in an obviously middle-class setting, washing her face, with the caption "Imagine washing a peach with colored and perfumed soap! Next to pure water, Ivory Soap is the purest and most innocent thing for a child's skin." At the bottom of the ad was the ever-present reminder that Ivory was 99 and 44/100 per cent pure and it floats.[17]

Old habits died hard, and well into the twentieth century both Ivory and its major competitor, Lever Brothers' Pears' Soap, utilized advertising that cautioned customers to beware of dangerous substitutes. A Pears' advertisement warned that "there are soaps offered as substitutes for Pears' which are dangerous,—so be sure you get Pears'." Ivory was even more explicit. "There are 100 Imitations," a 1906 ad declared, and "A dishonest grocer will give you one of these and say: 'This is Ivory!' or 'This is just as good!'. . . do not accept it unless it is stamped Ivory."[18]

Soap manufacturers utilized warnings and exhortations in an effort to ensure that customers requested and purchased the proper brand. Repeated requests by customers was the surest way to convince retail grocers to stock the product. Moreover, not only did advertisers stress the unique qualities of their products (particularly when other brands were in reality very close substitutes), but they also tried to reflect on the integrity and quality of establishments that failed to stock their particular brand. Pearline Soap, for example, printed a warning in their ads: "CAUTION: Peddlers and some unscrupulous grocers are offering imitations which they claim to be Pearline or 'the same as Pearline.' IT'S FALSE—they are not, and besides [they] are dangerous. Pearline is never peddled, but sold by all good grocers."[19]

Brand names and qualities associated by consumers with brand names imparted a distinction, however artificial it may have been, among essentially

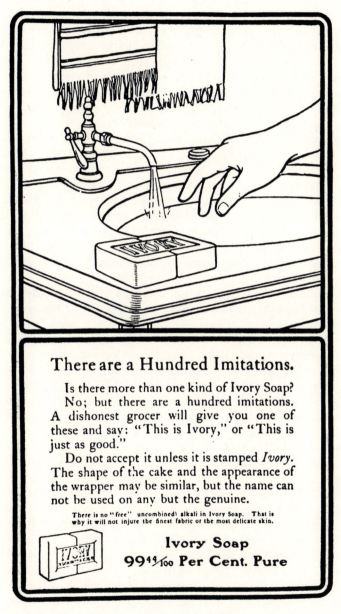

There are a Hundred Imitations.

Is there more than one kind of Ivory Soap?
No; but there are a hundred imitations.
A dishonest grocer will give you one of
these and say: "This is Ivory," or "This is
just as good."

Do not accept it unless it is stamped *Ivory*.
The shape of the cake and the appearance of
the wrapper may be similar, but the name can
not be used on any but the genuine.

There is no "free" uncombined) alkali in Ivory Soap. That is
why it will not injure the finest fabric or the most delicate skin.

Ivory Soap
99⁴⁵⁄₁₀₀ Per Cent. Pure

Reprinted from *Literary Digest*, May 26, 1906.

identical items. The implication was clear: if their grocer failed to stock Pearline, or Ivory, or Pears', or whatever brand was being advertised, the customer should find a better grocer. By the turn of the century, many ads instructed women to send their grocer's name if he did not carry the brand, and some offered free samples of the product as a reward. After World War I, the ominous warnings and bullying tactics largely subsided, and the warnings, replaced by "sold by leading stores everywhere," became a common caption. In fact, in the case of larger consumer durables, such as stoves and washing machines, potential customers were instructed to write the manufacturer for the name of the nearest dealer.

Ivory's major rival in advertising was Lever Brothers' Pears' Soap. In 1883, when Pears' began advertising in the United States, they already had nearly a century of experience in England. At a time when most American advertisers were utilizing small-column or at the most double-column advertisements, Pears' regularly purchased page or half-page ads. The ads were very large by American standards and they were unusually well illustrated. Not only was the Pears' campaign extensive, the copy was both attention-getting and imaginative; by 1903, John Powers could argue that "As a result of advertising, Pears' Soap is better known [in the United States] than England herself."[20]

Perhaps the most famous Pears' ads featured a baby in a bathtub reaching for a bar of Pears' Soap, with the caption "He won't be happy til he gets it!" The early caption, "Good morning, have you used Pears' Soap," suggested that the habit of morning bathing was something successful people expected. A mid-1880s ad in *Harper's* depicted a working man washing his face with Pears' Soap and the caption "Pears' Soapmakers by sealed appointment to H.R.H. the Prince of Wales." The basic appeal of Pears' advertising was captured in a turn-of-the-century ad featuring a drawing of a dirty, unshaven seaman standing on a dock scratching his head with a very surprised look on his face. Clearly he had missed his ship, but customers who used Pears' Soap for a morning bath would not miss theirs. The caption read "Whilst there's life there's soap," and the usual "Pears' Soap is matchless for the complexion."[21] The Pears' ad in the September 27, 1884, *Frank Leslie's Illustrated* commented that "if cleanliness is next to Godliness then soap must be considered as a means to Grace," and featured Henry Ward Beecher's picture and endorsement of Pears' Soap. In a testimonial in *Ladies' Home Journal* some five years later, Beecher suggested that clergymen should be willing to recommend "Moral Things" like soap. He concluded, "I am told that my commendation of Pears' Soap has opened for it a large market in the U.S. I am willing to stand by every word in favor of it I ever uttered."[22] While the soap manufacturers did not originate the cleanliness movement, nor were they the first to equate cleanliness with morality, they did embrace it with all the advertising skills they possessed.

Who will be the next President?

He wont be happy, 'till he gets it!

PEARS SOAP

Reprinted from *Overland Monthly*, July 1912.

Pears' pioneering efforts were rapidly copied. Changes in the layout and style of advertisements in part reflected the need of producers of essentially similar products to differentiate their wares. What occurred resembled a visual shouting match. Whereas a double-column ad attracted attention in the 1870s, by 1892 it took at least a quarter page to accomplish the same task. By the turn of the century, half-page ads were common and full-page ads not rare. During the first decade of the twentieth century, full and even double-page ads appeared, and by the end of World War I full-page ads were common, colorful, and clever. Illustrations, typically only a small drawing of the product or brand name in the early ads, became more complicated with time, placing the product in an attractive setting or in a story-telling situation; many included human models, and atmosphere and image situations were often added. The early soap ads featured long and generally crowded copy, with each advertiser attempting to convince the customer with long messages. The later ads tended to be less crowded and the arrangement of copy and size of type much more conducive to attracting the eye to key parts of the ad. The appeal was less to reason and more to creation of demand. As the business increased, the more intense competition became for the housewife's attention.

In contrast to the cleanliness theme and acceptability in polite society, some soap companies clung to the style of patent medicines during much of the nineteenth century. Cuticura, for example, continued throughout the period prior to World War I and after to advertise its products for their moderate medical qualities for most skin problems.[23] Lever Brothers' Lifebuoy Soap launched a campaign just after the turn of the century which featured Lifebuoy's disinfectant qualities, claiming that "If there is a taint of Typhoid, Cholera, or Diphtheria floating in the air or concealed in the clothing of the individual . . . Lifebuoy, with its germ-destroying agent, will remove the danger."[24] Escalating the campaign two years later, a Lifebuoy ad made the following boast:

Microbes kill about 15 million Human beings a year . . . Exhaustive experiments by some of the world's greatest scientists have proved that Lifebuoy Soap destroys the microbes of disease.[25]

Even Ivory occasionally found itself venturing into the medical arena; for example, a 1902 advertisement argued that Ivory should be used after exercise because "the skin, when 2,300,000 pores are opened by exercise, becomes extremely sensitive."[26]

Perhaps the success of patent medicine advertising and the widespread use of persuasion based on the consumer's fears and concern about health reflected the generally held public fear of diseases over which they seemed to have no control. Also, the success of the patent medicine industry after the Civil War had probably inspired the use of health as an appeal in advertisement for a wide range of products. The discoveries of Koch and Pasteur in Europe in the mid-1870s made its impact in the United States in the 1880s and 1890s, and American medicine was just beginning to reshape itself into a profession grounded in science. Indeed, as the period progressed, the change in the health appeal itself became obvious, from the outrageous claims of "health underwear" and patent medicines of the 1880s to the "scientific explanations" of the digestibility of cereals and Eskay's baby food and the germ killing properties of Lysol in 1920.

After the beginning of the twentieth century, negative health appeals, based on consumers' ignorance and fears, declined; even some heretofore "curative" soaps switched the nature of their advertising. Creative advertising could, rather quickly, change a product's image. For example, throughout most of the nineteenth century, Packer's Tar Soap had emphasized the curative properties of pine tar; indeed, at one time their advertising had suggested that the soap could cure lame horses. After the turn of the century, the curative approach was brushed aside for an encompassing appeal to beauty. An intricately drawn ad featured a young woman, casually dressed, playing contentedly on a mandolin, while the natural beauty of her hair was highlighted by the sun streaming through the open window behind her. The caption said simply "A sun bath after a shampoo with Packer's Tar Soap." Pine trees outside the window and pine clusters framing the picture reminded the reader of the soap's natural contents.[27]

The early ads for John H. Woodbury Company dealt with wrinkles, constipation, nervousness, overweight, freckles, dandruff, warts, pimples, oddly shaped heads, and arsenic poisoning. While Woodbury claimed that he could cure all these problems, either by the use of his soap or by special methods in his office, the implication of the ads was clearly that Dr. Woodbury's soap was the source of the "cures." After the turn of the century, Woodbury slowly shifted the appeal of their advertising to more closely conform to the appeal used by the rest of the industry. By 1906, beauty had become the key phrase in soap advertisements. Not to be left behind by the competition, the soap had been renamed "Woodbury's Facial Soap" well before World War I. In addition, the appeal had a frankly direct sexual overtone: "Woodbury's—for the skin you love to touch." The full-page color ad in the *Ladies' Home Journal* offered a copy of the picture of the handsome couple featured in the ad if the reader would send in a wrapper from a bar of Woodbury's Soap. More important, the advertisement promised beautiful skin and romance by using Woodbury's soap.

Somewhat to the surprise of the industry, the frankly emotional and sexual appeal worked. In many ways, assurance of romance was more deceptive than the old curative promises. But the approach sold soap. In the decade following 1915, Woodbury spent over $4 million on advertising, using the same basic beauty and romance theme, and its sales jumped to six times the 1915 level. Its major rival, Cuticura, decided to rest on its excellent reputation and retained the basic curative theme in its modest advertising campaign, on which the company spent only $70,000 in the same period that Woodbury spent $4 million.[28] Ivory, Pears', Woodbury, and the other brands demonstrated that the image projected, and not the product, provided the differentiation among essentially similar soaps. While the themes were many and varied, the general pattern of successful advertising shifted from being basically product oriented, that is, concerned with the virtues and qualities of the product (purity, utility, price, practicality), to being consumer oriented, that is, linked intimately with the individual, affording status or other desirable qualities such as beauty to the user.

Richard and Claudia Bushman, in their recent article on cleanliness in America, concluded that the cleanliness movement in the late nineteenth century did not originate with soap manufacturers, but that

they wholeheartedly exploited its commercial possibilities. . . . But through advertising, the industrialist propagated faith in soap as an essential of good health and refinement. Added to the pressures to conform to cleanliness standards in order to be respectable and healthy, the force of advertising made the culture of cleanliness nearly irresistible. In the course of a few generations, cleanliness habits were deeply ingrained in the American personality.[29]

By 1920, the advertising campaigns of the soap companies had succeeded beyond their early dreams. A mother could rely on the industry to help to educate her daughter in the art of self-beautification. A full-page color ad in *Ladies' Home Journal* that year pictured a mother and her maid fondly watching a little girl admire herself in a hand-held mirror with the message that "Rightly trained, the unconscious vanity of a little miss becomes the ingrained personal daintiness which is priceless to a woman." The caption admonished the mother to "Teach her that it is the frequent, regular use of Ivory Soap which gives her the lustrous hair, the clean smooth skin, and the spotless garments which she so innocently admires."[30] In other words the message seemed to be "mothers teach your daughters to use Ivory Soap."

With a few exceptions, the cosmetic industry and the advertisement of cosmetics is a twentieth-century phenomenon. Among those rare exceptions would be toilet articles such as dentifrices, shaving soaps, nostrums, and a few beauty aids. As was more generally the case, the trend in beauty aids was from a few products supposedly designed to fulfill a number of uses to a great variety of products made for more and more specific uses. As the products multiplied and diversified during the first decades of the century, advertising attempted to convince the American woman that she needed the products. Throughout the period, for example, Cashmere Bouquet Perfume was advertised extensively as a handkerchief perfume, with no suggestion that it might be applied to the body.[31] Sozodont dentifrice, for most of the last quarter of the century, conducted a major advertising campaign in *Harper's*, *Century*, and *Scribner's*, attempting to educate the public to use a dentifrice for healthier teeth and more pleasant breath. Dr. Lyon's Tooth Powder, which had used small, single-column space advertising since the Civil War, and Rubifoam Dentifrice mounted major campaigns only shortly before the end of the century. Various types of toothbrushes also advertised in a manner which suggested that oral hygiene was a relatively novel idea. For example, an 1876 advertisement for Crown Tooth Brushes in *Harper's Weekly* never mentioned dental hygiene, but assured the customer that the "bristles [are] warranted not to fall out or break-off while using"; the appeal was not designed to create demand by increasing the number of people who regularly brushed their teeth, but to convince the consumer of the perfection of a particular product.[32] In truth, the need for regular cleaning of the teeth with a brush and dentifrice was not widely recognized. As late as 1897, a *Printers' Ink* reporter referred to Sozodont as "an article of luxury."[33] Complexion soaps included Woodbury, Pears', Cuticura, Packer's Tar Soap, and Cobbs'. Barry's Tricopherous Shampoo and Ayer's Hair Vigor were almost alone in advertising in their category. Pozzoni's and LaBlanche's face powders and Dr. Hebra's Complexion Cream nearly completed the list of widely advertised cosmetics in the nineteenth century.

Diversification had not yet entered the strategies of most American business firms, and soap manufacturers continued to advise their customers against the use of cosmetics. A 1901 Ivory advertisement argued "Better to preserve a good clear natural complexion than to risk injury in attempts to improve upon it with cosmetics."[34] Hand Sapolio took up the cause with one of Artemus Ward's jingles:

> With paint and powder in Grandma's time,
> ye lady made great show.
> Today my lady makes up fine—with
> Hand Sapolio.[35]

In spite of the soap manufacturers' negative campaign, face creams, particularly cleansing or cold creams, gained popularity; and in 1907 Ivory Soap instructed women to use cold cream if they wished. "It has its value," the ad admitted, "But *to clean* the skin, you must use soap; pure soap . . . Ivory Soap."[36]

The potential market for toilet articles for men remained virtually untapped in the nineteenth century. With the exception of soap and perhaps dentifrices, the only advertising directed toward male consumers was for shaving soap. In the mid-1880s, J. B. Williams Company launched a campaign for the Williams Shaving Stick in small, three-inch single-column ads; by the end of the decade the campaign included full-page illustrated ads in national magazines. Williams' ad often featured a man using Williams Shaving Stick and obviously enjoying a shave, compared to having a most unpleasant shave with some other brand.[37] Colgate joined the campaign in the late 1890s with their own shaving soap. Presbrey claimed that the shaving soap and the Gillette safety razor in the early years of the twentieth century made daily shaving "a part of the toilet of even the mechanic," and resulted in "a nation of clean-shaven men." Perhaps Presbrey was correct, but one should not forget that during the first decades of the century, illustrated advertisements for women's products often included men, for the first time. Invariably, the men included were young, handsome, and clean-shaven. The upper- and middle-class world of the advertising agency and the accompanying image of success, whether in business or in romance, no longer included beards.[38]

In the first decades of the twentieth century, cosmetics available to American women multiplied. By 1905, the list of complexion soaps had lengthened, Fairy Soap and Palmolive Soap being notable additions to those promising clean, healthy, young and beautiful skin. Dentifrices seemed to multiply (Colgate, Caloz, Sanitol, to mention only a few), and toothbrushes became common. Both products promised clean, white, and beautiful teeth, and pleasant breath. Face creams, cold creams, and vanishing creams became a necessary part of the smart woman's toilet, and talcum powder ads stressed the variety of tints and scents, as well as purity and the intended uses of their products. Even Mum Deodorant began to place small discreet advertisements. Creams, soaps, shampoos, dentifrices, and face powders seemed to multiply beyond description as manufacturers sought advertising to differentiate and secure markets for their products in the face of growing competition from close substitutes. On the eve of America's entrance into World War I, Cutex cautioned women not to cut their cuticles but to use their Cuticle Remover, and by 1920 they could choose from three more Cutex products to whiten, polish, or highly polish their nails. The May 1919 issue of *Ladies' Home Journal* carried a full-page ad featuring a handsome young couple, with the caption, "There isn't a girl who can't have the irresistible, appealing loveliness of perfect daintiness . . . WITHIN THE CURVE OF A WOMAN'S ARM . . . A frank discussion of a subject too often avoided." The copy discussed the problem of perspiration odor and promised that the product, a deodorant named "Odorono," could spare a woman that embarrassment.[39] Personal hygiene and appearance had developed over the period into a near fad, or perhaps more aptly, a cult. What better industry in which to create demand where very little had existed?

Among popular magazines intended for women readers, *Harper's Bazar* appealed to the more cosmopolitan, style-conscious, upper-class readers. *Bazar*, in addition to featuring sketches of the latest Paris and London styles in hats, coats, gowns, and a variety of ladies clothing, carried more advertising than its middle-class rival *Ladies' Home Journal.* For example, while the *Journal* carried articles and patterns explaining how mothers could sew play clothes for their children, or remodel last year's dress, or make their own fashionable hats, the *Bazar* featured the latest Paris fashions and carried an advertisement for "Golden Hair Wash," which promised to lighten hair to a more attractive "Sunny Hue."[40]

For the most part the early ads promised to remedy or cure problems rather than to enhance natural beauty. As early as 1890 *Harper's Bazar* advertised products to remove unwanted facial hair; one ad featured a bearded lady with a heavy mustache and a goatee before treatment and promised to remove all the facial hair.[41] In another, Mme. Velais' ad urged the *Bazar* readers to write for information on how she could solve their problems:

Wrinkles, Black-heads, Pimples, Freckles, Pittings, Moles, and superfluous hair permanently removed. Flesh increased or reduced. Complexion beautified. The Form developed; hair, brows and lashes colored and restored.[42]

Few cosmetic firms suggested that the use of their products would cover up or change a woman's physical appearance; rather they promised to cure or restore the natural healthy appearance. LaBlanche Face Powder promised to "preserve a fine complexion and restore a poor one" as well as prevent sunburn, chapping, and roughness of the skin.[43] As late as 1905, Malvina Cream boasted that it "Cures freckles, sun-burn, pimples, ringworm, and wrinkles."[44]

The first rudiments of glamor appeal in cosmetic advertising appeared in the early twentieth century. For example, Lustr-ite, a brilliant and long-lasting nail enamel, placed advertising in the *Ladies' Home Journal* as early

Reprinted from *Harper's Bazar*, February 8, 1890.

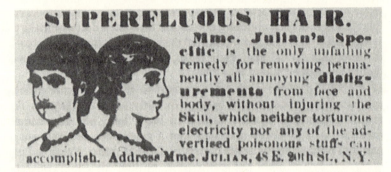

Reprinted from *Harper's Bazar*, February 8, 1890.

as February 1905. But the natural beauty, purity, and curative properties utilized as the major themes in cosmetic advertising did not give way until about 1914 when youth, polished glamor, and social acceptability became the dominant themes. Even the ads for hair depilatories no longer promised permanent cures, simply temporary relief.[45] By 1915, women reading *Harper's Bazar* could order Marchioness Rouge to "enhance" their beauty, or Dainty White, a liquid make-up, to cover any blemishes; or if they preferred, V. Darsy also carried a liquid cover-up, a very expensive import called Poudre Liqueflie at $3.15 a bottle; Violet Carate specially designed eye cream was available to enhance the beauty of the eyes; or they could simply order from Mme. Helena Rubinstein, who carried a "full line" of very modern beauty products, including Novina Eyelash Cream to darken the eyelashes, Valaze Beautifying Skinfood, various powders for dry, normal, or oily skin, an astringent, and a multitude of creams.[46] In 1914, Pears' Soap advised women that the way to prevent wrinkles and to appear younger was "to use Pears' Soap"; and three years later *Ladies' Home Journal* carried an ad for a complexion soap named "Sempre Giovine ('always young')."[47]

A Dr. Lyon's Tooth Powder advertisement in 1914 reminded consumers that, "Of ALL features, your smile can be most expressive of your personality, can have the greatest power to attract and charm. Teeth in fine condition, revealed by the smile, are proof of health care and personal refinement. Neglected teeth are a severe detriment."[48] A 1920 Cutex advertisement in *Ladies' Home Journal* illustrated a dominant theme in advertising directed at women. The ad pictured a well-dressed, obviously upper-middle-class woman looking critically at the fingernails of another (unaware) well-dressed, obviously middle-class woman, and the caption read "Every day, people judge you by your nails. 'How beautifully turned out, how correct' you thought—until you caught a glimpse of her nails. Then 'shocking' you said to yourself. And that one glimpse of her carelessly groomed hands left an impression that you never forgot."[49] By the end of

Every Day People Judge You by Your Nails

Have they the beauty they so easily can gain?

"HOW beautifully turned out, how correct," you thought—until you caught a glimpse of her nails.

Then, "Shocking!" you said to yourself.

And that one glimpse of her carelessly groomed hands left an impression that you never forgot.

Do you realize how easy it is to keep your nails lovely—so lovely that they

This method is the secret of the perfect, even cuticle of many fashionable women

lend you that assurance which comes from the knowledge that even the most critical eye can find nothing but immaculate perfection?

The secret of beautiful nails lies in the care of the cuticle. This is the most important part of a manicure. To cut the cuticle or force it back with a sharp instrument is ruinous. Such rough methods are the cause of most ragged, unkempt nails. The more you cut the cuticle the faster it grows. It becomes tough, thick, and hangnails appear.

You can have nails that add to your attractiveness

You can keep your nails lovely without injuring the cuticle. The Cutex way of manicuring will keep them always dainty.

Cutex is a harmless cuticle remover developed after years of experiment. Applied to the cuticle, it keeps the base of the nail smooth, firm, crescent-like.

It maintains the even, regular curve which Nature intended it to have.

Wrap a little cotton around the end of an orange stick (both come in the Cutex package), dip it into the bottle of Cutex and work it around the base of the nails, gently pushing back the cuticle. Instantly the dry cuticle is softened. Wash the hands, pushing back the cuticle with a towel. The surplus cuticle will disappear, leaving a firm, even, slender nail base.

If you like snowy white nail tips apply a little Cutex Nail White underneath the nails directly from its convenient tube. Finish your manicure with Cutex Nail Polish. For an especially brilliant, lasting polish, use Cutex Paste Polish first, then the Cutex Cake or Powder Polish.

If your cuticle has a tendency to dry and grow coarse, apply a bit of Cutex Cold Cream each night. This cream was especially prepared to keep the hands and cuticle soft and fine.

Give yourself this manicure regularly. Make it as much a habit as keeping your shoes shined. You will find that it is no trouble. It takes only about fifteen minutes a week to give your nails this complete manicure. But do not neglect this duty. Do not do it one week and forget it the next. It is true that one Cutex manicure makes your nails look lovely; but you cannot keep them

well groomed by irregular care. Give your nails a Cutex manicure regularly.

Just give your nails a few minutes' care once or twice a week, depending on how fast your cuticle grows, and they are always exquisite—smooth, shapely, a decided addition to your personal charm.

Cutex Cuticle Remover, Nail White, Nail Polish and Cold Cream are 35 cents. The Cuticle Remover comes also in 65 cent bottles. You can get Cutex in any drug or department store in the United States, Canada and in any chemist shop in England.

A little spraying of this tube—and your nail tips will stay snowy white

A manicure set for 20 cents

For twenty cents we will send you the Cutex Introductory Manicure Set, not as large as our standard set but containing enough of the Cutex preparations for at least six complete manicures. Use the coupon below. Your first manicure will be a delightful surprise to you. Address Northam Warren, 114 West 17th Street, New York City.

If you live in Canada, address Northam Warren, Dept. 103, 200 Mountain Street, Montreal, Canada.

Send you dimes for this manicure set

MAIL THIS COUPON WITH TWO DIMES TODAY

NORTHAM WARREN
Dept. 188, 114 West 17th Street
New York City

Name

Street and Number

City and State

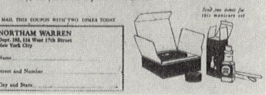

Reproduced courtesy of Chesebrough-Pond's USA Co., owner of the registered trademark CUTEX.

World War I, fear of social stigma and the desire for social acceptance were major themes in creating demand for cosmetics and toilet articles. Stuart Ewen in writing about advertising in the 1920s referred to the "commodity self," and suggested that, "Each portion of the body was to be perceived critically, as a potential bauble in a successful assemblage."[50] Ewen's conclusions applied with equal force to the previous decade. It was no longer acceptable for American women to meet the world with a clean gown and a well-scrubbed face. Social acceptability depended upon attention to every detail.

Advertisers also sought to convince American women that social status and acceptability depended as much on attention to every detail of their home as it depended on personal appearance. Sapolio, Enoch Morgan's Sons' cleanser, advertised throughout the last three decades of the nineteenth century as a general-purpose cleanser with a multitude of uses, from scrubbing pots and pans, to cleaning dishes and floors, to sharpening knifes, and even to cleaning false teeth and tombstones, featured a man looking at his image in the bottom of a pan, with the caption "It's cheaper and better than soap" for "General Household Purposes."[51] Under Artemus Ward's direction as advertising manager, Sapolio expanded both the scope and the appeal of its advertising. Ward pioneered in advertising designed to make Sapolio a household name. In 1892, he sponsored a Captain Andrews' Trans-Altantic voyage, in a fourteen-foot dory, in celebration of the voyage of Columbus four hundred years earlier. The voyage took three months to complete and was widely followed and reported on in the press, always with free publicity for Sapolio. One of Ward's most successful publicity ideas was the "Spotless Town" campaign at the turn of the century:

Allusions to Spotless Town became common on the stage, in newspaper text and cartoons, in public speeches and in political controversies, until the phrase got into the language as a synonym for cleanliness, order and perfection. . . . With the exception of the Ford automobile, no commercial product ever received so much secondary and free advertising as Sapolio got from . . . this campaign.[52]

Ward argued that people bought familiar products, and his basic philosophy was to make Sapolio a household name. By 1888, Ward had started a practice of accompanying each Sapolio ad with a jingle which "became so much a part of life that each new piece of this advertising copy was actually looked forward to by a multitude of people."[53] A very clever ad that year pictured two servant girls, one dressed up and leaving the house with a young man, the other scrubbing pots and pans:

> Two servants in two neighboring houses dwelt.
> But differently their daily labor felt,
> jaded and weary of her life was one,
> always at work and yet 'twas never done.

The other stepped out nightly with her beau—
BUT then She cleaned house with Sapolio.[54]

In addition to the jingles, which emphasized speed and ease of cleaning with Sapolio, a long list of possible uses accompanied the ads.

Even in the nineteenth century, Sapolio experienced stiff competition from its closest substitute, Bon Ami; in addition, two soap powders, Pyle's Pearline and Gold Dust, advertised extensively as general-purpose cleansers. The soap powder ads claimed that they were superior for washing dishes and laundry, and could be used for the same purposes as cleansers. By the turn of the century, Colgate's Octagon and Babbitt's had entered the competition. By 1905, both Armour and Swift introduced powdered cleansers, and that year Cudahy's Old Dutch powdered cleanser in a sifter-top can was introduced with an extensive national advertising campaign.[55]

In spite of the competition and thanks to an aggressive and clever advertising campaign, Sapolio sales boomed until 1906 when they began a slow but steady decline. Faced with declining sales and vigorous competition, especially from the powdered cleansers, Sapolio reverted to stressing economy in their ads. Advertising legends maintained that Sapolio sales declined because Enoch Morgan's Sons reduced their advertising expenditures. Actually, appropriations for advertising remained high for almost another decade. Rather than an illustration of the power of advertising, the decline of Sapolio is an example of the limitations of advertising. The decline of sales in Sapolio resulted more from failure to maintain the currency of their product in the face of increasing competition. Consumers simply preferred powdered cleansers in sifter-top packages. In addition, Sapolio continued to advertise as a general-purpose cleanser in an era of increasing specialization and competition.[56]

A reader of *Ladies' Home Journal* during the first decades of the twentieth century would have noticed the same profusion of advertisements for household cleaning items as for cosmetics. Soap companies introduced special items for laundry, such as the naphtha soaps, a field dominated by Fels and by Procter and Gamble. In 1910, N. K. Fairbanks, an old soap manufacturer, ran a full-page ad to illustrate its diversified line of soap products: Fairy Soap for the face, Gold Dust for general household cleaning, and Sunny Monday for the laundry. During the same year, Parson's Ammonia lectured housewives on the difference in their "household ammonia" and just "ordinary" ammonia. Old English Floor Wax promised clean and shining floors, and Wrights' Silver Cream performed the same tasks for the household silver. Within a few years, O-Cedar advertised a variety of floor and furniture polishes and mops, and Johnson's Liquid Wax promised to take the chore out of waxing floors and furniture. SaniFlush for cleaning the toilet bowl appeared, and Scott Tissues offered the ultimate convenience in disposable household towels.

Fear of social criticism and the need for acceptance was obviously not limited to a woman's person. Advertisers rushed to instruct women on every phase of their lives and to provide the products necessary for perfection. A clean house was as important as a clean body, and advertisers cautioned women to examine the shine on their furniture as closely as the shine on their noses. Household cleaning agents followed a path similar to cosmetics in their development, that is, from a few simple general-purpose products to a wide diversity of specialized items for specific purposes. By the end of World War I, a glance through the advertisements in those magazines directed primarily toward women made it apparent that the housewife had, or soon would have, a product specially made and perfectly suited for each and every cleaning task in her house. While many of these products may have been a great help to housekeeping, the promotions played too much on the fears and anxieties of women. The housewife learned through advertising that she had new standards of cleanliness to live up to if she wished to be considered a good wife and mother. Since so many products were available to lighten her load and to help her reach those new standards of social acceptability, there was no excuse not to do so. Having cleaned and polished all the dirt she could see, the homemaker (or in the advertisements her maid, of course) was now armed with Lysol against that which she could not see—the sinister and ubiquitous germ!

Although the national census did not enumerate cosmetics as a separate industry, the category of "drug, toilet and household preparations," in terms of value of the output for domestic consumption, increased from slightly over $40 million in 1879 to more than $765 million in 1920.[57] Department stores, such as Marshall Field's and Macy's, created entire new departments of cosmetics and usually located them in the most desirable location in the store. In addition, department stores often heavily advertised their cosmetics as lead items designed to attract women shoppers into the stores. While household cleaning items usually received less attractive locations, they too were often organized as separate departments. Drug stores and variety stores, such as F. W. Woolworth Company, generally featured their smaller versions of cosmetic departments with less expensive products but often had more extensive household products departments. In less than a generation, an entire industry had been created and its seemingly endless variety of products sold to American women.

In 1963, Betty Friedan, speaking of modern advertising, noted "As motivational researchers keep telling advertisers, American women are so unsure of who they should be that they look to this glossy public image [created by advertisers] to decide every detail of their lives."[58] As advertising shifted its function from informing the public to creating demand in cosmetics, as well as in a number of other consumer goods industries, it created an artificial need by creating doubt about old ways, about old products, about old values, and even about women's selves.

Medical cure-alls gave way to emotional cure-alls; and human relations, even love, acceptance, and confidence, were available through consumption. By implying that basic human needs could be satisfied by consumption of the tangible products of modern industry, advertising exacerbated the conflict between the values of an older America and the realities of modern industrial society. As Friedan suggested, the American woman may have gained materially through the substitution of consumption as an ethic replacing the older values, but she lost a large part of herself in the process.

4

LEISURE TIME FOR THE LADIES: BICYCLES, CAMERAS, APPLIANCES, AND OTHER LUXURIES

"Advertising doesn't cost!—It Pays"
(quote from empty billboard on Highway 51 near DeKalb, Illinois)

Readers of magazines in the last decade of the nineteenth century found what must have seemed, compared to only a few short years earlier, an incredible array of goods advertised. Interestingly, however, with only a few exceptions, the appeal of the advertisements had not kept pace with the assortment of goods and remained essentially unaltered. Only a few venturesome companies had followed the lead of the patent medicine and soap industry and patterned their advertising campaigns after either the direct and plain-spoken appeal advocated by John Powers or the flamboyant schemes of Artemus Ward. Certainly fewer still, if any, advertisers had anticipated Walter Dill Scott's stress on the power of emotional appeals in advertising. "Man has been called a reasoning animal," Scott wrote, "but he could with greater truthfulness be called the creature of suggestion."[1] Scott argued that advertisers should use the power of suggestion from external sources as opposed to internal reasoning to evoke the desired behavior—namely buying. Pictures or illustrations that provided examples of the use of the product, direct commands to buy, to return coupons, or to copy, or illustrations that produced emotions attached to use of the product were most influential. Actually, as Daniel Pope has argued, while the emotional and non-rational approach of Scott seemed directly contradictory to the "reason-why" approach of Powers, "it soon became clear that the distinction was slight." Indeed, "reason-why," as Pope concluded, also quickly became a method of persuasion designed to convince consumers to purchase a particular brand or product; the reason, however, did not necessarily need to be logical or real; it could easily be emotional.[2]

Figure 4.1
Growth of Consumer Industries by Major Categories, 1869–1919

Year	Consumer Semi-Durables (1,000,000)	Percent Growth	Consumer Perishibles ($1,000,000)	Percent Growth	Consumer Durables ($1,000,000)	Percent Growth
1869	665		1594		262	
		24.5%*		28.7%*		16.0%*
1879	828		1996		304	
		36.7%		45.5%*		64.0%*
1889	1132		2905		499	
		<-12.5%>**		0 %**		<-14.0%>**
1894	970		2916		429	
		41.6%**		31.0%**		47.8%**
1899	1374		3820		634	
		27.0%		35.0%**		30.0%**
1904	1746		5167		826	
		40.0%		33.9%**		46.7%**
1909	2447		6922		1212	
		10.7%**		19.4%**		29.5%**
1914	2709		8296		1578	
		159.0%**		109.6%**		159.5%**
1919	7019		17392		4075	

*Growth [decline] per decade.
**Growth [decline] per 5 years.

Source: U.S. Department of Commerce, Bureau of the Census, Historical Statistics of the United States: Colonial Times to 1970, Part II (Washington, D.C., 1975), 699–701.

Production of consumer durables, which included household furniture, heating and cooking apparatus, vehicles, jewelry, watches, clocks, and silverware, as well as musical instruments, bicycles, cameras, and household appliances and supplies, increased dramatically from the decade of the 1880s and the early 1890s. The panic in 1893 produced a rather sharp depression in both consumer semi-durables and consumer durables, with neither classification recovering until immediately prior to the turn of the century. The rate of increase in the production in both categories of goods accelerated in the twentieth century.[3]

Pianos, organs, bicycles, cameras, and indeed many appliances introduced in the nineteenth century undoubtedly represented luxury items to most American consumers. Amazingly, Frank Presbrey, in a long section discussing the various advertising campaigns conducted at the close of the nineteenth century by manufacturers of literally dozens of consumer items including patent medicines, soaps, prepared foods, cameras, bicycles, silverware, watches, and even automobiles, included only a short page and a half

NEW STYLES

Mason & Hamlin Cabinet Organs, Resonant,

WITH IMPROVEMENTS Patented June 21 and Aug. 23, 1870.

☞ The CABINET OR-GANS made by this company are of such universal reputation, in Europe and America, that few will need assurance of their superiority. They have uniformly been awarded highest premiums at Industrial Exhibitions, and are declared the BEST INSTRUMENTS OF THE CLASS by musicians generally.

The MASON & HAMLIN ORGAN CO. announce, this month, new styles of their instruments, containing the important improvements for which patents were recently granted them; also, a FURTHER REDUCTION OF PRICES on many styles. A NEW ILLUSTRATED CATALOGUE, with full information, is ready, and will be sent free to any one desiring it.

Warerooms, 596 Broadway, New York; 154 Tremont Street, Boston.

Reprinted from *Harper's Weekly*, October 22, 1870.

on "the earliest luxury advertising." It is difficult to explain why Presbrey, writing at the end of the "Jazz Decade," listed only pianos, organs, and phonographs as household luxuries. Diamonds, silverware, jewelry, playing cards, and other apparent luxuries were advertised alongside the pianos, organs, and phonographs. His rationale for selection of luxury items escapes explanation. Perhaps Presbrey was simply recognizing the obvious facts that musical instruments throughout the nineteenth century had depended on more than local markets and that the industry never attempted to create a mass market through advertising campaigns addressed to lower- and lower-middle-class consumers. Although Presbrey insisted that "Large-scale advertising of musical instruments was inaugurated by the Steinway in 1894," he well knew that musical instruments were among the most frequently advertised products in magazines and periodicals throughout the late nineteenth century.[4]

Estey, Mason & Hamlin, Ivers and Pond, S. D. & H. W. Smith, and Geo. A. Prince, as well as Steinway and a number of other organ and piano firms, advertised extensively in the last quarter of the nineteenth century. As early as 1870, Mason & Hamlin advertised regularly in *Harper's* with a double-column, one-eighth-page illustrated ad.[5] Readers of either *Godey's* or *Peterson's* could hardly help but have been familiar with the Estey, which featured an elaborate ad with two angels playing horns and the caption "For Power and Purity of Tone, Durability and Finish, They [Estey Organs] Are Unrivaled." On more than one occasion the facing page of the same issue contained a quarter-page ad for Beatty's pianos and organs.[6] Beatty's advertisements featured the price; Marchal & Smith Piano Co. headlined "NO AGENTS," with the price and a guarantee; Mason & Hamlin noted that organs were becoming more popular and affordable and that 70,000 had sold the previous year; while one smaller firm, Geo. A. Prince Co., claimed to have 54,000 in use. While advertisements for pianos and organs appeared more often in the more prestigious journals, popular magazines and newspapers also included numerous advertisements for a wide variety of musical instruments and sheet music as well as for books on how to play each and every instrument.

Like most nineteenth-century advertisements, leisure, luxury, and appeals to social status were simply not present. Indeed, the appeal utilized in musical instrument advertisements closely resembled that of the sewing machine ads which often appeared on the same page of the periodical. In an advertisement for their piano in the October 12, 1872, issue of *Harper's Weekly*, Knabe & Co., one of the leading musical instrument manufacturing firms, featured an illustration of their imposing-looking factory in Baltimore, with very little copy accompanying the picture. In addition to this rather common tactic used frequently by sewing machine and other durable consumer goods manufacturers of featuring an impressive factory in their advertising in an effort to impart an air of stability for the particular firm, the copy simply claimed that Knabe organs and pianos were "unequaled" and "unrivaled." Pianos, organs, sewing machines, lawn mowers, and other durable goods were described as the famous, the superior, the best, the guaranteed, and the certified, and, like the sewing machines, they were simple to use, durable, and practical. For example, in 1870 Mason & Hamlin featured in their copy an announcement that they had recently incorporated new "patented" improvements into their instruments and reminded customers that "The cabinet organs made by this company are of such universal reputation, in Europe and America, that few will need assurance of their superiority." In addition, the company offered a "FURTHER REDUCTION OF PRICES."[7] Ten years later, Mason & Hamlin, in a style that had remained almost unchanged, again advertised their new styles for the season. The new instruments incorporated "important improvements" and the ad reminded customers that "the usefulness of cabinet or parlor organs is shown by the fact that seventy thousand are sold yearly in the United States." The copy continued to mention prices and to boast that Mason & Hamlin were "the best."[8]

Although the manufacturers of pianos and organs advertised widely, the ads appeared designed to compete within the industry and made little attempt to increase the total demand. In that sense Presbrey was correct; Steinway's 1894 campaign did represent both a significant increase in the volume of musical instrument advertising and an attempt to make owning a piano a symbol of good taste and social status. However, the four-page insertion was hardly directed at creating mass markets.

Musical instruments, especially major instruments such as the piano and the organ, were much too expensive for popular consumption. Faced with limited local demand, manufacturers of major musical instruments had long competed in national markets. Mason & Hamlin listed a wide variety of organs for churches and schools, and a smaller "superb drawing room style" instrument at prices ranging from $200 to $510. Smaller organs, of "less capacity" in "plainer cases" listed for $51 to $200 and "upward." In the same magazine, Beatty's pianos sold for $297.50, and the same company's smallest organ for only $65. Both companies offered trial examination and national delivery of their instruments.[9] Nearly a decade later, *Godey's* carried an advertisement for the Beethoven Piano Organ Co.'s "Ideal" organ, which normally sold for $125, and was "now on sale for only $62.50."[10] At the upper end of the price scale, an expenditure of the magnitude of $500 represented more than double the average per capita income for a year and even at the lowest prices was over a third of the average annual income (see Figure 1.9). A 1909 advertisement for Baldwin pianos captured the appeal of most piano and organ campaigns. Pictured were three women at a Baldwin piano, one in a sixteenth-century costume, one in eighteenth-century dress, and one in a modern and very stylish twentieth-century gown, with the simple caption "BALDWIN—the best for centuries."[11] The setting was luxurious, the gowns elegant, and the appeal was clearly to upper- and middle-class customers. It obviously made little sense to use advertising in a futile effort to create mass markets in an industry that enjoyed extremely limited economies of scale and when the price of pianos and organs remained beyond the means of the average American consumer.

Manufacturing of musical instruments, especially large complex instruments such as pianos and organs, was both labor intensive and required highly skilled workers; hence the industry did not lend itself to inexpensive mass production or enjoy significant economies of scale. Writing in the late 1890s, William Steinway lamented the fact that Americans no longer constituted the majority of "piano artisans," but skilled workers had to be lured to this country from Germany. Steinway noted some blamed this on the fact that the United States no longer had an effective "apprentice law in force in any of the States." Actually, he argued, such a law would make little difference since American youths were no longer willing to serve a six- or seven-year apprenticeship before being allowed to enter the trade. The innovations in the production of pianos and organs during the nineteenth century improved the quality of the instruments but did not decrease either the skill or the labor costs involved in production. Musical instrument manufacturing in the nineteenth and early twentieth centuries simply was not a decreasing cost industry in the sense that sewing machines, clocks, watches, and bicycles were.[12]

Few industries embraced as quickly or as completely the notion of large-scale production, closely tied to an aggressive marketing program, utilizing "labor-saving machinery for producing perfect and interchangeable parts," as the clock and watch industry.[13] Even before the Civil War, American manufacturers had seized control of the market from English and Swiss producers, and it was not until the Swiss "adopted American methods and machinery" in the latter part of the nineteenth century that Swiss watches re-entered the American market. In 1895, Edward Howard, president of the E. Howard Clock Company, commenting on the large-scale operations required to remain competitive, argued that only ten major American clock companies and only eight watch companies did business "on an extensive scale."[14] David Hounshell pointed out that unlike the firearms industry which sought to manufacture arms with interchangeable parts, "the clock industry . . . desired above all to turn out vast numbers of cheap clocks. . . . When markets seemed to sag or competition pushed too hard, clock manufacturers introduced a new model."[15] Faced with competition from products such as "The Celebrated Imitation Gold Hunting Watch," the more reliable firms stressed brand-names and the dependability of their brands. Seth Thomas, Waterbury, New Haven, Waltham, Elgin, Ingersoll, Howard, and Hamilton all conducted extensive advertising campaigns in the nineteenth century. Although clock and watch advertisers emphasized the variety of styles, and style became increasingly important at the turn of the century, the major theme was the quality associated with dependable brand names. For example, Waltham Watches, certainly one of the most widely advertised brands, secured the endorsement of that ubiquitous endorser Henry Ward Beecher, who assured consumers that his Waltham Watch had "run more steadily, evenly and accurately than its foreign competitor [a superlative English Watch]."[16] Actually, unlike many other products, clock and watch manufacturers had operated as a decreasing cost industry with a dependence on advertising and national markets throughout most of the last half of the nineteenth century.

Unlike musical instruments and watches and clocks, the advertising of phonographs for home entertainment is a twentieth-century phenomenon. Although Edison secured the basic patent for his machine in 1878, work on the electric light delayed the development of a practical machine until the last decade of the nineteenth century. In the meantime, the Columbia Graphophone Company was attempting to market their instrument for office use as a dictating machine. Edison announced their machine for sale as early as 1893, but it was not until a decade later in a double-page ad in the *Saturday Evening Post* that the promotion of the Victrola as a home musical instrument started. The ad featured the famous dog listening to the phonograph with the caption "His Master's Voice."[17] Like many new inventions, the early advertising sought to reassure potential customers of the dependability, the solid construction, and the practicality of the machines. A 1915, full-page, color ad in the *Overland Monthly* placed the Victrola in an attractive social setting, with the price listed in a very inconspicuous fashion and with the caption "The instrument that brings you the world's best music in all its beauty."[18] By the beginning of the second decade of the century, the appeal had shifted to the popularity and social status associated with owning a Victrola. Sales boomed.

The last decades of the nineteenth century witnessed the development of a large number of vastly improved or new mechanical appliances such as the phonograph. Advertisements filled the popular magazines for such items as "The Bennett Telephone," designed for "short private lines"; and the Keystone washer, which clamped on any sized tub and which was guaranteed to "wash cleaner, easier, and with less injury to clothes than any other in the world." Keystone also produced a clothes wringer, which the company advertised with almost identical copy as that used for the washer. The Massachusetts Organ Co. in Boston advertised the "Phonographic Piano—A Most Wonderful Invention" and the Organita, "The Most Wonderful Musical Instrument in the World."[19] Both the piano and the organ utilized strips of perforated paper like the early versions of the player piano, but a closer inspection would reveal that they more closely resembled music boxes than full-sized pianos and organs. Appliances such as Jewett's Refrigerator, Adams & Westlake's "non-explosive oil stove," and the Hull Vapor Cook Stove appeared in the *Harper's Weekly* advertising.[20] Among the ads for patent medicines, musical instruments, lawn mowers, and various mechanical devices were occasional industrial and even institutional advertisements. Companies such as the Westinghouse Machine Co. of Pittsburgh advertised their "Westinghouse Automatic Engine" and their central stations for incandescent systems; the American Bell Telephone Company published warnings to consumers (probably of the Bennett telephone) that the patents granted to Thomas A. Edison "embrace all forms of microphone transmitters and carbon telephones."[21] Readers of *Godey's, Peterson's, Frank Leslies'*, or *Harper's* magazines during the decades of the 1880s and '90s had no doubt become acclimated to the wondrous new products being continually introduced through the advertising pages of their favorite periodical. Even the most jaded consumers would probably have noticed the boom in bicycle advertising and the advertising campaign introducing the Eastman Kodak camera.

In his study of the development of mass production in the United States, David Hounshell argued that by 1880, the Singer Sewing Machine and the McCormick Reaper began to dominate their respective markets. Both introduced production techniques that allowed them to enjoy increasing benefits from the lower production costs associated with economies of scale. Unable to compete, a number of rival firms "turned to a different line of manufacturing—notably to the bicycle—in order to use their manufacturing plant." "Beginning in the late 1880s," Hounshell noted, the bicycle craze "reached fever pitch by 1895-96 and then collapsed entirely in 1897."[22]

For Presbrey, of course, almost complete credit for creating demand for bicycles went to advertising. Citing advertising expenditures for Monarch Bicycles, Presbrey argued that Monarch spent "a few thousand in 1893" and sold 1,200 machines. In 1894, the figure was $20,000, with 5,000 bicycles sold, and the next year, Monarch spent $75,000 and sold 20,000 machines. In 1896, only three years after the firm started their campaign, Monarch allocated $125,000 for advertising, with $10,000 going into catalogs and $10,000 for a bicycle racing crew that toured the country participating in bicycle races under the Monarch name. The remaining $105,000 went into newspapers and magazines, and the company sold 50,000 bicycles. Specifically, Presbrey credited the Columbia and the Victor safety bicycles with mounting the advertising campaigns "that set the famous 'bicycle craze' going. In ten years, systematic advertising by these and a score of other companies . . . made one person in seventy in the United States a 'devotee of the wheel.' . . . They swarmed in city, street and country road, single and tandem, *and to the advertising man presented an inspiring picture of the results of full-schedule, large-scale advertising.*"[23] While Presbrey willingly credited advertising with creating the craze, he pointedly ignored the bust.

In 1876, at the Centennial Exhibition in Philadelphia, Albert A. Pope, a Boston businessman who would become known as the "father of the bicycle," saw an English-made bicycle. A year later Pope ordered a machine constructed for his personal use; it "was made entirely by hand, and cost the somewhat extravagant sum of $313."[24] Pope felt that the design of the "ordinary or high bicycle" limited its demand to "those brave men whose courage and love of the sport could not be dampened by the occasional header." With the development and introduction of the safety bicycle (two equal-sized wheels) in 1887, cycling became an activity to be enjoyed by "any one who is able to walk . . . boys and girls . . . men and women."[25] Albert Pope threw himself into the promotion of bicycling: he supported *Bicycling World*, a semiweekly magazine that reported on American cycling activities. He sponsored poster contests and induced noted artists to enter them; he arranged exhibition tours of the posters, and he supported the League of American Wheelmen in its legal battles to get the bicycle classified as a transportation vehicle and hence be permitted to use the public roads. Pope became involved in the Good Roads movement, seeking more and better roads in the United States. Beginning in 1883, Pope was one of the moving personalities in convincing the bicycle trade to hold a series of exhibitions, the first of which was in Springfield, Massachusetts; by 1894 both New York and Chicago held annual bicycle trade shows. The exhibitions attracted hundreds of exhibitors and agents and thousands of interested spectators.[26]

The promotional and advertising efforts of Pope and his fellow bicycle manufacturers paid handsome dividends. The demand for bicycles escalated. By the middle of the 1890s, consumers had their choice of a wide variety of such well-advertised brands as Cresent, Columbia, Waverly, Victor, Gladiator, Acme, and Windsor. The bicycle proved so influential that it spawned new products, such as the bicycle shoe and corset; it influenced dressing styles for women; and even Ivory Soap attempted to capitalize on the craze by claiming that Ivory was an excellent bicycle chain lubricant. For women, the bicycle craze proved somewhat emancipatory: vigorous outdoor activity for women became more acceptable, and for the first time advertisements illustrated women outside the home in a non-domestic setting.

Up to 1887 and the introduction of the safety bicycle, probably no more than 250,000 machines had been produced in the United States, primarily by the Pope Manufacturing Company. In early 1893, a bicycle insurance company estimated at least one million bicycles were in use. Pope himself estimated the 1895 output at more than 550,000 and predicted that at least "fifty per cent more will be made and sold in 1896" by the 200 bicycle manufacturers in the United States.[27] Bicycle production, while requiring a good deal of skilled labor in some operations, such as the wheel assembly, lent itself well to cost-saving innovations and was a decreasing cost industry. Moreover, as Hounshell skillfully demonstrated, the industry was effective in innovating for cost reduction. Even in the throes of the Panic of 1893, the bicycle industry prospered. However, when the census of 1899 reported that over 1.1 million bicycles had been produced that year, the decline had already commenced. Five years later, fewer than 250,000 machines were manufactured, and the 1910 census indicated that only slightly over 160,000 machines had been produced during the previous year.[28] In Hounshell's words, "the market for bicycles simply vanished."[29] Bicycle manufacturers did not cease to advertise, but all the advertising in the world would not have rekindled the demand. If the bicycle craze testified to the power of advertising, its demise after 1897 testified to the impotence of advertising to build or even sustain demand in the face of shifting fashions and changing technology.

In retrospect, Hiram Percy Maxim, a pioneer in the construction of the automobile, offered the best explanation of the demise of the bicycle as a major means of transportation. Maxim noted that the railroad "created a new demand [for transportation] which it was beyond the ability of the railroad to supply. Then it came about that the bicycle could not satisfy the demand which it had created. A mechanically propelled vehicle was wanted instead of a foot-propelled one, and we now know that the automobile was the answer."[30] The bicycle craze also produced a willingness, even a desire, on the part of the American consumer to accept new products and to expect continual improvements in those same products.

Of all the advertising campaigns at the end of the nineteenth century which sought to create demand, establish a brand name, and secure a national market for that product and brand name, none proved more successful than the Eastman Dry Plate and Film Company's campaign for their "Kodak." The campaign, which started in 1888, emphasized the ease of taking photographs and the small, convenient size of the Kodak. The ads illustrated the Kodak in a variety of settings, "abroad," on board ship, and at family outings, and emphasized that "the finest pictures may be taken by persons with no knowledge of the art."[31] With the Kodak, Eastman made photography practical and available to amateurs. For $25, the customer got a Kodak loaded for one hundred pictures and "a division of labor is offered. . . . The operator need not learn anything about photography. He can 'press the button—we do the rest.'" When the picture had been taken, the operator returned the entire camera and Eastman reloaded the camera and processed the pictures.[32] The rapid growth and development of amateur photography led to the slogan "You press the button and we do the rest," being modified within a year by the addition of "or you can do it yourself," in recognition of the fact that many amateurs were developing their own film. By 1892, Eastman recommended the new improved Kodak with easy-to-operate features designed specifically for women, and by 1905 the Brownie folding camera offered many additional automatic features for the amateur photographer. So successful was the Eastman campaign that the word "Kodak" was adopted into the language as a synonym for camera. Convinced that this was counterproductive, Eastman adopted another slogan, "If it isn't an Eastman, it ISN'T a Kodak."[33]

Eastman ads during the early decades of the century continued to emphasize improvements in the Kodak and to stress the popularity of both the Kodak and amateur photography. Slogans such as Eastman's "If it isn't an Eastman, it ISN'T a Kodak" provided another way to lend familiarity to the product, and made it not just another product but a familiar fixture in the popular culture. Luxury and recreational products were relatively rare in the nineteenth century, but at times their popularity took on the proportions of "fads." Certainly, the rapid acceptance of such items reflected an important aspect of popular culture. Advertising, in selling the material objects of the fads or crazes, such as the bicycle and camera, on a national scale created homogeneity in America's leisure and recreational habits as in other areas.

One of the most persistent themes in advertising addressed to women throughout the period of 1880 to 1920 was the notion that regardless of the household product or appliance being advertised, it would greatly reduce the labor involved in cooking, cleaning, sewing, washing, scrubbing,

"KODAK"

Is our Registered and common-law Trade-Mark and cannot be rightfully applied except to goods of our manufacture.

If a dealer tries to sell you a camera or films, or other goods not of our manufacture, under the Kodak name, you can be sure that he has an inferior article that he is trying to market on the Kodak reputation.

If it isn't an Eastman, it isn't a Kodak.

EASTMAN KODAK COMPANY,
ROCHESTER, N. Y., *The Kodak City.*

Reprinted from *Saturday Evening Post*, May 25, 1912.

Take a
KODAK
with you

Catalogue free at your dealer's, or by mail.

EASTMAN KODAK CO., ROCHESTER, N. Y., *The Kodak City.*

Reprinted from *Saturday Evening Post*, May 16, 1914.

or whatever. Many early ads, especially for household cleansing agents and appliances, spent most of the copy extolling the product's labor-saving virtues. Later advertisements contained the same theme, but added a personalized element and often appealed to the need to be a "good" wife and mother. In spite of the fact that women, even middle-class women, were seeking and finding employment outside the home in unparalleled numbers, advertisers never suggested that the new labor-saving appliances and products would be especially helpful to working women. Yet, as James McGovern, writing about the changes in women's manners and morals in pre-World War I America, noted, the "great leap forward in women's participation in economic life came between 1900 and 1910."[34] Moreover, the "great leap" accompanied a restructuring of the role of women in the economy, "with women leaving roles as domestics and assuming positions affording more personal independence as clerks and stenographers."[35] Advertisers failed to reflect in their marketing programs the new economic realities for women; without exception the women depicted in advertisements were either upper-class homemakers or domestics, and the appeal most often was to more leisure time, and to being a better wife and mother.

By 1910, leisure time and outside activities were the supposed reward for using the various labor-saving products, and the woman who did not use them was "old fashioned" and failed to "keep up with the times."[36] An 1888 ad for Empire Wringers stated, "Buy the wringer that saves the most labor . . . saves half the labor of other wringers and costs but little more." As an added incentive, the ad concluded that "Empire does not grease the clothes."[37] A Western Electric Vacuum ad in 1914 pictured two women in spheres, one with a broom, one with a vacuum, with the caption "Woman in her newer sphere." The copy praised the "new way" of cleaning over the "sweep and dust age" and concluded that "There is a new sphere for the woman in the home as well as in the broader activities of her life, and nothing so revolutionizes the dull routine of her household work as the Western Electric Vacuum Cleaner."[38] The following year, advertising copy for vacuum cleaners in *Cosmopolitan* suggested that the new electric vacuum cleaners allowed the housewife to "Push the Button—and Enjoy the Springtime!"[39] Advertising copywriters (almost overwhelmingly men) drew heavily on the labor-saving themes in their efforts to convince customers of the virtues of each appliance. Perhaps they even believed their own copy.

James R. McGovern suggested that "Statistics on money expended on those industries which reduced home labor for the wife (Figure 4.2) suggest that women in middle-income families gained considerable leisure after 1914."[40] McGovern noted that the "tone and content of advertising in popular magazines" tended to confirm his analysis, especially when "compared with advertising at the turn of the century."[41] Recent studies by Ruth Cowan, however, suggest that really only the nature of the work shifted.

Figure 4.2
U.S. Population Compared to Consumption of Related Household
Items ($1 million)

	1909	1914	1919	1923
Population (1,000,000)	90	99	104	112
Percent Increase		10%	5%	8%
(a) Canned fruits & Vegetables	$162	$254	$575	$623
Percent Increase		57%	126%	8%
(b) Cleaning & Polishing Preparations	$ 6	$ 9	$ 27	$ 35
Percent Increase		50%	200%	30%
(c) Mechanical Appliances (refrigerators, sewing machines, washers, cookers)	$152	$175	$419	$535
Percent Increase		15%	139%	28%
(d) Electricity in Household Operations	$ 83	$132	$265	$389
Percent Increase		59%	101%	47%

Source: James R. McGovern, "The American Woman's Pre-World War I Freedom in Manners and Morals," Journal of American History, 55:321 (September 1968). Reprinted by permission.

Certainly, the conclusion that the introduction of special-purpose household items and appliances and the further finishing of clothing and foods resulted in substantial leisure time for women is a serious oversimplification of what really happened. To quote Cowan:

we do have various time studies which demonstrate somewhat surprisingly that housewives with conveniences were spending just as much time on household duties as were housewives without them—or, to put it another way, housework, like so many other types of work, expands to fill the time available . . . mechanization of the household meant that the time expended on some jobs decreased, but also that new jobs were substituted, and in some cases—notably laundering—time expenditures for old jobs increased because of higher standards. The advantages of mechanization may be somewhat more dubious than they seem at first glance.[42]

Given that McGovern's work covered the pre-World War I period, while Cowan convincingly demonstrated that the "drastic changes in patterns of household work" occurred after World War I, it seems clear that in this

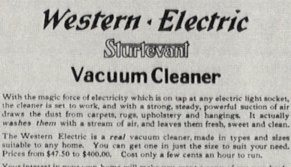

Woman in Her Newer Sphere

The "new way" of housecleaning eclipses the ache and fatigue and long hours of the sweep-and-dust age. The Western Electric Vacuum Cleaner brings brightness into the home, banishes the dust-clouded, danger-laden conditions of the past. There is a new sphere for the woman in the home as well as in the broader activities of her life, and nothing so revolutionizes the dull routine of her household work as the

Western · Electric

Sturtevant

Vacuum Cleaner

With the magic force of electricity which is on tap at any electric light socket, the cleaner is set to work, and with a strong, steady, powerful suction of air draws the dust from carpets, rugs, upholstery and hangings. It actually *washes them* with a stream of air, and leaves them fresh, sweet and clean.

The Western Electric is a *real* vacuum cleaner, made in types and sizes suitable to any home. You can get one in just the size to suit your need. Prices from $47.50 to $400.00. Cost only a few cents an hour to run.

Your interest in your own home will make you want a copy of our new book, "The Clean Way to Clean." It describes the correct principles of cleaning, and the approved modern methods of applying them. Ask for book No. 14-A P.

There is an opportunity for agents to represent us in some unoccupied territories.

WESTERN ELECTRIC COMPANY

Manufacturers of the 7,500,000 "Bell" Telephones

New York	Atlanta	Chicago	St. Louis	Kansas City	Denver	San Francisco
Buffalo	Richmond	Milwaukee	Indianapolis	Oklahoma City	Omaha	Oakland
Philadelphia	Savannah	Pittsburgh	Minneapolis	Dallas	Salt Lake City	Seattle
Boston	Cincinnati	Cleveland	St. Paul	Houston	Los Angeles	Portland
New Orleans						

EQUIPMENT FOR EVERY ELECTRICAL NEED

Reprinted from *Ladies' Home Journal*, April 1914.

area McGovern's conclusions were based on the false image created by early appliance advertising.[43]

Not until 1910 was electrical current for domestic residences standardized in the United States. Only at that juncture could the manufacturers of electrical appliances prudently make the sizable investments needed for mass-production facilities. Electrical appliance prices fell markedly in the twenty years following the standardization of electrical power. In addition, manufacturers introduced new devices and continually improved their older products in an effort to secure product differentiation. Electrical motors, which could be attached to fans, sewing machines, and even washing machines, made their appearance in the nineteenth century. Toasters, irons, hot water heaters, and other heating devices were available by 1910. Before the United States entered the war, electric vacuum cleaners, sewing machines, and washing machines were on the market. Electric refrigerators and even dishwashers had been developed, but as Ruth Cowan pointed out, they "were little more than toys for the very rich—as they tended to be either extremely expensive or extremely unreliable."[44] While the electrical appliance industry, as a mass-production decreasing cost industry, was essentially a phenomenon of the 1920s and 1930s, however, women consumers had been conditioned by a generation of advertising to expect new products and continual improvements in the style and performance of old.

Thrift, always a cherished American value, remained one of the dominant themes in appliance advertising throughout the nineteenth century, along with quality, dependability, and durability.

By the second decade of the twentieth century, quality had succumbed to style, built-in obsolescence had replaced durability, and social acceptance meant more than dependability. Economy, rather than thrift, became a virtue, and the upper- and middle-class American housewife practiced thrift by purchasing new products that were "economical." Indeed, appeals to economy seemed to grow almost in proportion to the apparent affluence depicted in the advertisements. Economy, however, as defined by American businesses in their advertisements, did not mean saving; rather it meant "getting your money's worth on your purchases."

In 1885, the Baldwin Dry-Air Refrigerator assured customers that the Gold Medal received by the Baldwin Company at both the New Orleans Exposition and at the Mechanics Fair in Boston certified its quality, as did the Bronze Metal for Superiority awarded by the American Institute in New York City. Moreover, the Baldwin was the choice of such famous institutions as the United States Army and a large number of hospitals and colleges.[45] The Lowell Washer offered to refund the purchaser's money if the customer did not agree that the washer "did better work, easier and in less time."[46] As late as 1905, the Detroit Jewel Gas Ranges advised their customers to insist on ranges with the company's trademark as an assurance of quality.[47] Even Singer Sewing Machine, when their machine won the Grand Prize for sewing machines at the 1900 Paris Exposition, ran a full-page advertisement with the "announcement," but Singer shifted themes. Not only was the Singer functional, it was stylish; the cabinet came in oak or walnut and could be ordered to match "any surroundings"; in addition, the Singer Cabinet Table Model was perfectly at home in the bedroom or the parlor.[48] The 1905 Baldwin Refrigerator came in 140 styles in ash, oak, or soft wood and would match any decor.[49] In a 1910 ad entitled "The Link to Perfect Dressmaking," there were three scenes: in the first, a woman is shown selecting a fabric; in the second, she is sewing the fabric; and in the third, she is wearing a very stylish finished dress. More importantly, all the scenes have Singer Machines in the background to make sure that the consumer equated the Singer with style. Ten years later, three children are depicted having a tea party on a Singer Sewing Machine in an obviously middle-class parlor and the actual machine is not shown.[50] By the beginning of the 1920s, style had indeed replaced function.

While a good many of the new appliances did, indeed, offer housewives added convenience, the early refrigerator (icebox), while the only device available to urban households to keep food refrigerated, was a veritable nuisance. Housewives had to arrange for ice to be delivered, to clean up the puddles of water left after a delivery, to continually empty the container into which the ice dripped, and to endlessly clean the inside to prevent mold and mildew from forming in the damp interiors. Early advertisements played on these shortcomings, and individual manufacturers offered a variety of improvements to remedy each defect. For example, the McCray Refrigerator offered the convenience of outside ice delivery through a panel in the wall and provided a hose to drain the water to the outside.[51] The Leonard Cleanable Refrigerator featured a porcelain water cooler and a pure white porcelain enamel interior for easy cleaning, while its rival the Monroe advertised "rounded porcelain corners," which ensured complete and easy cleaning; indeed, the ad promised that the Monroe "with a cloth wrung from hot water becomes germlessly clean." Not to be outdone, the White Frost Sanitary Refrigerator boasted white porcelain inside and out. The entire cylinder-formed box stood on old-fashioned bathtub-like legs and featured a water cooler reservoir on top.[52] The Bon Syphon stressed that their product "keeps up a vigorous circulation of air between the provisions and the ice chambers by which all the impurity-laden moisture is condensed on the ice and drawn off through the drain."[53] Almost all the advertisements included information on the recent improvements, such as glass linings, revolving doors, or the mechanics of air circulation in the new models. Most offered free booklets on the proper use and care of refrigerated food. Each company promised housewives that their brand would economize on ice and reduce loss of perishable foods. Economy was emphasized, but it was an economy of wise consumption, not of thrift.

While the early vacuum cleaners promised "thrift" in reducing the labor of inefficient corn brooms, in truth the first machines offered little improvement. As late as 1913, the Bissell Electric Suction Cleaner was acclaimed for weighing only *thirty-three* pounds. The 1909 hand-operated Ideal Vacuum claimed to be so easy to operate that an eight-year-old would find it no challenge, and it cost only $25; those with electric motors cost only $55 and $60 for direct and alternating current, respectively; unfortunately, the Ideal appeared heavy, crude, and cumbersome.[54] By 1915, the Franz Premier Electric Cleaner cost only $25 and weighed only nine pounds.[55] The Electric Sweeper-Vac emphasized that electricity did all the work and the machine was so light and easy to use that a woman should actually feel rested after vacuuming. The same company used an illustration of a small girl using the vacuum. The copy suggested that operating a vacuum was play for a child as well as training for her future.[56] The labor-saving qualities of the appliance was only one appeal used in ads. Women were also lectured on the need to be modern, to buy the latest models, and to keep up with their friends and neighbors. A 1920 advertisement for the Electric Sweeper-Vac captured that theme with an illustration of a gathering of very stylishly dressed women grouped around a bride admiring a vacuum cleaner. The caption assured women that the vacuum was the "Best of all her gifts" since "the heaviest load of all her household duties has been lifted from her shoulders by the Electric Sweeper-Vac."[57]

The Hoover Suction Sweeper Co. in 1920 ran a series of ads depicting the Hoover in a variety of settings: in front of a fireplace, in front of a dining room table, in front of a piano, in front of a bassinette, and in front of a Christmas tree loaded with presents. The caption stated, "The Hoover: it beats—as it sweeps—as it cleans." The copy explained that using the Hoover saved labor as all three functions—beating out embedded dirt, sweeping clinging litter, and suctioning to remove surface dirt—were performed at the same time.[58] In each of the ads, the Hoover was placed in a very stylish, upper- or middle-class home, and like most vacuums advertised, the Hoover was purported to be both labor-saving and economical. Potential customers were informed that modern housewives knew that vacuums not only kept their homes cleaner, but that they helped preserve rugs and fabrics, cost less than one "professional renovation," and lasted a lifetime. And in 1915, the Eureka Electric Vacuum Cleaner Company's easy payment plan made all this possible for only a few cents a day.

In the unlikely event that the housewife was not familiar with an appliance, almost every firm offered instruction booklets and many a free trial. Baldwin Dry-Air Refrigerators sent free circulars on how to store food and keep it fresh and odorless, while the White Mountain Freezer Company included with the purchase of any ice cream freezer a free recipe booklet entitled "Frozen Dainties," which explained how to make ice cream, sherbets, and water ices. For those customers thinking of buying an icebox, the Grand

Rapids Refrigerator Company would mail a free booklet and a sample piece of porcelain to guide them in selecting the best product.[59] Detroit Jewel Gas Ranges offered a free cookbook with over fifty recipes, and the Bon Syphon staged a "Novel Recipe Contest" complete with prizes and promised to share the recipes with their customers.[60] The rising school of "scientific homemakers," home economists, women's magazine writers and editors, and even the government offered advice on how to cook, clean, care for children, dress, eat, and most of all how to consume with economy.

Many appliance dealers, department stores, and hardware stores, taking a lesson from the Singer Sewing Machine Company, arranged free demonstrations and lessons for customers. In 1905, the Simmons Hardware Company in St. Louis, no doubt taking notice of various department stores' activities held during the previous year in conjunction with the St. Louis World's Fair, announced an "Exposition Week" beginning March 21st, but with events all year. Some thirty-eight demonstrations were scheduled, with experts from many appliance factories on hand to explain their products. The Majestic Coal and Gas Range representative demonstrated baking bread in a gas oven, while the expert for the Volex Sewing Machine taught "moss embroidery, Hatenburg and Mexican draw work." Ladies were invited to meet their friends and relax in the new reception and waiting room. The public was invited to attend a chrysanthemum show and a performance by a noted soprano as well as attend the demonstrations.[61] Not to be outdone, a couple months after the Simmons Exposition Week, the Charles Suda Hardware Store, the John E. Dooly Furnace Co., and the Laclede Gas Light Company all announced illustrated demonstrations and lectures on cooking with gas.[62] Certainly, through the flower shows and musical performances as well as the demonstrations, this was intended to lure customers into the various stores. Regardless of the motivation and more to the point, countless staged events such as these provided ample training for women consumers in the art and economy of consumption.

Appeals to labor-saving and style, even when connected to the need to be "up-to-date" and not "old fashioned," were increasingly supplemented by playing on the concern of housewives about the health and welfare of their families. For example, a 1910 ad for the Monroe Icebox claimed that most other brands had corners and cracks that were almost impossible to clean, hence "here particles of food collect and breed countless germs. These germs get into your food and make it poison, and the family suffers—from no traceable cause." In the same magazine, the McCray Icebox copy used words such as "spoiled," "unpleasant odors," "unsanitary," and "sickness" to describe competing appliances and "clean," "wholesome," "safest," and "most economical" in describing the McCray. Appeals to sanitation were not limited to iceboxes. Vacuum cleaner advertisements often emphasized that germs bred in dirt and warned housewives to protect their families by avoiding dirt-carried diseases. The Ideal Vacuum Cleaner

Write for Our Free Book on
HOME REFRIGERATION

This book tells how to select the home Refrigerator, how to know the poor from the good, how to keep down ice bills, how to keep a Refrigerator sanitary and sweet — lots of things you should know before buying ANY Refrigerator.

It also tells all about the "Monroe," the Refrigerator with inner walls made in one piece of solid, unbreakable, White Porcelain Ware an inch thick and highly glazed with every corner rounded. No cracks or crevices anywhere. The "Monroe" is as easy to keep clean as a china bowl.

Always sold
DIRECT and at Factory Prices.
Cash or monthly payments.

Most other Refrigerators have cracks and corners which cannot be cleaned. Here particles of food collect and breed countless germs. These germs get into your food and make it poison, and the family suffers—from no traceable cause.

The "Monroe" can be sterilized and made germlessly clean in an instant by simply wiping out with a cloth wrung from hot water. It's like "washing dishes," for the "Monroe" is really a thick porcelain dish inside.

The high death rate among children in the summer months could be greatly reduced if the Monroe Refrigerator was used in every home where there are little folks.

The "Monroe" is installed in the best flats and apartments, occupied by people who CARE—and is found to-day in a large majority of the VERY BEST homes in the United States. The largest and best Hospitals use it exclusively, The health of the whole family is safeguarded by the use of a Monroe Refrigerator.

When you have carefully read the book and know all about Home Refrigeration, you will know WHY and will realize how important it is to select carefully. Please write for book to-day.

MONROE REFRIGERATOR CO.   Station 8   Cincinnati, O.

Reprinted from *Literary Digest*, June 11, 1910.

The Best of All Her Gifts

Longest to be remembered is

The ELECTRIC SWEEPER-VAC

WITH·MOTOR·DRIVEN·BRUSH

She cannot soon forget either the gift or the giver.

The reason is easily seen, since the heaviest load of all her household duties has been lifted from her shoulders by the *Electric Sweeper-Vac* with its motor driven (not muscle driven) brush.

Whether it is rug, mattress, upholstery or drapery cleaning, electricity does it for her.

With the *Electric Sweeper-Vac*, she does not have to do part of her cleaning by hand and part by electricity.

Electricity does it all for her, producing powerful suction and properly speeded brush action.

Two machines in one—sold at the price of one!

Yes, the two accepted types of vacuum cleaners now on the market are fully embodied in the *Electric Sweeper-Vac*, and it costs no more than some of the one type kind.

Either type in the *Electric Sweeper-Vac* is at instant command by one turn of That Lever.

Turn That Lever to the left and you have the type that cleans by suction alone.

Turn That Lever to the right and you have the combination type that cleans by the same powerful suction, plus motor driven brush.

Light weight, easy operation, freedom from adjustment, reasonable price, and many other useful features, make the *Electric Sweeper-Vac* the cleaner for you.

Ask for the most elaborate book ever written on vacuum cleaners.

PNEUVAC COMPANY, Department I, **Worcester, Massachusetts**

Reprinted from *Literary Digest*, June 26, 1920.

warned that, "Any physician will tell you that summer's dirt is laden with the germs of disease." Of course, the Ideal promised to keep "everything clean, wholesome, sanitary, and sweet." What woman could fail to protect her family?[63]

"If I had to choose one word to characterize the temper of women's magazines during the 1920's," Ruth Cowan observed, "it would be 'guilt.' "[64]

[G]uilty if their infants have not gained enough weight, embarrassed if their drains were clogged, guilty if their children go to school in soiled clothes, guilty if all the germs behind the bathroom sink are not eradicated, guilty if they fail to notice the first signs of an oncoming cold, embarrassed if accused of having body odor, guilty if their sons go to school without good breakfasts, guilty if their daughters are unpopular because of old fashion, or unironed, or—heaven forbid—dirty dresses. In earlier times women were made to feel guilty if they abandoned their children or were too free with their affections. In the years after World War I, American women were made to feel guilty about sending their children to school in scuffed shoes. Between the two kinds of guilty there is a world of difference.[65]

If anything, Cowan is too modest in her analysis. The guilt she so aptly described as pervading the advertisements of the 1920s underlay much of the advertising of the previous two decades. Indeed, by the 1920s, American women had been conditioned by more than a generation of advertising communications increasingly based on the appeal of the need to conform in individual consumption. When modern advertising was able to equate consumption of an article being marketed to social status and approval, it tapped a very deep American insecurity in society and a deadly pressure to conform. Under such conditions guilt, even the guilt of non-consumption, is the natural result of the fear of non-conformity.

A 1900 ad for Brunswick-Balke-Collender Billiard Tables employed even more blatant guilt tactics that charged mothers to "Keep Your Boys at Home." By providing a pool table at home, a good mother could keep her boys out of the pool halls.[66] In VanCamp Beans advertisements the company stressed the ease of using their products by picturing the hard (old) way of preparing beans and the new (easy) way, arguing that modern women take advantage of modern technology; otherwise, "One might as well spin her own linen, weave her own carpets, make her own soap—as they did in the olden days." The appeal for mothers to be modern and utilize labor-saving products unfortunately was accompanied by an assurance that VanCamp Beans were prepared in a sanitary and scientific fashion and ended with the warning that no housewife could do as well and should never deprive her family of the best.[67] By the end of the war, mothers were frequently warned about the mental health of children who were forced to face the world without the "right" breakfast, the "proper" shoes, or any other item necessary to conform. An ad for Slipova Clothes for children warned mothers that "There is a direct relation between your children's

A
Champion
of
Woman's
Rights

—the right to
freedom
from household
drudgery

—the right to
a clean home
and leisure to
enjoy it

—the right to
spotless floors and
walls, shining pots
and pans, etc.,
without the penalty
of tired arms
and aching back

Old
Dutch
Cleanser

insures all
this to every
woman

Its many uses and
full directions on

Large Sifter-Can

10c

Reprinted from *Ladies' Home Journal*, July 1910.

mental state and the clothes they wear."[68] Obviously, a hefty measure of guilt was in store for any mother who failed to take the advice offered in all these and many other ads.

By and large, national advertising ignored real-world events such as the Panic of 1893 or the Spanish-American War, and even the passage of the Pure Food and Drug Act and the truth-in-advertising movement, both of which undoubtedly exercised a great deal of influence on advertising. Nevertheless, little specific mention of either event intruded into national advertising. Only America's entry into World War I, which united the nation behind the war effort, gave advertisers an uncontroversial issue to use in their appeals. The suffrage movement, which should have appealed to advertising's major audience, on the other hand, was fraught with controversy, and advertising agencies tended to shy away from the possibility of offending any consumer. What few ads referred to the suffrage movement, and they were even less numerous than might be expected, tended to relate suffrage to the labor-saving theme. Women found little support for their movement from within the ranks of manufacturers and advertising agents; what few ads did touch on women's issues were at best innocuous and at worst offensive only to liberated women. No doubt, advertising executives counted the latter as extremely rare. An "Old Dutch Cleanser" ad appearing in the middle of the suffrage movement, for example, was headed "A Champion of Women's Rights," and the copy went on to list those rights as "the right to spotless floors and walls, shining pots and pans," and so forth.[69]

The advertisements that employed a "liberating" theme were even more disturbing than those that ignored the issues. Liberation, in the hands of advertising copywriters, paid lip service to feminine liberation and still managed to keep the woman confined to her traditional role in the home, outfitted with the new "conveniences of industry." While the women depicted in advertisements were freed from a certain amount of household drudgery and awarded a significant role in the consumption ethic, the notion of a woman's proper place being in the home went unquestioned and was, in fact, reinforced by advertising themes. "Here lay a festering contradiction of modern womanhood," Stuart Ewen concluded, "one which would emerge in years to come as reinvigorated feminism."[70]

5

TRADEMARKS AND BRAND NAMES—SELLING THE IMAGE

Advertisements are now so numerous that they are very negligently pursued, and it is therefore become necessary to gain attention by magnificence of promises, and by eloquence sometimes sublime and sometimes pathetic. Promise, large promise, is the soul of advertisement.

—Dr. Samuel Johnson, January 20, 1759,
in the *Idler* as quoted in the *Encyclopedia Americana* (1967) I:161

One of the most striking transformations in the American economy during the twentieth century has been the decline of the relative share of employment in production and the growth in service sector employment. At the same time, distribution seems to have increased or at least maintained its relative share in the economy during most of this century. In a major study of the role of distribution in the American economy, Harold Barger concluded that while the number of persons engaged in the commodity-producing industries more than doubled in the eighty years following 1870, the number engaged in the distribution of these commodities increased twelvefold. As Figure 5.1 illustrates, distribution's share of the total labor force increased from 6 per cent to nearly 10 per cent in the period 1870 to 1920; at the same time, the share involved in commodity production fell from 70 per cent to 57 per cent.[1] In addition, output per man-hour in commodity production rose more than twice as fast as in distribution, meaning that all other things being equal, the costs of production declined more than twice as fast or increased less than half as fast as the costs of distribution.

Actually, Barger suggested that while the share of the retail sales dollar consumed by distribution costs between World War I and 1950 remained "with remarkable regularity" around 37 percent, there had nevertheless been a slow but definite increase in distribution's share of the retail costs

Figure 5.1
Percentage Distribution of the Labor Force by Industry, 1870–1920

	1870	1880	1890	1900	1910	1920
Commodity production and construction	75.8	75.7	71.4	68.5	64.1	62.3
Commodity production	70.0	70.9	65.3	62.7	57.8	57.0
Construction	5.9	4.8	6.1	5.8	6.4	5.3
Service	24.2	24.3	28.6	31.5	35.9	37.7
Commodity distribution	6.1	6.7	7.7	8.6	9.3	9.9
Other service	18.0	17.6	20.8	22.9	26.5	27.9
Total	100.0	100.0	100.0	100.0	100.0	100.0

Source: Harold Barger, *Distribution's Place in the American Economy Since 1869*, National Bureau of Economic Research No. 58 (New York, 1955), 6. Reprinted by permission.

during the *preceding fifty years*. Moreover, since this occurred at a time when transportation costs displayed a secular decrease, other factors in the distribution process must explain the rise in proportional costs.[2] Barger made a convincing case that at least part of the rise in distribution costs could be attributed to urban growth and to the fact that products previously consumed on the farm or household products consumed in the home must now be processed and sold in distant markets. Increased finishing prior to the final purchase also accounted for additional costs, as did credit, further retail packaging, delivery, customer conveniences, and services offered at the point of sale.[3]

In spite of the relatively low gains in man-hour productivity in distribution and the demand for more services, retail and wholesale margins remained remarkably constant. At least part of the explanation lies in the fact that some of the increased costs were passed back to manufacturers in the form of additional processing and packaging. Coffee, sugar, butter, flour, spices, beans, and crackers, to say nothing of liquids such as molasses, vinegar, and even whiskey, had been purchased in bulk and then repackaged by retailers throughout most of the nineteenth century. As Barger concluded, many of the new costs associated with packaging, processing, or even services were not passed on to the retailer. More and more manufacturers absorbed these costs. For the most part, manufacturers have been willing to assume the responsibility of packaging as a means of gaining product differentiation through distinctive packaging of essentially similar products such as sugar,

Figure 5.2
Retail Margins by Kind of Store, 1869–1919 (per cent of retail value)

	1869	1879	1889	1899	1909	1919
Grocery, independent	18.0	18.5	19.0	19.5	19.5	19.5
Grocery, chain	--	--	--	--	17.0	18.0
Meat	29	29	29	28.0	26.8	25.8
Candy	35	35	35	35	35	35
Department	--	--	22.2	25.6	29.3	32.8
Mail order	--	--	24.4	25.0	25.6	26.2
Dry goods	18.7	18.7	19.2	21.4	27.0	29.0
Variety	--	--	--	31	33.3	34.7
Apparel	21.1	23.2	25.4	27.5	29.6	31.8
Household appliances	37	37	37	37	37	37
Vehicles	23	23	23	23	23	23
Automobile accessories	--	--	--	--	26.5	26.5
Filling stations	--	--	--	--	22.0	14.0
Hardware	25.2	25.2	23.7	22.2	23.6	25.0
Bars	46	46	46	46	46	--
Drugs	28.4	28.4	30.2	31.8	33.6	34.6
Liquor	35	35	35	35	35	35
Cigars	33.0	33.0	31.8	30.4	29.0	27.4
Jewelry	31.7	31.7	31.8	31.9	33.8	38.2
Cameras, luggage, toys, and sporting goods	38.6	38.0	37.2	36.5	35.8	35.2
Other	17.5	17.5	17.8	18.1	18.7	19.0

-- = not applicable.

Source: Harold Barger, *Distribution's Place in the American Economy Since 1869*, National Bureau of Economic Research No. 58 (New York, 1955), 81. Reprinted by permission.

coffee, rice, beans, spices, and whiskey. Packaging and further finishing products, especially food products, allowed manufacturers to advertise the packaging and the convenience of their products.

National magazine advertising reflected both the growing use of distinctive packaging to differentiate similar products and the accelerated use of brand names and trademarks on the part of manufacturers and processors. Separated by both time and distance from the producer, consumers became more and more dependent on brand names to ensure real or perceived

Figure 5.3
Wholesale Margins by Kind of Business, 1869–1919 (per cent of wholesale value, except adjustment)

	1869	1879	1889	1899	1909	1919
Grocery, independent	11	11	11	11	11	11
Meat	13	13	13	13	13	13
Dry goods	14	15	16	17	18	18
Apparel	16	16	16	16	16	16
Household appliances	20	20	20	20	20	20
Vehicles	10	10	10	10	10	10
Automobile accessories	--	--	--	--	25.0	25.0
Gasoline and oil	--	--	--	--	18.0	16.0
Hardware	19	19	19	19	20.0	22.0
Liquor	14.5	14.5	14.5	14.5	14.5	14.5
Drugs	10	11	12.2	13.6	15.2	16.6
Cigars	8	8	8	8	8	8
Jewelry	24	24	24	24	24	24

-- = not applicable.

Source: Harold Barger, *Distribution's Place in the American Economy Since 1869*, National Bureau of Economic Research No. 58 (New York, 1955), 84. Reprinted by permission.

quality. For business firms selling in a market characterized by growing competition for consumer loyalty, brand names offered a relatively easy method to gain product differentiation, ensure customer loyalty, and even increase their share of the market. Not surprisingly the last decade of the nineteenth and first decade of the new century witnessed the very rapid expansion of the use of national brand-name advertising.

Free-standing, like a ghostly apparition of a breast-plate from a medieval armour for a lusty Rubenesque woman, Warner's Rust-Proof Corset floated against a garden background with a nude child in hip boots spraying water on it. The advertising copy dwelt on the "patented" rust-proof features of the corset. In addition, the ad mentioned that the new designs "with low bust, bias cut, give the stylish figure effect with ease and comfort."[4] With the exception of the emphasis on the brand-name and rust-proof feature, Warner's turn-of-the-century advertisement typified earlier corset advertisements. Warner Corsets launched their advertising campaign in the 1870s and, as Frank Presbrey noted, "led in wearing apparel" advertisement during the late nineteenth and indeed much of the early twentieth century.

Actually, Presbrey's count of the leaders in national advertising during the 1890s revealed that three corset makers, three shoe companies, and two underwear firms, with the exception of Earl & Wilson Collars, constituted all of the clearly identifiable apparel firms included in the survey.[5]

Writing in 1929, Presbrey, an unabashed admirer of large-scale advertising campaigns, noted that the physical appearance of the W. L. Douglas Shoe ads had scarcely changed since the adoption of the brand-name in 1885. The ads featured a woodcut of W. L. Douglas' head, and the copy read "W. L. Douglas $3 shoe for Gentlemen, the only fine seamless shoe in the world made without tacks or nails." Presbrey's praise of both brand-name corset and shoe advertising some thirty-five years after the ads appeared indicated the very slow development of advertising for men's and women's wearing apparel. The growth of both the men's and women's ready-made apparel industry, in spite of their rather primitive beginnings and the slow development of national advertising for wearing apparel, revealed some of the very real limitations of the power of advertising as well as some of the fundamental shifts in the American economy.

While an analysis of the major national advertisers in 1893 indicated that more than half of the large-scale firms which spent money on advertising were patent medicine proprietors, twenty years later, these patent medicine promoters had been largely replaced. In fact, only seven of all the original 104 firms, regardless of product, remained on the list of large advertisers: Quaker Oats, Armour, Cudahy, Procter & Gamble, American Tobacco Company, P. Lorillard, and Remington Typewriters. Amazingly, as Daniel Pope pointed out, "among leading national advertisers, there was far more turnover in the twenty-five years before World War I than in the nearly seventy-five years since then."[6]

The firms engaging in large-scale advertising in the first two decades of the twentieth century tended to cluster in five industries—food processing, chemicals (mostly soaps and cosmetics), automobile manufacturing, tire producers, and tobacco companies, all of which relied heavily on brand-name advertising. In spite of the overly enthusiastic claims of the advertising professionals that the product itself was unimportant and that with a proper advertising campaign they could "sell dishwashers or refrigerators to Eskimos," the fact remained that not all products lent themselves to marketing through national advertising. More importantly, the period provided ample evidence that intensive advertising of brand-names could neither successfully create nor even sustain demand for products in the face of consumer resistance.

Generally speaking, consumers are more apt to rely on brand-name recognition and advertising when the cost is not a significant portion of their income and where there is little other basis for comparison or product judgment. Unlike these "convenience items," if the cost of a product is significant either in terms of the consumer's budget or in terms of the risks of a lack of social acceptance, consumers are much more likely to shop around. In making purchases in these categories, consumers are more apt to make comparisons based on product characteristics and on personal and peer judgment than to rely on advertising. Finally, in cases where instructions on the use of a product, or service, or further finishing are significant, the retailer "assumes a larger share of the task of differentiating one maker's product from another. In these cases, national advertising by manufacturers is likely to be diminished."[7] Convenience products accounted for at least one-half of the products ranked among the largest national advertising campaigns in terms of expenditures in 1914. However, some of the other, more expensive items, such as appliances and automobiles, were in the process of winning acceptance and building vital product differentiation and customer recognition through their brand-name advertisements. It is of great significance that, as Pope concluded, "Of those pre-World War I national brands that have remained heavy advertisers for over six decades, roughly two-thirds are convenience products."[8]

Clothing, in particular women's and adolescents' clothing, cannot be classified as convenience products; however, ready-made clothing for men, women, and children provided excellent examples of further finishing of products by the manufacturers. The invention of the sewing machine, the experience gained by manufacturers of uniforms during the Civil War, and the improvements in cutting clothes to fit, as well as the increasing industrial and urban development all spurred the growth of the men's ready-made clothing industry during the last quarter of the nineteenth century. By 1875, for example, Montgomery Ward & Co. carried a fairly complete line of men's clothing. A survey of the men's clothing business indicated that during the last two decades of the century, it was "possible for any man or boy, from any walk of life, to obtain, at a reasonable cost, a well-fitting suit of clothes."[9]

National advertising for ready-made clothing also provided an excellent study on the limitations of national brand-name advertising to create demand. In particular, purchases of women's and children's clothing depend greatly on fashion, personal tastes, the advice of friends, and retail sales personnel. In clothing, the risk of social disapprobation for incorrect purchases may be the highest of all consumer goods. All of these conditions and unpredictable shifts in fashion have severely limited the ability of manufacturers to create demand for specific items. Nevertheless, advertising brand-name ready-made clothing followed a familiar pattern and at least helped to create an environment conducive to a consumption ethic.

A survey of advertising in *Harper's Weekly* from 1864 until 1900 revealed a slow but steady growth in clothing ads. During the last decade of the century, clothing consistently ranked in the top four categories of advertised products, usually surpassed only by educational opportunities, food, and books and publications in total number of ads per issue. However, throughout the nineteenth and into the twentieth century, the category was dominated by ads for specialty items such as shoes, hats, undergarments, collars and cuffs, and men's suits and overcoats.[10] In 1899, the *Press and Printer* tabulated advertisers who regularly advertised in popular magazines and ranked wearing apparel third among all categories. For the most part the advertising copy employed throughout the last quarter of the nineteenth and early twentieth century emphasized the desirable features of the specific brand such as durability, availability, fit, and price. Although this would change rapidly, especially in the case of women's apparel, the period witnessed little attention to style or attempts to create new markets.[11] In truth, men seemed to pay little attention to style. To quote Paul Nystrom, "men were more inelegantly and more shabbily dressed during this period [1870–1900] than they had been at anytime before. . . . This was likewise the period during which factory-made clothing secured predominance over tailor-made clothing. . . . By the end of the century, the factory-made clothing was the equivalent in style as well as workmanship of the tailor-made clothing of the preceding periods."[12]

In spite of the advances in the art of advertising other consumer products, such as soap, toilet articles, and bicycles, ads for men's clothing evidenced only modest change during the period. Even in the early twentieth century, national advertising for men's clothing very seldomly attempted to create additional demand; rather, the ads assured consumers of the fit and desirable qualities of name brands. An attractive, well-designed, two-full-page ad for Arrow Collars and Shirts in the *Saturday Evening Post* in 1912 simply assured men that Arrow Collars both added "a note of individuality to your attire" and were favored by fashion. The shirts, for "$1.50 and more," afforded men the "pleasing distinction imparted by garments that fit, styles that are correct, and fast-color patterns that are correct."[13] As late as 1914, Hart, Schaffner & Marx based the appeal of their fall line of men's clothing almost entirely on the quality associated with the name of their products. To be sure, potential customers were assured that Hart, Schaffner & Marx clothing was fashionable, and the advertising was modeled in a manner to imply that it was the proper clothing for upper-class successful men, but the copy argued that men should insist on Hart, Schaffner & Marx suits because they lasted longer. Smart businessmen knew that "Quality always won the battle for business growth: Men soon find that 'cheap' clothes are usually expensive."[14] Nothing in the ad seemed designed to increase the total demand. If a man needed a suit, then indeed he was well advised to purchase a Hart, Schaffner & Marx, but nothing in the ad even suggested the need for a new suit simply to be fashionable. It is striking that while the development of the men's ready-wear clothing industry preceded women's by nearly a generation, women's apparel manufacturing rapidly caught up, and both were well-developed industries by the time of America's entry into the war in 1917. Yet national advertising for men's apparel designed to build

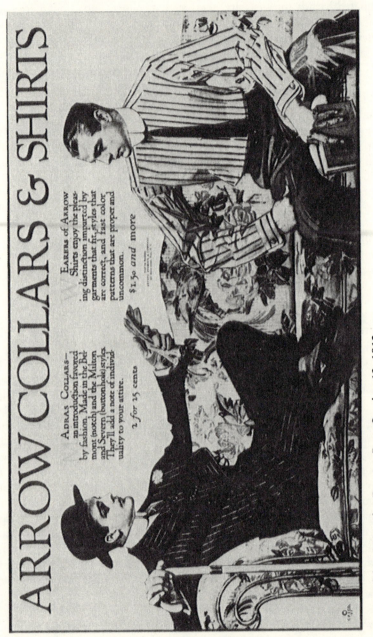

ARROW COLLARS & SHIRTS

ARROW COLLARS—an introduction favored by fashion. Made in the Belmont (notch) and the Milton and Severn (buttonhole) styles. They'll add a note of individuality to your attire.

2 for 25 cents

WEARERS of Arrow Shirts enjoy the pleasing distinction imparted by garments that fit, styles that are correct, and fast color patterns that are proper and uncommon.

$1.50 and more

Reprinted from *Saturday Evening Post*, October 12, 1912.

national markets and create additional total demand simply failed to develop in the pre-World War I era, and advertising for women's apparel remained in its infancy.

To be sure, urban newspapers carried extensive retail advertising that featured men's, children's, and women's apparel. Designed to lure customers to shop in particular stores, these generally assumed that the demand already existed and avoided mentioning brand names, dwelling instead on the newness and availability of large stocks of fashionable women's apparel. Urban retail advertising undoubtedly led national manufacturers in advertising in women's apparel. While the early retail ads tended to stress price, fit, and quality in their copy, vague references were always made to "up-to-date" style. Stores in Midwestern cities, for example, advertised the arrival of "the latest eastern fashions," even though Europe remained the fashion capital to be emulated by stylish American women. Advertisements for the St. Louis department store of Scruggs, Vandervoort, and Barney in 1880 proudly announced the arrival of goods personally selected by Mrs. Vandervoort during her recent European trip. The ad promised that the "latest Paris styles" included in the goods would certainly please the "refined and highly cultivated tastes" of St. Louis women.[15] In the competition to attract customers to their stores, local merchants and department store managers stressed price reductions, sales, arrivals of new shipments, and the availability of large stocks in their women's ready-to-wear ads. Specific brand names or even seasonal changes of stock were seldom mentioned, rather the ads assured women shoppers that the store had the latest style. By 1915, even the major department stores and women's specialty shops had shifted the appeal of their ads. Brand names were almost always stressed, with the emphasis on "quality and fashion." One store, capitalizing on the post-World War I slenderness trend in fashion, advised customers that "no matter what your type of figure, there is a Redfern [corset] which will subdue its faults and bring out its best lines."[16]

In nineteenth-century women's apparel advertisements, the appeal tended to vary according to the type of garment being advertised. Corset and underskirt ads appealed primarily to usefulness; in the case of corsets, health and elegance dominated the copy. While the appeal to purity and health was most often associated with patent medicines, foods, and toilet articles, not even clothing escaped. An 1888 ad for Dr. Warner's Health Underwear captured all the themes:

Made of pure Camel's hair and fine Australian wool.
   It is the best underwear made.
   It is the most durable.
   It is free from all dye.
   It will not irritate the skin.
   It has special electric properties.

It is a protection against colds, catarrh, rheumatism, and malaria.[17]

The manufacturers of suits, skirts, and shirtwaists emphasized that women should be properly and well dressed whatever the occasion and usually guaranteed the fit of each item. The ads equated up-to-date fashion with style, almost always listed prices, rarely mentioned beauty, and refrained from references to sex appeal. During the first two decades of the twentieth century, national magazine advertising for women's apparel increased, the products diversified, and the appeal shifted further away from health, durability, and price to style and elegance.

Style was not unheard of in the 1880s, but it ran a very poor second to other appeals. By 1896, a mail order clothing house advertised that "stylish women everywhere say that our catalogue is their guide."[18] Less than a decade later, the connection between "style" and brand-names had become much more authoritative, and deviation from style became a serious social blunder. A tailor-made corset firm claimed that their "a la Spirite corset" was necessary for "the woman of fashion." A rival firm warned style-conscious women that only their brand "well defines a small waist and rounding contour, curving the hip line in precise conformity to the *dictates* of fashion."[19] In a two-full-page ad, beautifully illustrated with models wearing the latest fashions, the National Cloak & Suit Company, which claimed to be the "Largest Ladies' Outfitting Establishment in the World," urged women in the March 1909 *Ladies' Home Journal* to write for their "National" Spring Style Book. The firm guaranteed low prices, the latest styles, and complete satisfaction, or the customer's money would be refunded and National would pay the "express charges both ways."[20] A Wooltex ad carried the warning even further: "Dame fashion," the ad warned, "will not smile on the woman who deviates from the *law of style*."[21] By 1910, advertisers were insisting that self-confidence depended on being stylish. That year, a Kabo Corset ad advised women that "Your confidence in your appearance depends more on the corset you wear than anything else."[22] Gossard Corsets printed a full-page illustrated ad on the inside front cover of *Harper's Bazar* that pictured a youthful model in an obviously upper-class setting with the caption, "the luxury of a Gossard corset is now shared by women in every walk of life."[23]

Changes in style during the last two decades of the nineteenth and the first two of the twentieth centuries reflected a general "liberating" trend in women's lives. The period began with women literally bound up with corsets, bustles, high-button shoes, and pounds of material in long full skirts. Corset ads indicated the degree of discomfort in their own overzealous claims of comfort and health. With the bicycle fad of the 1890s came bloomer pants and "bicycle" (presumably more comfortable) corsets. By 1910, maternity skirts, blouses, and corsets appeared in small ads, and as early as the outbreak of World War I, less confining underwear was

Reprinted from *Ladies' Home Journal*, October 1905.

commonly advertised. Very modestly styled (dress and bloomer style) bathing suits appeared in fabric and talcum powder ads by the beginning of the second decade of the century. And during the same period, Ped Outing and Play Shoes (a type of tennis shoe) began advertising. Swimsuit ads, by 1920, bared women's arms and legs. The suits somewhat resembled the more modern, one-piece styles; sport dresses were advertised, dress lines became slim, and hemlines crept up to a daring nine or ten inches above the floor. The average American woman depicted in advertising was by no means a "flapper" in 1920, but she had come a long way from corsets and bustles.

When skirts shortened after 1915, a new emphasis on hosiery resulted, and one of the first full-page hosiery ads captured the current fashion trend in slenderness with the copy "Those silken inches of hosiery that twinkle 'neath your skirt must be smooth and perfect fitting if you are to have slender, graceful ankles."[24] Like slenderness, by the time America entered the war, youth had become linked to style and fashion. A 1917 ad referred to "that slim, youthful silhouette which the latest French fashion decrees," and that same year, a fashion catalogue offered "useful hints to matrons who still demand models possessing youth and grace—who still delight to wear styles that are undeniably smart and metropolitan."[25] Even prior to World War I, advertisers of women's ready-made clothing played on the fear of being out of style or not keeping up with fashion. An early National Cloak and Suit Company ad advised women that "In attending a fashionable function she [a considerate lady] pays her hostess a compliment of presenting herself tastefully and artistically."[26] The appeals made little attempt to increase demand for any one style or fashion; rather they assured American women of social acceptability by consuming the brand of clothing being advertised.

"Advertising men and business managers who pride themselves on their ability in sales promotion and on their ability to influence consumer demand may not like this statement," Paul Nystrom concluded, "but there seems to be very little to indicate that any important trend of fashion has ever been changed by any form of sales promotion."[27] Even Nystrom agreed that while advertising may have failed to sell fashion trends, it succeeded in selling the need to be fashionable. A careful observer remarked that "the nation had made the conversion from home-made to factory-made clothing before the outbreak of the First World War."[28] The two statements are not incongruent; while national advertising had not been able to sell specific fashions and style, it had been successful in gaining acceptance for an entire industry. Indeed, the extent to which the production of clothing had escaped the home was illustrated in 1917 in a series of ads for the Women's Institute of Domestic Arts and Sciences. The ads featured a troubled looking woman asking herself, "Am I really fair to my husband?" The answer, of course, was "NO!" She should learn to make her own clothes at home, and save her husband the expense of ready-made clothing.[29]

The changing role of women from producers to consumers, as well as the growth of urban markets, was also reflected in the rapid development of the processed food industry. As more and more prepared foods became available, a greater variety in the diets of urban dwellers became possible, and women were supposedly freed from long hours in the kitchen for more leisure and creative activities. At the same time, they gave up the creative and self-reliant aspects of feeding their families and more and more found themselves forced to rely on distant food processors. Until the last years of the nineteenth century, there was little advertising of food products that could be considered prepared, nearly ready-to-eat, or main-dish foods. The overwhelming majority of advertised products were food ingredients (e.g., Pillsbury's Flour, Baker's Chocolate, Royal Baking Powder, and Magic Yeast), flavoring extracts (e.g., vanilla, Armour's Extract of Beef), condiments (e.g., Heinz ketchup, sauces, and pickles), or drink mixes (e.g., coffee, tea, cocoa, and Hires Root Beer). Infant or invalid foods (e.g., Lactated Food) were also available.

By 1896, VanCamp Boston Baked Beans made the prepared instant meal, however bleak it may have been, a possibility. At the turn of the century, Swift and Company promised that its brand names meant uniform quality in meat products, regardless of where they were purchased, and National Biscuit Company claimed that their unique packaging made the same thing possible for their crackers and cookies. More infant foods appeared (e.g., Eskay's and Imperial Granum), and breakfast foods flourished (Ralston, Quaker Oats, Hornby's Oats, Pettijohn's, Cream of Wheat, and Shredded Wheat). Once introduced, the number of brands and types of breakfast foods seemed to multiply. In addition to breakfast foods, Campbell's Soup had become a large national advertiser by 1905.

The variety of foods and the number of brands being introduced to the American woman by 1910 must have seemed overwhelming. Many of the early advertisers of single products had developed diversified lines of products which they marketed under their brand name. For example, Franco-American, a producer of prepared soups in the 1890s, quickly developed an entire Franco-American line of soups, entrees, potted meats, and even plum pudding. Pillsbury's Flour not only advertised its "Best" flour, but by 1907 their ads included their "Best" cereal. By the end of World War I, Armour had such a diversified line that it advertised its brand name more than its products, which included items as unrelated as sausage and grape juice.

To accompany growing product lines, firms expanded unique packaging. Welch's Grape Juice came in convenient, individual-size bottles and Hawaiian Pineapple came in cans. Easily and quickly prepared desserts such as Minute Tapioca and Jell-O in small packages were common. As in other consumer products, food products became more tailored to specific users. For example, whereas in 1888 flour was flour, by 1917 there was not only a variety of flour brands to pick from, but also types, such as cake flour (e.g., Swansdown) and pancake flour (Aunt Jemima). Evidence of the degree to which the food industry had convinced women to turn the preparation over to industry appeared in a 1920 ad for Sunkist Orange Marmalade, which claimed that in the Sunkist kitchens the marmalade was "Cooked by Women in the genuine 'Home Way.'"[30]

In an effort to convince consumers to purchase food items prepared by distant producers, early advertising for food products placed almost total emphasis on the purity of their brand. Throughout the last quarter of the nineteenth century, Royal Baking Powder Company's campaign consisted of "never lagging iteration of the name and the purity phrase . . . Royal Baking Powder—Absolutely Pure." By 1900, the president of the company estimated that any potential rival would be forced to spend $15 million to capture Royal's market. Two competitors, Dr. Price's Baking Powder and Cleveland's Baking Powder, also advertised but "never with the thorough system of Royal" and were finally absorbed by Royal, which, given the significant barrier to entry by rivals, completely dominated the market.[31] The demand for Royal Baking Powder would decline, not because of competition, but with the decline in home baking. The trademark of Baker's Cocoa and Chocolate, "La Belle Chocolataire," painted by a French artist in the late eighteenth century, appeared with monotonous frequency on quarter-page ads in popular magazines from the 1880s onward. The few lines of copy accompanying the famous woman with the tray almost always stressed the purity of Baker's and often warned that other cocoas "have been doctored by the addition of alkali, starch, malt, kola, hops, etc."[32] Given that advertisers were attempting to persuade customers to purchase food products often manufactured or processed in distant and unknown places, the emphasis on brand identification is understandable, and in the absence of federal standards for purity, the stress on purity is hardly surprising. Often accompanying, and sometimes combined with, the purity appeal were exaggerated claims about the health benefits associated with the consumption of the various products.

Advertisement for cereals, already a strong competitive industry with rival firms engaged in selling essentially similar products, seemed at times in the late nineteenth century to rival patent medicines in their copy. Shredded Wheat claimed "Stomach Comfort in Every Shred" and noted that it was "the cleanest and purest cereal food made."[33] Hornby's Oatmeal, with the brand name H—O, started their campaign with the slogan "Eat H—O"; their trademark featured Oliver Twist holding out his bowl and saying "I want some more." An endorsement by James A. Garfield, the ex-president's son, carried the caption "'If the power to do hard work is not talent, it is the best substitute for it.' If you are not talented, don't fret, you can obtain power by eating the peerless H—O."[34] As the market for cereals expanded, the competition intensified and advertisers sought ways to differentiate their products. Puffed Rice and Puffed Wheat were "shot from guns," while Quaker Oats claimed that "Forty million dishes are now served every month."[35] Since many of the cereals were substantially the same, cereal companies depended on brand advertising to differentiate their product from competitors'. Kellogg, for example, stressed that their Toasted Corn Flakes packages always had the signature of W. K. Kellogg, and a 1908 full-page ad in the *Ladies' Home Journal* featured a very determined-looking young lady, with the caption "Excuse me—I know what I want and I want what I asked for—TOASTED CORN FLAKES—Good Day."[36]

All cereals attempted to appeal to women's maternal feelings. Kellogg ads almost always featured children and stressed that Kellogg's Corn Flakes provided children a nourishing breakfast; mothers need not worry about making their children eat a good breakfast because children loved "the crispy flakes and . . . their delicate flavor."[37] Not to be outdone, Grape-Nuts played on guilt and fear and warned mothers that children needed the proper breakfast. "Improper food," mothers were warned, "makes . . . [children] rickety, dull and peevish," but they had no need to worry if they served Grape-Nuts, which of course made children strong, healthy, and intelligent.[38]

Of course, cereals were far from alone in stressing the health-related benefits of their consumption; all advertisements for prepared foods, ingredients, or drinks emphasized their nutritional value. Many of the food ads that saturated the pages of popular magazines like *Ladies' Home Journal*, *Literary Digest*, and *Saturday Evening Post*, included practical ideas and helpful hints for the hard-working housewife, mother, and hostess. Some offered free recipes and instructional booklets or free samples to introduce new products. In addition to educating the consumer about new products, the advertisements made clear that since the woman's role as wife, mother, and homemaker made the care and nurturing of the family her responsibility, she was obligated to be informed, modern, and up-to-date about new products her family might need or enjoy. Men were rarely portrayed, and when they were it was almost always as the happy consumer of the item. Neither references to nor pictures of helpful husbands were included in the advertising. Since it was simply assumed that the family's health was the woman's responsibility, ads for prepared foods played on this concern by stressing the purity of the ingredients, the sanitary conditions of preparation, and the scientific testing involved, as well as the illness and maladies that careful, "modern" mothers could avoid by serving their particular brand.

Since it was the mother's duty to guard and protect the health of her family, it is not surprising that guilt and fear emerged as prevalent themes in many food product ads. True, few food companies went as far as Hygeia Nursers in 1917 when their ad warned mothers that "Just one unclean bottle may bring fatal results." Having frightened the poor mother to near panic, the ad went on to allay her fears by assuring her Hygeia Nursers

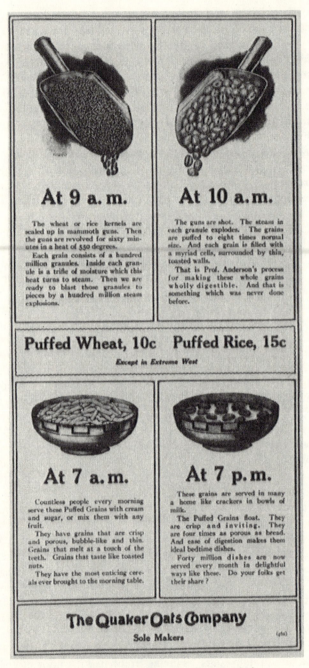

Reprinted from *Literary Digest*, October 4, 1913.

were so easily cleaned that even "a servant" could be trusted to the task.[39] Milk companies often claimed that only cow's milk, which was, after all, close to natural mother's milk, was healthy for an infant. And an ad for Holstein's Cow's Milk even went so far as to argue that the vigor and vitality of the Holstein breed could be passed on to the infant that drank Holstein milk.[40]

Not only infants deserved a woman's concern. A Salada Tea ad stressed that tea should be served to the sick because "Neither the stomach or the nerves of the sick are strong enough to endure coffee." In fact, the ad implied that only tea, not coffee, should be served in the home since "Tea is a stimulant and a sedative [at the same time] and is more refreshing than coffee and the after effects are soothing to the nerves."[41] Horlick's Malted Milk got into the act by claiming that it was better than either coffee or tea.[42] With all the competition from tea, coffee companies fought back, claiming that their particular brand never caused upset nerves or any other ill effect. Barrington Hall Coffee noted that while other coffees, which were crushed or ground, might be harsh and cause nervousness, their "steel cut" coffee did not. But claims were not enough. Barrington Hall proved their point with the "scientific" explanation which claimed that in their process "the berry is *cut* into small uniform particles and the little oil cells are not crushed as in grinding."[43]

Welch's Grape Juice, an extensive advertiser, claimed to be a healthful tonic, while Chiris Olive Oil bragged that "Olive Oil Drinkers Have Firm Flesh, Perfect Digestion, and Clear Complexions."[44] Not to be outdone, Dole Pineapple Juice claimed that it was a health food often prescribed by physicians for stomach, intestinal, and throat problems. Earlier, Horlick's Milk had informed women that it was a "nourishing, easily assimilated food in impaired digestion, satisfying without leaving any distressed feeling."[45] Huyler's Candies came scientifically blended, and Shredded Wheat Biscuits were produced in the "cleanest, finest food factories."[46] In 1910, a Heinz Strawberry Preserves ad offered the worried housewife the ultimate assurance. Heinz, the ad announced, belonged to the American Association for the Promotion of Purity in Food Products. With those credentials, clearly the housewife need not worry about serving her family Heinz brand products.[47]

Starting with Uneeda's praises for its individually packaged crackers, food processors gave special attention to packaging. In the twentieth century, reduction in the cost of using "tinned" cans, a technique that had been available, but costly, since the antebellum period, solved the major problem in securing hermetically sealed products. Products canned in glass jars, which were fragile, proved difficult to transport over long distances and retain the seal. More importantly, improvements in the process and decreasing costs in using tin cans made canned goods a mass consumption commodity.[48] Heinz, for example, argued that its "improved tins . . . [not only] reduce the price of the finest preserves, but . . . [also] prevent deterioration from exposure to light and permit perfect sterilization, difficult with glass." The 1910 Heinz ad continued to practically eulogize the tin can, claiming that it was "sealed without solder and is further protected on the inside by golden enamel, proof against heat and the natural acids of the fruit, thus making it a food-container superior to all others."[49] Never modest in their claims, a 1920 National Canners Association ad reached the point of suggesting that from the time of creation, Providence intended that the earth's metallic resources be shaped into tin cans! Not only did nature "hold in trust the tin can in its original elements . . . awaiting the hand of man to bring it forth," but she also provided food to fill the cans, so that the two essentials could "rise from the earth and meet again" to "triumph in 'the miracle on your table.'" Moreover, the ad also made it clear that American business deserved the credit for the "miracle," claiming that "The tin can of commerce was not born in a day or without great industrial travail." Indeed, housewives were admonished to think of the tin can for "what it really is . . . a wonder of the times . . . [and] a monument to patient achievement in our personal interests."[50] Business had become the keeper of nature's blessings, the maker of miracles, the guardian of the cherished belief in progress, as well as the housewife's best friend.

By the second decade of the twentieth century, the assortment of canned and prepared foods available to the American housewife was staggering. The appeals employed by advertisers as brand names established reputations, while certainly retaining the claims to purity and health, shifted to convenience and quality. Shredded Wheat claimed that only the best selected wheat grains were used. Sunkist Oranges were "seedless," "firm," "tender meated," as well as the sweetest and juiciest. Heinz Baked Beans claimed that their beans were "brown, mealy, and tender—delicious" and really baked, not steamed like some of the other brands.[51] VanCamp Beans countered that their beans "excel beans baked at home." However, they hastened to assure women that "the fault does not lie with you, but solely with your lack of facilities."[52] It was the steam oven that made VanCamp Beans better than home cooked. Another VanCamp ad pictured the hard (old) way of preparing beans versus the new (easy and modern) way and argued that the housewife "might as well spin her own linen, weave her own carpets, make her own soap—as they did in the olden days."[53] By 1916, Campbell's Soup ads informed women that "Good soup is the key to good living." The full-page and full-colored ads in *Saturday Evening Post* also advised women that in the "countless American homes" that served Campbell's Soup, house-keeping became "home-keeping."[54]

Most prepared food companies offered free recipes and instructions to assure customers that they need not fear committing an error in their use. Many times, rather nebulous authorities, such as "prominent chefs" or cooking authorities or simply "those who know," were invoked to assure

The Hard Way

Pick over the beans the day before, and soak them over night.

Boil them next day in two waters—not less than an hour and a half. Then bake them three hours.

One must keep the stove going full blast half a day—just for a dish of beans. It's about as much trouble as roasting a turkey.

Then serve the beans before they sour—the sooner the better. And serve them until they're used up.

When beans are wanted again, repeat the 16-hour process of soaking, boiling and baking.

That is the old way—the hard way.

One might as well spin her own linen, weave her own carpets, make her own soap—as they did in the olden days.

The Easy Way

Take the can from the shelf and pour the beans on a plate. Put the slice of pork on top.

The meal can be served in a jiffy.

If you want the beans hot, heat the can before opening. They'll taste then as though they came direct from the oven.

Keep a dozen cans on hand—a dozen meals always ready. When guests drop in unexpectedly there's something good to serve.

Three to five meals a week—among the best meals you have—are thus prepared without any trouble.

A skilful chef has done all the work for you, and it costs less to employ him than to do it yourself.

That is the Van Camp way.

The Nitrogen in Beans

It requires a rare soil, rich in nitrogen, to grow good navy beans. For beans are 23 per cent nitrogenous.

Van Camp's come from Michigan. They are picked out by hand from the choicest beans that grow. They are so choice that they cost us last year, on the average, $2.25 per bushel.

Such beans are 84 per cent nutriment. They are richer in food value than meat or eggs or cheese.

For our sauce we use the Livingston Stone tomatoes—the whole solid tomato, ripened on the vine.

This tomato sauce costs us five times what common sauce would cost. But, when you taste Van Camp's with this tomato sauce baked in, you know why we pay the price.

There is no other way to get such baked beans as you get when you buy Van Camp's.

We Multiply the Heat

Van Camp's beans are baked in steam ovens. The heat applied is 2 1-2 times as great as a dry oven applies to the middle beans in a dish.

Because of that heat, Van Camp's beans digest as home-baked beans never do. That's why Van Camp's don't ferment and form gas.

And Van Camp's beans are not crisped like your home-baked beans. They are not broken and mushy, but nut-like and whole. That is the way people like them.

One can't bake such beans without a steam oven—without years of experience—without the rarest skill.

That's why millions of housewives have adopted Van Camp's, and the people they serve are glad of it.

Please think what they gain in convenience—what they save in trouble and time. Then find out how good Van Camp's are.

Van Camp's
PORK AND BEANS
Three sizes: 10, 15 and 20 cents per can

Van Camp Packing Company, Established 1861 Indianapolis, Ind.

Reprinted from *Ladies' Home Journal*, March 1910.

The National dinner-call

In countless thousands of American homes the daily call to dinner is also a call to *Campbell's Soups*.

And this widespread custom of eating these wholesome soups once a day at least is among the best things that ever happened to the national health and welfare.

Good soup is the key to good living

Not only is it an inviting dinner-course but it is the best of appetizers; a valuable assistance to digestion; a most efficient promoter of health and vigorous condition. Good soup plays a part in the re-enforcement of the human organism which no other food can perform so well.

The best demonstration of this is found in the nourishing, body-building effect of *Campbell's Soups*.

Look at their attractive variety—

The favorite *Campbell's Tomato Soup*—full of appetizing zest, rich yet delicate, a tempting overture to the most important dinner. Campbell's popular *Vegetable Soup*—a wonderfully well-balanced combination of meaty beef stock with choice vegetables. *Campbell's Ox Tail Soup*—a thick, savory, substantial soup that is almost a meal in itself. *Campbell's Clam Chowder*—delicious and invigorating. So on down the whole attractive list—a soup for every taste and every occasion.

Summer is just the time when you get a particular benefit from these palatable soups. Their strengthening properties always help to fortify the constitution against enervating heat. Almost no effort is required to prepare them for the table.

You cannot do better than keep a supply handy on the pantry shelf.

21 kinds   **10c a can**

Campbell's Soups

LOOK FOR THE RED-AND-WHITE LABEL

Reprinted from *Saturday Evening Post*, July 15, 1916. Reprinted with permission of Campbell Soup Company.

women that they could not do as well by cooking themselves. In spite of what was then an unparalleled movement of women out of the home and into the work force, advertisers of prepared foods made no attempt to use the convenience and labor-saving features of their products to appeal to working women. For American business firms, the woman's place remained in her home and the image of working women had no place in their advertising campaigns. In 1917, Purity Cross Cream Chicken à la King never mentioned in their advertisements that their product offered a quick, easy, and convenient meal after a busy day at work; rather, the appeal emphasized that it was "The Choice Delicacy at the Dinner of the 'Four Hundred.' "[55] What woman could ask for more?

Alongside the prepared food ads in national magazines, advertisements for soft drinks, beer, wine, and various kinds of whiskey and tobacco products appeared in increasing numbers. The patterns of appeal employed varied greatly, but there was little indication that these products would eventually dominate much of modern national advertising. Beer, wine, and distilled liquor producers would, of course, reluctantly cease their attempts to create demand and build national markets during prohibition, but they would become some of the largest advertisers in the period following the repeal of the Eighteenth Amendment. In the 1920s, soft drinks, led by Coca-Cola, and the tobacco industry, primarily featuring cigarettes, together with the automobile industry, would dominate and set the tone for advertising throughout most of the decade. In each industry, the precedents and the patterns used to create demand, while perhaps immature, were clearly in place by the end of World War I.[56]

As early as the 1870s, both Ayer's and Hood's promoted their sarsaparilla primarily on the basis of its supposed medical properties. According to the copy sarsaparilla cured scrofulous, humor in the blood, ulcers, catarrh, consumption, neuralgia, sciatica, rheumatism, general tired feeling, and even pimples. In addition, Hood's claimed to purify the blood and was an excellent Spring tonic.[57] However, by the first decade of the twentieth century, soft drink advertising stressed brand-name identification. Clicquot Club, a major producer of beverages, soft drinks, and mixers, advertised its sarsaparilla along with a line of ginger ale, root beer, lemon soda, and other flavors simply as a refreshing, non-alcoholic beverage.[58] Carbonated and various other kinds of mineral waters, along with malt extracts, malted milks, and even fruit drinks, followed the familiar pattern of sarsaparilla during the late nineteenth century in advertising primarily as health tonics. Vichy Celestins Water, for example, claimed to settle the stomach and cure liver complaints, gout, and dyspepsia, while Buffalo Lithia Water was a general tonic and cure-all.[59] Within a few years after the turn of the century, without dropping a claim to being generally healthy and "good for you," the primary appeal in bottled water advertisements shifted to brand names as a guarantee of purity as a drinking water and as a mixer for alcoholic

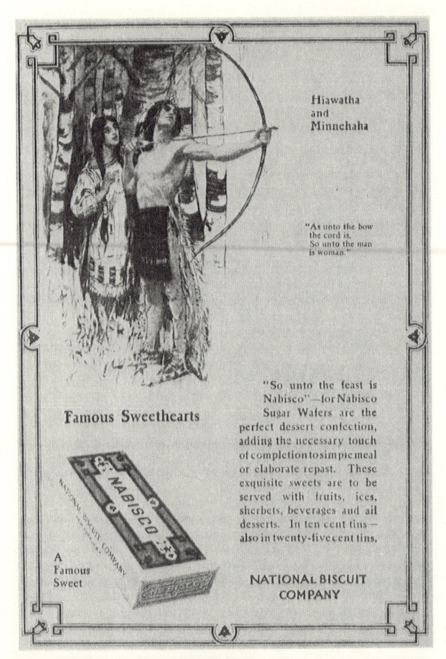

Reprinted from *Overland Monthly*, July 1912.

beverages. In 1903, for example, Deerfield Water suggested that a good hostess served Deerfield because "as a table water . . . [it] is delicious" and it "blends perfectly with all beverages."[60]

In the period between 1890 and 1920, advertisements for beverages moved from an emphasis on the medical and therapeutic value of the products to an appeal based on their individual taste and refreshing quality. Frank Presbrey suggested that by 1920, what he termed the "soda-counter habit," or the social acceptability associated with the consumption of soft drinks in a social setting, had been inculcated into the social fabric of Americans. As usual, Presbrey attributed most of the change to the power of advertising, and as usual he overstated the influence of advertising.[61]

Actually, soda fountains had long been a part of the American scene. In 1895, when Chauncey Depew edited his *One Hundred Years of American Commerce*, he selected soda fountains as one of only one hundred American industries to include in his two-volume study. Not surprisingly, Depew asked James W. Tufts, President of the American Soda-Fountain Company, to write the essay. Tufts, who in 1863 had built and patented a soda-fountain apparatus for use in his Boston drugstore, estimated the number of apparatus in use in this country at the time he wrote his essay as conservatively between 50,000 and 60,000.[62] "The Centennial Exhibition at Philadelphia afforded an opportunity not to be overlooked for advertising the soda-fountain and popularizing soda-water as a beverage," Tufts noted. Together with Charles Lippincott & Company, Tufts paid $50,000 for the exclusive privilege of serving soda water at the Exhibition. He later noted that the business, while not profitable, was "enormous, and . . . proved a valuable advertisement."[63] In 1891, Tufts, A. D. Puffer & Sons, Charles Lippincott & Company, and John Matthews Apparatus Company, the four largest manufacturers of soda-water equipment, organized the American Soda-Fountain Company as a holding company. The new firm held over 200 patents and enjoyed a clear dominance of the soda fountain, carbonated-water equipment industry. The significance of the position of the American Soda-Fountain Company is amply illustrated by Tufts' remark that he had recently completed a machine, based on his patented "Cataract," that was "entirely automatic, and adapts its output to the demands made upon it by the bottlers." The recently completed machine, constructed for Charles E. Hires Company of Philadelphia, was capable of turning out over 40,000 bottles of carbonated beverage in a ten-hour working day.[64]

Up until the turn of the century, most carbonated beverages were made, sold, and consumed at the local soda fountain. Indeed, a great deal of "plain" carbonated water mixed with ice was sold by the glass as a refreshing drink. Enterprising druggists also mixed various flavored syrups with the ice and carbonated water to offer their customers a wide variety of "sodas." For the most part, these flavored syrups were produced locally and often concocted by individual druggists, merchants, or even farmers. Occasionally, as in the case of Charles E. Hires' root beer, a local syrup gained a considerable reputation. Hires' contribution, to quote Presbrey, "was a demonstration that through advertising" a soft drink could develop a national market.[65] Hires started advertising in the *Philadelphia Public Ledger* in the late 1870s and only slowly expanded his campaign into newspapers and magazines with national circulation. By the last decade of the nineteenth century, Hires regularly ran quarter or half-page ads in *McClure's, Harper's, Ladies' Home Journal,* and *Frank Leslie's Illustrated.* The Hires ads, which featured the brand name, had a clean, crisp appearance; they used strategically planned open-spaces and cautioned customers to insist on *Hires* Root Beer. At a cost of only twenty-five cents for enough flavoring for five gallons, Hires was "the purest, most delicious, health giving beverage possible to produce."[66]

Coca-Cola—"Coke," a name that would become synonymous with soft-drinks and whose advertising would emphasize youth, social acceptance, and "smartness," started its advertising campaign by distributing cards reading "Good for a Coca-Cola for you and your friend." Potential customers seeking to redeem the cards at a local soda fountain obviously demanded that the fountain stock and serve Coca-Cola. In addition, the company printed signs and posters and produced trays, glasses, and other soda-fountain paraphernalia all with the Coca-Cola logo, and within a few years a Coca-Cola clock was distributed which quickly became a common sight in drugstores and soda fountains all over America. Throughout most of the first two decades, Coke concentrated its advertising efforts on achieving brand name recognition and creating demand for the product at soda fountains.

"Hott? [sic], Tired? Thirsty?" asked a typical Coca-Cola ad in 1909; "COCA-COLA is Cooling . . . Refreshing, Thirst-Quenching."[67] The relatively few ads that Coca-Cola placed in the popular national magazines had a surprisingly modern appearance. The most prominent feature of the usually simple but eye-catching ads employed by Coca-Cola was the name, always with the logo and a slogan accompanied by simple, direct copy that suggested that Coca-Cola was refreshing, thirst-quenching, delicious, and available for "5¢ everywhere." Although the company conducted an effective advertising campaign for their syrup, the campaign did not make extensive use of magazines and newspapers as an advertising media until about 1906 when Coca-Cola was generally available in bottles as well as through soda fountains.[68] In 1901, Coca-Cola boasted an advertising budget of only about $100,000, and as late as 1908 it amounted to only $500,000, of which a relatively small portion was spent on magazine and newspaper ads; twenty years later, Presbrey estimated that Coca-Cola's yearly expenditures on advertising had grown to $5,000,000.[69]

While Coca-Cola concentrated its early efforts on the soda-fountain trade, one of its major competitors in the soft-drink business, and by far the largest advertiser in national magazines, was Clicquot Club. Although the Clicquot Club Company produced a variety of flavors, including birch beer,

Reprinted from *Harper's Weekly*, June 26, 1909.

root beer, sarsaparilla, lemon sour, and orange phosphate, the advertising campaign stressed its brand of "Extra Dry" Ginger Ale. Unlike both Hires Root Beer and Coke, Clicquot Club, which as the ads always pointed out was pronounced Klee-ko club, slanted its advertising toward home consumption. For example, a 1915 *Saturday Evening Post* ad featured an obviously perplexed woman in an evening gown asking, "What shall we serve our guests?" At the same time, her smiling husband, dressed in formal evening clothes, is being informed by the Clicquot Club Eskimo child to serve ginger ale. "Go down to the ice box and bring up a big, frosty bottle or two of sparkling Clicquot Club Ginger Ale," the copy suggested, and to make sure you have plenty on hand, "order a case today from any 'good' grocery or druggist."[70] While the Clicquot Club advertising copy noted that it was sold at "most" soda fountains, the "great place for Clicquot is in the ice box at home." In addition, after 1915, the ads emphasized that "It mixes well with almost anything."[71] Although Clicquot Club engaged in an extensive and aggressive advertising campaign and claimed to be "sold nationally—all over America," the equation of ginger ale as a mix in alcoholic drinks and the emphasis on home consumption may, in retrospect, have been a mistake. More importantly, unlike the Coke ads, which stressed the sociability and what Presbrey called the "smartness" of drinking a soft drink with friends, there was little or nothing in the appeal employed by Clicquot Club that increased the total demand.

Like many other commodities in the nineteenth century, whiskey had been purchased in bulk by storekeepers from local distillers and retailed to their customers by the quart or gallon with little or no reference to the distiller's name. As late as 1895, James E. Pepper, president of James E. Pepper & Co. distillers in Lexington, Kentucky, noted that the number of stills in operation at the time "appears nominally very large, approaching 1000, while actually the bulk of the output is produced by less than a tithe of that number."[72] Pepper acknowledged the growing concentration in the liquor industry into fewer and larger operations but declined to offer any suggestions about its impact on consumption, pleading that the "history of the large combination of American distillers" was too recent and too complicated for him to offer any analysis.[73] By the last decade of the nineteenth century, advertisements for particular brands of wines and liqueurs and various brands of whiskey appeared in some popular magazines, especially magazines such as *Harper's Weekly* that catered to an upper- and middle-class clientele. The pattern of advertising and the type of appeal used closely resembled those for other consumer food products. For example, in August 1897, an advertisement for Hunter Baltimore Rye, "The best whiskey in America," noted that "leading Physicians" had endorsed Hunter's for "ladies *obliged* to use a stimulant."[74] That same month, G. F. Heublein & Bro. urged readers to try their "Club Cocktails," "A better cocktail at home than is served over any bar in the world." Customers could take their choice of Manhattan, Whiskey, Tom Gin, Martini, Holland Gin, or Vermouth and York. Surprisingly, an adjacent ad for Londonderry Lithia Water employed a much more modern and sophisticated appeal:

CLUB MEN, as everybody knows, are satisfied with nothing less than *the best*. They are men of wide experience and of keen, cultivated, critical taste. . . . Therefore, the fact that Londonderry Lithia Water is to be found among the staple articles of supply of *every leading club in the United States* must be convincing evidence of its superiority.[75]

Although the volume of advertising for whiskey, wine, and liqueurs increased during the first decade of the twentieth century, the appeal used was to secure brand recognition and did little to increase the total demand. For example, a 1903 full-page ad for Red Top Rye Whiskey, one of the most frequently advertised whiskeys, advised consumers to "Try a Red Top High Ball," and the copy then described the proper method to mix a high ball. Not only did the ad fail to suggest that serving or drinking a high ball was fashionable, it never even suggested that the drink would taste good.[76] G. F. Heublein & Bro., another frequent advertiser, suggested that if you were

Reprinted from *Harper's Weekly*, March 4, 1905.

going to have a cocktail, "Don't be prejudiced against bottled cocktails until you have tried the club brand."[77]

As late as 1905, a full-page ad for "Old Beechwood" whiskey closely resembled the patent medicine ads of a quarter-century earlier. The cluttered and crowded ad featured a picture of Col. C. L. Applegate, vice president of Vogt-Applegate distillers of Old Beechwood, a picture of the still, and four large quarts of Old Beechwood. The caption promised "4 full quarts of Old Beechwood for $3.00," while the copy indicated that Col. Applegate would include his "copyrighted" book, *All About the Making of Whiskey*, and a free fifth quart of Old Beechwood with every order. The fact that customers were assured that Old Beechwood was "shipped in a plain box with no marks to indicate contents" provides a clear illustration of the inability of distillers to increase total demand by appealing to social approval or status in the consumption of liquor.[78] Earlier that year, alongside an ad for Red Top Rye which promised purity and bouquet, a small column ad for Gin-Seng-Gin, "The Gin with a push," promised that it "Gives you courage" and cures rheumatism, kidney, bladder, and nervous troubles.[79]

During the first two decades of the twentieth century, advertising, except for some marginal success with beer, never succeeded in popularizing the consumption of alcoholic beverages. Not all popular magazines even accepted liquor ads, and in those that did, such as *Harper's Weekly*, the volume of advertising for wines, liqueurs, and whiskey displayed only modest, if any, increase in the period. A full-page, inside back-cover ad

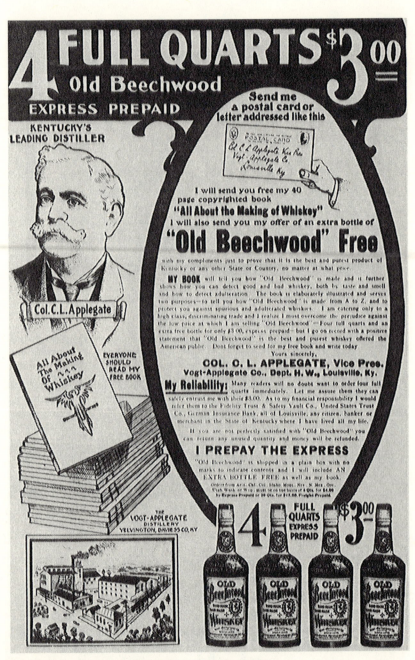

Reprinted from *Harper's Weekly*, October 28, 1905.

for Old Pepper Whiskey in the March 6, 1909, issue of *Harper's Weekly* illustrated the rather primitive state of liquor advertising. The ad featured a white man, dressed as a colonial gentleman, being served Old Pepper Whiskey by a Black servant, with the caption "To be sure of getting real 'Old Pepper' whiskey familiarize yourself with this label"; an arrow pointed to a bottle of Old Pepper. The copy, which read like nineteenth-century patent medicine ads, stressed brand identification and warned customers to beware of counterfeits or imitations. "Every good dealer in the United States," the ad insisted, "has the genuine Old James E. Pepper in stock, or he can get it for you without trouble." Should any dealer refuse to stock Old Pepper, the company would supply the whiskey for $5 a gallon in "plain packages."[80] The continued willingness of distillers to supply alcoholic beverages directly to consumers in plain, unmarked packages indicated the degree of social disapprobation associated with the consumption of liquor, and advertising never really attempted to overcome this stigma. The social disapprobation rendered social status as an appeal to increase the consumption of alcohol useless, and indeed prior to World War I the industry was never able to substantially increase the total demand.

In 1895, in an essay on the American brewing industry, Fred Pabst, president of Pabst Brewing Company in Milwaukee, predicted that "beer is to become, if it is not already, the national beverage of the United States."[81] That same year a full-page *Harper's Weekly* ad stressed brand-name recognition in announcing that "2 trains, 15 carloads of Pabst Milwaukee Beer are shipped daily." The scant copy accompanying the ad also emphasized that *Pabst Beer* was the best because it sold the most, and "public opinion is incontrovertible."[82] Two years later, a full-page illustration entitled "Perry's Victory" announced that "Perfection in brewing is reached in America." The copy, apparently to follow the nautical theme, compared the human body to a ship in a dead calm: "The nerves, the muscles and the mind in summer are at the slack"; however, no reason for concern, Pabst Malt Extract, the "Best" Tonic, promised to "take up the slack" and bring "her safely to the dock."[83] The ad was accompanied by a testimonial from W. R. Franklin, M.D., of Rockford, Illinois, who had for fourteen years prescribed Pabst "Best" Tonic for his patients with amazing results.[84]

Fred Pabst noted that in 1895 there were over 2,200 breweries operating in the United States, most of which brewed for local markets, and only a very few "gigantic" firms that produced over a million barrels annually for national markets. Two of the giant breweries, Pabst and Schlitz, advertised extensively in the early years of the twentieth century. For the most part, the ads stressed brand names. Surprisingly little beer advertising stressed the social acceptability of beer consumption. For the most part, beer ads tended to resemble earlier patent medicine ads in attempting to induce increased consumption. Indeed, in 1903, a full-page back-cover *Harper's Weekly* ad

Reprinted from *Harper's Weekly*, February 9, 1895.

Figure 5.4
Production of Beer, Cigars, and Cigarettes, 1870–1919

Year	(1) Population (million)	(2) Beer (1000 Bbls)	Ratio 1:2	(3) Cigars (1,000,000)	Ratio 1:3	(3) Cigarettes (1,000,000)	Ratio 1:3
1870	39.9	6,600[1]	6:1	1,183	1:30	16	7:1
1880	50.3	13,300[1]	4:1	2,510	1:50	533	1:10
1885	56.7	19,200[1]	3:1	3,294	1:58	1,080	1:19
1890	63.0	27,600[1]	2:1	4,229	1:67	2,505	1:40
1895	69.6	33,600	2:1	4,099	1:59	4,238	1:61
1900	76.1	39,500	1.9:1	5,566	1:73	3,878	1:51
1905	83.8	49,500	1.7:1	6,748	1:80	4,477	1:53
1910	92.4	59,500	1.5:1	6,810	1:74	9,782	1:106
1915	100.5	59,800	1.7:1	6,599	1:66	18,945	1:188
1917	103.3	60,800	1.7:1	7,560	1:73	36,323	1:351
1919	106.5	27,700	4:1	8,097	1:76	53,865	1:505

[1]Listed in Census as "Fermented Malt Liquor" until 1891.

Source: U.S. Department of Commerce, Bureau of the Census, *Historical Statistics of the United States: Colonial Times to 1970* (Washington, D.C., 1975), I:8–9; II:690–691.

for Schlitz pictured a man talking with his doctor while the copy listed the doctor's reasons for recommending Schlitz:

It is good for anybody. The hops form a tonic; the barley a food. The trifle of alcohol is an aid to digestion. And the custom of drinking beer supplies the body with fluid to wash out the waste. People who don't drink beer seldom drink enough fluid of any kind. A great deal of ill-health is caused by a lack of it.[85]

Two years later, a similar ad carried essentially the same message, "Schlitz Beer is Good for You."[86] As late as 1909 Pabst continued to emphasize health in its advertisements. Pabst, a full-page back-cover ad claimed, was an invigorating beer because of the tonic properties of hops, an ideal home beverage because it contained "a very small percentage" of alcohol, and was "a truly temperate drink, invigorating and healthful."[87]

As Figure 5.4 illustrates, advertising by major breweries proved only marginally successful in increasing total demand for beer. In 1870, the United States produced about one barrel for each six people. By 1890, production had increased to approximately one barrel for every two people. From this level, production rose only marginally to one barrel for every 1.5 persons in 1910 despite strong advertising campaigns, and from that time onward a slow decline began. By the middle of the second decade of the century, the social disapproval of drinking, which would result in prohibition, proved too influential for advertising to exert any appreciable effect on demand.

Indeed, even in the first decade of the twentieth century, it is questionable if advertising campaigns exercised as much influence as the growth in urbanization did in the marginal increase in demand for beer. As Thomas C. Cochran pointed out, it is interesting to note that most customers preferred to drink their beer in the social atmosphere of the tavern, yet national advertisers never dared to exploit the social status or social acceptance of beer drinking in their advertisements. This was, perhaps, largely because drinking beer in local taverns was frowned upon by the temperance movement, which often enjoyed the support of the middle and upper classes. The Pabst Brewing Company had actually invested in saloons, which as Cochran noted might have increased sales, but "It was an expensive way to do it."[88] Since beer drinkers preferred to drink in taverns and, as Daniel Pope suggested, they picked the taverns without "great concern for the brands of beer on tap," to promote direct sales of individual name brands to customers would prove necessary in the long run because "brewers' brand name advertising alone could not pull the product through independent retail channels on terms satisfactory to the brewers."[89] Nor could national advertising, in the face of social reform, increase beer consumption in any significant fashion.

6

I'D WALK A MILE FOR A CAMEL

You induce people to use more things than they naturally desire—the more useless and undesirable the article, the greater the advertising effort needed to dispose of it. . . . It follows, of course, that advertising men thrive most richly in the service of utterly useless commodities like tobacco or under-arm pastes, or in a field where there is a hopeless plethora of goods, such as soap or whiskey.

—Michael Wilde's oration
in Herman Wouk's *Aurora Dawn;*
Or The True Story of Andrew Reale, 111

If national advertising proved less successful than might have been expected in winning brand loyalty and significantly increasing the total demand for beer, the advertising agencies could take great delight in the success of tobacco advertising campaigns. Throughout the period from 1870 to 1921, tobacco consumption displayed a long-term secular increase. Per capita consumption more than doubled from 2.9 pounds in 1870 to 7.18 pounds in 1920. However, the patterns of usage shifted. For example, in 1870 the United States produced about 30 cigars for every inhabitant. By the turn of the century, this had increased to approximately 73 per person—a figure that would increase only slightly during the next two decades. On the other hand, only one cigarette for every six persons was produced in 1870, and it was not until 1910 that the United States produced and consumed more cigarettes than cigars (see Figure 6.1). Most important, cigarette smoking increased, but cigar smoking did not decrease. Indeed, cigar consumption peaked in 1917 before it began a slow, but steady, decline. On the other hand, cigarette smoking experienced a consistent and remarkable growth from almost nothing in 1870 to nearly 500 per capita in 1919.[1] Most important, the increase in cigarette smoking came not from converted cigar smokers but from new users, and no small portion of this growth in the

Figure 6.1
Per Capita Consumption of Tobacco Products in the United States, 1900–1921

Year	Large Cigars, Number	Small Cigarettes, Number	Cigars, Pounds	Cigar- ettes, Pounds	Chewing Tobacco, Pounds	Smoking Tobacco, Pounds	Snuff, Pounds	Total, Pounds
1900	70.5	34.9	1.33	-0.14	2.39	1.31	0.20	5.37
1902	77.7	33.6	1.47	.13	2.28	1.51	.23	5.62
1904	82.0	39.4	1.57	.15	2.22	1.80	.25	5.99
1906	84.4	44.5	1.65	.16	2.16	2.01	.27	6.25
1908	78.2	61.0	1.57	.22	2.06	2.07	.25	6.17
1910	76.7	93.7	1.59	.34	2.17	2.30	.34	6.74
1911	77.8	107.8	1.65	.40	1.98	2.23	.31	6.57
1912	77.6	139.0	1.65	.49	1.96	2.28	.33	6.71
1913	80.1	163.7	1.72	.60	1.96	2.27	.34	6.89
1914	75,3	168.5	1.67	.62	1.84	2.28	.31	6.72
1915	71.4	180.6	1.58	.67	1.77	2.36	.33	6.71
1916	76.1	250.4	1.71	.93	1.90	2.37	.34	7.25
1917	80.1	340.7	1.79	1.29	1.98	2.34	.34	7.74
1918	72.0	366.0	1.65	1.39	1.76	2.25	.36	7.41
1919	69.0	426.4	1.61	1.59	1.53	2.17	.34	7.24
1920	79.8	418.8	1.87	1.56	1.43	1.98	.34	7.18
1921	64.3	470.1	1.50	1.72	1.19	2.05	.33	6.79

Source: Adapted from Neil H. Borden, *The Economic Effects of Advertising* (Chicago, 1942), 215–216. (Taken from U.S. Department of Agriculture, Statistical Bulletin No. 58, *First Annual Report on Tobacco Statistics, 1937* [May 1937], p. 100 and Statistical Bulletin No. 67, *Annual Report on Tobacco Statistics, 1938* [1938], p. 79.) Reprinted courtesy of Neil Borden.

rate of cigarette consumption can be attributed to advertising. "Smoking," as Neil Borden argued, "is a social habit."

The form of smoking adopted by an individual is undoubtedly influenced largely by emulation ... as accepted social leaders adopt a usage, emulation provides a basis for its spread. ... Cigarette advertising has made much use of this motive of emulation. Well-known personages have been pictured using cigarettes; their testimonials have been presented. Advertising illustrations have pictured people worthy of emulation. Thus has advertising provided a force to speed up a usage that undoubtedly would have reached considerable magnitude without advertising.[2]

Actually, advertising proved relatively ineffective in increasing consumption by existing smokers; rather, advertising converted non-smokers to smokers. "Once adopted," Borden argued, "usage tends to be habitual and persistent."[3]

The American Tobacco Company dominated the modern history of the tobacco industry; from its formation in 1890 until its court-ordered dissolution in 1911, the Company controlled the cigarette, smoking tobacco, plug tobacco, and snuff market in the United States.[4] Prior to the development of an efficient, effective cigarette-rolling machine by James Bonsack in 1881, cigarettes, like cigars, were rolled by hand. Since the economies of scale available to large producers were severely limited, most cigarettes were produced in the numerous small tobacco factories. The Bonsack machines, which James Duke leased in 1883 and rapidly put to use in cigarette production, could roll 100,000 to 120,000 cigarettes a day, the equivalent of forty to fifty laborers rolling by hand. Although Duke enjoyed a favorable contract for the machines, which guaranteed him a cost 25 per cent below his competitors', the cost of rolling alone represented too small a fraction of the total costs to allow significant price competition. It did, however, greatly increase the production capacity of the cigarette factories that employed the machines. Faced with potential overcapacity of essentially a similar product, "the competition expressed itself chiefly in the form of expensive and sometimes elaborate advertising."[5] In 1889, James Duke, for example, allocated $80,000, 20 per cent of his gross sales, to advertising. Toward the end of the 1880s, the tobacco industry faced surplus production capacity, expensive competition, and a decline in the rate of growth of the demand. As Glen Porter noted, "Cooperation became an ever more appealing and logical solution, and, once more, James Duke led the way."[6]

From its organization in 1890, an American Tobacco Company absorbed over two hundred rival firms to gain control of the cigarette and smoking tobacco industries. The formation of the Continental Tobacco Co. and the American Snuff Co. allowed American to extend its control over the plug and snuff tobacco business. Despite the organization of the American Cigar Co. in 1901, and an expensive and determined effort by Duke, control of the cigar business eluded the trust. In 1904, concern over the activities of the Bureau of Corporations and the anti-trust division of the Department of Justice led Duke to scrap the Consolidated Tobacco Company (a holding company) and merge all of the firms into the American Tobacco Company. After the Supreme Court ordered its dissolution in 1911, the Trust divided into several firms, including the new American Tobacco Company, R. J. Reynolds, Liggett & Meyers, and P. Lorillard and Company. The oligopoly

of these large firms replaced the near-monopoly of the old American Tobacco Company.[7]

Formation of the American Tobacco Company trust did have the immediate effect of reducing advertising. However, from 1890 to 1895 the
consumption of tobacco fell. Actually, from 1895 to 1900, the period when
Duke was exerting a major effort to dominate the cigar business, the number
of cigarettes consumed declined by more than a half billion. Faced with
declining sales, competition from rival firms not in the trust, foreign brand
competition, and the need for maintaining brand-name loyalty among the
smoking public, the trust resumed advertising.[8] In 1884, prior to the organization of the trust, Duke had purchased 400,000 chairs, had his advertising
painted on the back, and supplied them free to tobacco retail shops. Much
of the advertising budget of the American Tobacco Company (trust) during
James B. Duke's presidency stressed coupons and premiums as promotional
devices. In the 1890s, when tobacco consumption slumped, as much as
four-fifths of the total advertising budget of the trust went into premiums
and coupons.[9] Even after the turn of the century, the largest portion, by
far, of the American Tobacco Company advertising budget continued to
go into promotional prizes, and cigar and smoking-tobacco advertisements.
For example, on one occasion Duke paid $300,000, a huge expenditure for
the time, to have a single brand of American Tobacco Company cigars
advertised on billboards in cities and towns across the United States. In
1907, Percival Hill, who succeeded James B. Duke as president of the Trust,
contracted for the advertising space on the Fifth Avenue (New York) horse-
drawn trolleys for "Bull Durham" smoking tobacco. Large signs of the
"Bull" in full color and "in all his roaring bullishness" appeared on the
Fifth Avenue buses, and New Yorkers were "horrified" by the huge pictures of what "was all too obviously a bull."[10] Local authorities arrested
the drivers and confiscated the signs. The legal case went all the way to
the Supreme Court. Amidst great publicity, the "Bull" was banished from
Fifth Avenue. Nevertheless, for the duration of the tobacco trust, national
magazine advertising remained relatively light and concentrated on cigars
and smoking tobacco.

For the first decade of the twentieth century cigar advertisements, whether
for Cortez Cigars, "Made in Key West for Men of Brains," Brunita,
Brunswick, and Bossy Cigars, "A good cigar at any price," or El Principe
de Wales, "Now King of Havana Cigars," utilized the same basic appeal.
Each brand of cigars claimed to be the "best," the "mildest," "hand rolled"
from the "finest tobacco," and the least expensive.[11] The ads attempted
to convince cigar smokers to smoke a particular brand and little effort
was directed to winning new consumers. Nothing in the ads equated
cigar smoking with social status or acceptance. In 1899, the American
Tobacco Company advertisement, a quarter-page *Harper's Weekly* ad that
introduced their new "little cigar," "Between the Acts," stood out as an

exception. The copy suggested that busy and obviously successful men could find time to enjoy the small cigars and "not only save half your cigar money but experience a new enjoyment in smoking."[12]

In 1912, Rob't Burns Cigars, in a series of half-page ads in *Saturday Evening Post*, suggested that "For Your Health's Sake" smoke Rob't Burns. The copy of the first ad in the series announced that subsequent "Smoke Talks" would dwell on the "*wrong* of *strong* cigars," and went on to explain that in choosing what cigar to smoke, "the effects upon your nerves, your heart and your brain" should be considered. The solution in each of the ads in the series was not to stop smoking, but to smoke THE MILD Rob't Burns.[13] As late as 1916, Rob't Burns Cigars continued to advertise "Why the Right Smoking Pays." Preaching moderation as the key to good living, the copy advised smokers to exercise moderation in their choice of cigars:

"Don't over-eat or over-play or over-work or over-smoke"—those are the rules! The man who moves with the modern trend obeys them. He "passes up" heavy cigars. He chooses the goodly tasting, milder kind that *soothes*. He smokes increasingly the ROBERT BURNS.[14]

The caption of a United Cigar Store Company ad in 1918 asked rhetorically "Who discovered the Ricoro?" The answer, from one businessman to another, came back, "An Efficiency Engineer discovered Ricoro."[15] The copy suggested that just because one could afford expensive 15¢ to 25¢ cigars was no reason to smoke them when Ricoro, "the 'self-made' cigar," sold for less. The ad suggested that smart and successful self-made *men* who understood the need for efficiency smoked cigars and would choose Ricoro. Social status as an appeal entered cigar ads just as the demand for cigars started a secular decline. Faced with a falling demand tobacco companies sought to increase consumption by winning new smokers and like other attempts to reverse fashion trends, advertising proved unequal to the task.[16]

The Supreme Court order in 1911 brought about a dissolution of the American Tobacco Company trust, which in turn produced a resurgence of cigarette and smoking-tobacco advertising. While the trust had advertised, the campaigns had stressed brand recognition through billboards, tobacco store signs and furnishings, and local newspaper ads. As Daniel Pope has pointed out, only after the trust became concerned about the Justice Department did its advertising shift to increasing the total market for tobacco products. True, the campaign sought to build brand loyalty, but the trust controlled such a high share of the total sales that for the most part it was a waste of effort to spend money enticing the smokers of other brands. Coupons and premiums remained the major promotional devices for trust cigarettes.[17] Competitive, non-trust brands, primarily Turkish tobacco cigarettes, advertised on an occasional basis throughout the trust period. For example, in 1900, Egyptian Deities Cigarettes took a full page in *Harper's Weekly* because "THERE ARE IMITATIONS OF THE BOX AND LABEL OF 'EGYPTIAN DEITIES,' " and customers were warned to insist on having the genuine product.[18] The copy described the "purer, finer tobacco" and "better workmanship" used in making Egyptian Deities, which "can be found in every first-class club." In an interesting reflection of the relative popularity of the two, smokers were assured that Egyptian Deities was "the only cigarette that is acceptable and satisfying to a 'cigar smoker.' "[19] The following year, the manufacturers of Egyptian Deities introduced their new brand "Turkish Trophies" with a full-page, back-cover ad in *Harper's Weekly*, featuring a portrait of a woman in Turkish costume holding a package of the cigarettes, but not smoking.[20]

Not surprisingly, tobacco companies, once machine production of cigarettes made the industry a decreasing cost industry, were not content to compete for the same market; the shift in appeal evidenced itself four years later, when the makers of Egyptian Deities and Turkish Trophies advertised "Carlton Club, the Exclusive Cigarette." The copy simply announced, "*Men* who appreciate Turkish tobacco at its best smoke Carlton Club."[21] Later that same year, Murad cigarettes appealed to the "exquisite tastes" of "connoisseurs" in their ads.[22] Pall Mall Famous Cigarettes, in a full-page, back-cover ad, which never mentioned the qualities of the cigarette, based the appeal entirely on social status. In a delightful bit of "snob appeal," the company announced that because of their "many patrons traveling abroad" on steamships, including the *Baltic, St. Louis, Kaiserin, Amerika, Adriatic, Minnetonka, Rotterdam*, and *Lusitania*, or for that matter any "first-class" steamers of the White Star, Cunard, Red Star, American, Atlantic Transport, Hamburg-American, or Holland-American Lines, Pall Mall had made arrangements so their loyal customers could now purchase Pall Malls on board the ships. More important, the on-board Pall Malls were packaged in special containers designed to protect the cigarettes against the "moist, salt air of the ocean."[23]

"The Smoke of the Smart Set," declared a full-page, richly illustrated advertisement in the *Saturday Evening Post*, "is not the ready-made or even ready-made-to-order kind." The foreground of the ad featured two handsome, formally dressed men, one smoking and handing the other a package of "Bull" Durham to roll his own cigarette. In the background, chic women dance with men in formal attire, and the copy reinforced the scene by informing the reader, "Smart men of fashion everywhere—clubmen, connoisseurs, bon-vivants, millionaire sportsmen" roll for themselves with "Bull Durham."[24] In a similar ad the following year, which pictured two well-dressed men in a club-like setting, smoking and rolling their own cigarettes to the admiring glances of women passing by, the copy insisted that the preference of "connoisseurs" such as these "has made it smart, fashionable, correct to 'roll your own.' "[25] With most of the

Reprinted from *Harper's Weekly*, September 21, 1901.

PALL MALL
FAMOUS CIGARETTES

❡ The proprietors take pleasure in announcing to their many patrons traveling abroad that these famous cigarettes can now be obtained on board the following steamships:

Mauretania	*Lusitania*	*Adriatic*	*Amerika*
Baltic	*Deutschland*	*Lucania*	*St. Paul*
Carmania	*Oceanic*	*Rotterdam*	*Cedric*
St. Louis	*Minnetonka*	*New York*	*Campania*
Teutonic	*Philadelphia*	*Caronia*	*Minnehaha*
Kaiserin Auguste Victoria		*Majestic*	*Zeeland*

and on board all the first-class steamers of the White Star, Cunard, Red Star, American, Atlantic Transport, Hamburg-American and Holland-America Lines.

❡ Owing to the effect of the moist, salt air of the ocean on tobaccos, the PALL MALL FAMOUS CIGARETTES sold on board these steamships have been specially packed in hermetically sealed tin cartons, and will therefore reach the consumer in the same state of excellence as on land.

"A Shilling in London
A Quarter Here"
Either on Board

Reprinted from *Harper's Weekly*, March 20, 1909.

smoking tobacco market captured by "Bull Durham," a brand retained by the American Tobacco Company after the dissolution order, Liggett & Myers introduced its "Duke's Mixture" granulated roll-your-own cigarette tobacco. The advertising campaign emphasized the "Virginia leaf" tobacco in the mixture and tried to impress potential customers by assuring them that the tobacco had a long history and the mixture was unique. Both claims were true, but then all domestic smoking tobaccos were "unique" mixtures, and all had Virginia Bright Leaf tobacco in the mixture. In addition, Liggett & Myers introduced "Velvet" pipe tobacco in a "tin" in an effort to capture some of the market. Although the pipe tobacco would ultimately enjoy some success, "Duke's Mixture" found difficulty in selling in a declining market long dominated by "Bull Durham."

In 1918, Percival Hill, president of the American Tobacco Company, announced that "Our Government has requested that we put at the disposal of the War Department our entire output of Bull Durham tobacco. And we have complied—fully, gladly. For whatever the Government wants, whatever it needs, it must have from us and from you fully and with a generous heart."[26] Hill had gained the upper hand on his major competition. The War Department had made a similar request of "Duke's Mixture," but Hill's "announcement" seized the publicity advantage and made excellent advertising copy. The full-page "announcement," for which the American Tobacco Company paid, concluded, "I know that you will not forget the little muslin sack—gone for the present on its mission of hope and inspiration to our boys in the trenches. 'Bull' will come back, with ribbons of honor. Have no fear."[27] Actually, the "Bull" came back to a market now dominated by cigarette smokers, and the demand for roll-your-own cigarette tobacco never recovered.

A year before the dissolution of the American Tobacco trust, in 1911, the U.S. Commissioner of Corporations estimated the total advertising expenditures for the largest portion of the tobacco industry to be slightly more than $13 million, of which cigarettes accounted for about one-third of the expenditures. By 1913, only two years after the dissolution, total advertising for the industry exceeded $25 million, with cigarette advertising amounting to over $13 million.[28] Estimates of the advertising expenditure for cigarettes, cigars, and smoking tobacco alone exceeded $75 million in 1931. The consumption of cigarettes reflected the explosion in advertising expenditures. By 1916, the per capita consumption of cigarettes stood at 250; during the next thirteen years it rose to nearly a thousand for every man, woman, and child in the United States.[29] The real surge in ready-made cigarette smoking occurred during World War I. Actually, as Neil Borden noted, "A slowing down of the rate of consumption [of tobacco] increase had set in before the first World War." Indeed even after the War, the per capita consumption of tobacco remained stationary for the next two decades. As important as Borden's observation was, it should not obscure the fact that an even more significant transformation assured the demand for tobacco products. The consumption of the finished-tobacco product increased rapidly. Chewing tobacco, smoking tobacco (pipe and tobacco to roll cigarettes), and cigar tobacco consumption fell; snuff remained constant; but ready-made cigarette consumption rose to fill the void.[30]

World War I proved the turning point in cigarette smoking. James Wood observed that "The British 'fag' had been a wartime fixture even before the entry of the United States into the conflict."[31] Both the Army and the Navy distributed cigarettes and smoking tobacco, and the public was encouraged to send tobacco to servicemen. No doubt, the ready availability of cigarettes and smoking tobacco popularized the habit. The pace of service life encouraged short smoking breaks, and the tension and strain promoted the use of tobacco. Certainly the war helped to break down local prejudices and social restrictions on personal behavior. The low price of cigarettes made them popular with servicemen and only a few years' usage was necessary "to bring widespread acceptance of this form of smoking among the young men of the nation."[32]

The pace of urban industrial life that the returning servicemen found awaiting them also promoted the short smoke of cigarettes as opposed to the more leisurely smoking of pipes and cigars. In many ways, the growth in the demand for ready-made cigarettes followed the similar pattern of clothing and food in further finishing products prior to ultimate consumption. The identification of cigarette smoking with youth and the heavy advertising campaigns which featured the "right" kind of people smoking in prestigious social settings also undoubtedly helped promote cigarette smoking.

Not all was smooth sailing for tobacco-product manufacturers, however. Even in the first two decades of the twentieth century, cigarette smoking encountered considerable unfavorable publicity. In 1914, Henry Ford, in press interviews and in a pamphlet he published, attacked cigarette smoking on both moral and physical grounds. Ford announced that he would refuse to hire cigarette smokers and insisted it was a sure sign of moral degenerates. Thomas Edison, who joined Ford in the attacks on cigarette smoking, blamed most of the harmful effects on the burning wrapping paper, which, he charged, "has a violent reaction on the nerve centers, producing degeneration of the brain cells, quite rapidly among boys." Edison, in a surprisingly modern conclusion, argued that, "Unlike narcotics, this degeneracy is permanent and uncontrollable."[33] In spite of the fact that Ford and Edison, two of the best-known men in America, were joined by such influential groups as the W.C.T.U. (Women's Christian Temperance Union) as well as such noted personages as John Wanamaker, Marshall Field, and Connie Mack, their protests against cigarettes attracted only short-lived attention in the popular press.[34] The significance of the failure of the attacks on tobacco usage in general and cigarette smoking specifically should not go unnoticed. Neil Borden, in discussing the growth of demand for cigarettes in his classic study on the economic effects of advertising, argued that the failure of the opposition to cigarette smoking to gain an audience had profound significance:

Undoubtedly the weakening of taboos and prejudices against cigarettes has been one of the most important factors in widening consumption among both men and women. . . . Ever since its introduction tobacco has suffered from a social prejudice which at times has brought organized proselyting against its use and widespread laws curbing its sale or use. Among tobacco products, the cigarette, particularly, has been subject to attack. . . . The best evidence of the extent and intensity of the prejudice is the fact that 14 states passed statutes between 1896 and 1921 prohibiting the sale of cigarettes. The last of the laws was not repealed until 1927. All states [in 1947] except Texas have laws prohibiting the sale of cigarettes to minors. Such prejudices against tobacco usage have their basis in beliefs and sentiments coming from medicine, religion, and morality. The disappearance of these prejudices rests in part in changes occurring in medicine, religion, and moral attitude. The campaigns of testimonials featuring well-known personages and the picturing of the "right" kind of people smoking have undoubtedly had an influence in breaking down such prejudices.[35]

The tobacco industry, then as now, did not accept attacks passively. Nor did the advertising agencies which handled the tobacco companies' accounts accept public criticism gracefully. Too much money was at stake. In 1877–1878, N. W. Ayer & Son, one of the early, large, and successful advertising agencies, received less than 5 per cent of its business from tobacco advertisements. Sandwiched in rank order between musical instruments and schools and colleges, the revenue from tobacco, which ranked at best twelfth in terms of income, played an as of yet insignificant role in the company fortunes. By the turn of the century, more than 7 per cent of Ayer's income came from tobacco advertising and it now ranked only slightly behind patent medicines and dry goods and clothing. More importantly, tobacco represented the fastest growth category of clients. In 1921, income from tobacco advertising ranked first and contributed nearly 23 per cent of Ayer & Son's income. Indeed, the advertising placed for tobacco exceeded the total for all commodities two decades earlier.[36] Not surprisingly, the agency itself looked with considerable disfavor on newspaper attacks on the tobacco industry. Ralph Hower, in his study of N. W. Ayer & Son, noted that while he found no evidence that the agency had ever sought to force inclusions of news or editorial material, it did seek, with success, to "have news items or editorial opinions suppressed." In 1904, an Ayer executive speaking to a group of publishers made a statement which Hower concluded represented the firm's philosophy "then and today":

In the handling of the advertising of the American Tobacco Company we have not infrequently been urged by the business department of the newspapers to give them a certain advertisement, and immediately after the advertisement appeared there was inserted either in the editorial or news items a direct attack upon the product thus advertised. . . . I contend that if this is the case, the advertising department of the paper ought to refuse to insert the advertisement. In other words, it is neither fair nor businesslike to take a man's money for an advertisement and then use the reading columns of the paper to destroy the value of his investment.[37]

More importantly perhaps, Hower went on to point out that such overt efforts by advertising agencies to control the news or editorial content of media were no longer common because "publishers are more careful about biting the hand that feeds them," and editors have "learned to make precautionary expurgations to forestall criticisms."[38]

Forestalling criticism through censorship proved effective in blunting social criticism of cigarette smoking, but the rival companies created by the dissolution of the American Tobacco Company trust found themselves in the unfamiliar water of unprotected markets. Each new company, eager to establish its brands, sought first to establish brand-name recognition, then to secure a larger share of the market as well as to increase the total demand. Advertising budgets for cigarettes multiplied.

In 1914, R. J. Reynolds developed a mild, blended cigarette specifically designed to appeal to as broad a taste as possible so as to compete with the many local ready-made cigarettes then on the market. After pretesting in several cities to ensure customer acceptance, a full-scale advertising campaign was launched in newspapers across the nation. The first ad announced "The camels are coming," with no mention that Camels were a brand of cigarettes. The second ad, again with no mention of the product, read "TOMORROW there'll be more CAMELS in this town than in all of Asia and Africa combined!" The third ad, complete with a picture of the Camel Cigarette package, announced "Camel cigarettes ARE HERE!"[39] The copy developed two themes which would be consistent in Camel advertising throughout the decade. The first insisted that the blend of Turkish and Domestic tobacco was milder and more favorable than either tobacco alone. The second theme, in an obvious effort to differentiate Camels from American Tobacco Company cigarettes, informed smokers that Camels offered neither coupons nor premiums: "Smokers realize that the value is in the cigarettes and do not expect premiums or coupons."[40]

In addition to extensive newspaper advertisements where most of the early advertising campaigns concentrated, Reynolds utilize posters and tobacco-shop accouterments, some national magazines, and a good deal of outdoor advertisements to advertise Camels. A story, probably the figment of an advertising man's imagination, suggests that the most famous slogan in advertising history originated when a man approached a sign painter working on an outdoor ad for Camels and asked for a cigarette. Upon receiving a Camel, he supposedly said, appreciatively, "Thanks—I'D

WALK A MILE FOR A CAMEL!" Camel's well-conceived and carefully implemented plan produced results; by the end of World War I, Camels were the leading ready-rolled cigarette in the market.[41]

Camel's increasing dominance of the ready-made cigarette market encouraged rival companies to start advertising campaigns. George Washington Hill, Percival Hill's son and an unabashed admirer of the power of advertising, decided to copy R. J. Reynolds and compete for the machine-rolled cigarette market with one brand of blended tobaccos designed to appeal to the broadest possible tastes. Hill chose Lucky Strike, a brand name registered in 1871 for smoking tobacco and still marketed by a subsidiary, R. A. Patterson Tobacco Company, as pipe tobacco.[42] In choosing Lucky Strike, Hill gained the advantage of starting his campaign with some brand recognition carried over from the earlier advertisement. For example, a very attractive 1912 ad for Lucky Strike smoking tobacco carried the caption "Lucky Strike Tobacco makes the pipe smoker welcome." The ad featured a group of well-dressed and obviously successful men smoking cigars and cigarettes in the club car of a train; in the foreground a man is loading a pipe with Lucky Strike tobacco. The copy read, "The fragrant, cheery, *quality*-aroma of Lucky Strike Tobacco is a friendly introduction for the pipe user to *any* company of smokers."[43] Seizing on the fact that all tobacco was heated in the processing, Hill coined the Lucky Strike slogan "It's Toasted." In January 1917, Hill launched a massive advertising campaign. Focusing on newspapers, posters, and outdoor signs, the ads featured the "It's Toasted" theme. The illustration showed a slice of bread on a fork being beautifully toasted over an open fire. The copy suggested that the toasting, without actually saying it, was unique to Lucky Strike, enabling it to capture the flavor of the tobacco for the smoker.[44] For the most part, the emphasis in the early Lucky Strike campaign, like Camel's, focused on brand recognition.

Not only former tobacco trust companies intensified their advertising in the period following the dissolution. Indeed, in many ways the non-trust companies, who, since the trust had largely controlled the supply of domestic tobacco, had been forced to utilize imported Turkish tobacco in their cigarettes, found themselves in a fiercer competition than before the dissolution. For one thing, the companies organized at the dissolution of the trust now seemed to be paying more attention to the growing ready-made cigarette market as opposed to an entire line of tobacco products. Given the scrutiny by the Justice Department, the trust had little incentive to eliminate these small, competitive companies. More important, the massive advertising campaigns for Camel and Lucky Strike shared a common emphasis that blended tobacco made better cigarettes than pure Turkish tobacco.

A 1915 advertisement in *Harper's Weekly* featured a couple on a moonlight drive in a stylish convertible; a well-dressed man is smoking and a chic woman is driving. The slogan "Just like being in Cairo" is supplemented by

Reprinted from *Harper's Weekly*, September 18, 1915.

the copy "Mogul Egyptian Cigarettes." The ad places cigarette smoking in a romantic and "smart" setting.[45] Later that same year, an ad for "MURAD, *The* Turkish Cigarette" claimed that Murads "on sale" were "The Foremost High-Grade Cigarette in the World." Obviously, this distinction "could never be mere chance"; rather, it had been attained only by the "Delicious, Exclusive, Wonderful Taste of Pure Turkish Tobacco" in Murad. The illustration featured four men, all smoking, and an attractive young woman at a tennis or country club.[46] Again, the ad placed cigarette smoking in a "smart" social setting.

Certainly the cigarette companies and their advertising agencies stayed "ever-lastingly at it" in their efforts to capitalize on the increased customer preference for ready-made cigarettes. In 1925, two years before the American Tobacco Company broke the taboo and launched the first advertising campaign directed toward women and featuring women smoking in social settings, approximately 75 billion cigarettes were consumed by American smokers.[47] The big three, R. J. Reynolds (Camel), Liggett & Myers (Chesterfield), and the American Tobacco Company (Lucky Strike), accounted for over 82 per cent of the 75 billion. Camels led with 34 billion, followed by Chesterfields with 20 billion, and Lucky Strikes sold over 13 billion.[48]

Advertising agencies, some of which had earlier refused to handle liquor advertising for "moral" reasons, threw themselves into the campaigns, reaping large profits and enthusiastically claiming success at every increase in their clients' sales. The inclusion of women in the smart social settings illustrating cigarette ads led *Printers' Ink*, in 1919, to warn against "an insidious campaign to create women smokers."[49] Although the overt campaign of American tobacco companies' advertising to bring the "gift" of cigarette smoking to American women would have to wait until the middle of the next decade, the techniques to accomplish that task were in place even before World War I. The efforts of the independent companies and the massive advertising campaigns accompanying the brand wars of the major tobacco firms formed after the dissolution capitalized on and helped promote, but did not create, the shift in tobacco consumption from other forms to ready-made cigarettes. The shift to cigarettes resembled a long-run fashion curve. Causes of fashion shifts remain hazy, but emulation, imitation, and the desire for social approval are "potent motivating forces in bringing about consumption change of the kind involved in fashion cycles."[50] In employing those very appeals which they knew were "potent motivating forces," in exerting unscrupulous and inexcusable economic pressure on the media to censor or dampen legitimate social concerns about the consumption of tobacco, and in deliberately seeking to extend the market to non-smokers, cigarette companies and their advertising agencies must share the blame for increasing the use of a deadly substance by the American consumer.

7

ADVERTISING COMES OF AGE

SOPO SAVES SCRUBBING—NUTRAX FOR NERVES—CRUNCH-
LETS ARE CRISPER—NOURISH NERVES WITH NUTRAX—FAR-
LEY'S FOOTWEAR TAKES YOU FURTHER.... The presses, thun-
dering and growling, ground out the same appeals by the million: ASK
YOUR GROCER—ASK YOUR DOCTOR—ASK THE MAN WHO'S
TRIED IT—MOTHER'S! GIVE IT TO YOUR CHILDREN—HOUSE-
WIVES! ... HUSBANDS! ... WOMEN! ... Whatever you're doing,
stop it and do something else! Whatever you're buying, pause and buy
something different! Be hectored into health and prosperity! Never let
up! Never go to sleep! Never be satisfied! If once you're satisfied, all
our wheels will run down. Keep going—and if you can't, Try Nutrax
for Nerves!
    Lord Peter Wimsey went home and slept.
               —Dorothy L. Sayers, *Murder Must Advertise*, 88

Frank Presbrey once predicted that advertising "practitioners" of the 1980s
would regard the entire history of advertising up to the automobile as unimportant. It was "The automobile [which] provided the big opportunity,"
he argued, for advertising to reveal itself as a force in American society,
"A force comparable to steam, electricity and—the automobile." Waxing
eloquent, Presbrey concluded that:

Successful advertising of the motor car set at rest all doubts as to the ability of the
average American to acquire an article of luxury when the pleasure of possession is
convincingly pictured to him, and opened the way for a class of advertising that
has in a quarter of a century revolutionized American living habits and given us
the highest standard of living any people ever enjoyed. Besides the automobile
other mass selling tasks were obviously capable of accomplishment. A long line of
new luxuries and comforts that in the nineteenth century were not for the ordinary

family have been developed and made a part of the family possessions as a result of confidence that mass distribution can be obtained.[1]

As usual, Presbrey overstated the case. Certainly no one, not even Presbrey, argued that automobile advertising reached its full maturity during the first two decades of the twentieth century. As Roland Marchand has clearly illustrated, it would be another decade before the planned obsolescence of yearly model changes, and before the concept of owning two and three automobiles by families, would be introduced into the consumption ethic.[2] Still, by 1920 the pattern was in place, and the appeal was less on the utility of the product than on the social gratification associated with the ownership of a particular automobile. What Presbrey and other advertising professionals suggested was that the size, the scale, and the success of automobile advertising indicated the acceptance and maturity of advertising as a major force in the American economy. More than that, as David Hounshell has aptly demonstrated, automobile production by the Ford Motor Company represented the logical culmination of the movement toward mass production in this country and presented the best illustration of the great potential of decreasing-cost industries to meet the demands of mass consumption.[3] In selling the automobile, advertising and American industry came of age.

Automobile advertising, like the automobile industry, underwent a major transformation in a very short period. During the waning years of the nineteenth century, popular magazines attracted little paid automobile advertising. The public, although already fascinated by automobiles, had yet to be convinced that the new machines would work, much less that they would prove practical. Since many of the early builders of automobiles came from the bicycle business, it was not surprising that "bicycle trade papers were automobile trade journals before an American car was sold."[4] In 1895 the *Cycle Trade Journal* became *The Cycle and Automobile Trade Journal*, and *The Horseless Age* appeared. That same year, Charles E. Duryea, a bicycle manufacturer from Peoria, Illinois, inserted a notice in *The Horseless Age* that he made "motor wagons." Duryea's notice, which appeared two years after an article in the *Springfield* (Illinois) *Evening Union* reported that he was building a horseless carriage, may have been the first advertisement for an American automobile. Following a pattern established by bicycle manufacturers, early motor car builders relied heavily on free publicity to advertise and introduce their new product to consumers.

Automobile races, like the earlier bicycle races, proved extremely popular and provided free advertising. More important, the events served to break down the popular preconceptions and prejudice about the early automobiles. Duryea won the first American automobile race, from Chicago to Evanston and back, on Thanksgiving Day, 1895. More than a hundred vehicles had entered the race, but only six showed up and only two finished the race. In spite of the few contestants and the fact that Duryea's winning time for the 54 miles was 7 hours and 53 minutes, the winning vehicle received great publicity.[5] For example, the "Duryea Motor Wagon," the vehicle which won the great Chicago race, opened Barnum & Bailey's Greatest Show on Earth at Madison Square Garden in 1896, and hundreds of thousands saw the same "Wagon" in the circus's street parades and when it was displayed in the menagerie tent.[6] For more than a decade, racing, both speedway races and cross-country durability events, attracted tremendous attention to the new automobiles.

Newspapers followed the events closely and devoted headlines, as well as pictures and long stories, to each race. Duryea won both the New York City to Irvington and return race sponsored by *Cosmopolitan* and the London to Brighton race in 1896. A year later Alexander Winton drove from Cleveland to New York on almost impassable roads in ten days, a feat that astounded newspaper readers. Four years later an Oldsmobile averaging ten miles an hour made the trip from Detroit to New York in only seven and a half days. In 1901, Henry Ford beat Winton in a challenge race at Grosse Point in a ten-mile race. Both automobiles received a great deal of publicity, Ford for a winning time of 13 minutes and 23.8 seconds and Winton for covering a mile in the record time of 1 minute and 14.4 seconds. Impressed by the excellent publicity, Ford immediately started construction of new racing cars. In 1903 one of them, Ford's "999" driven by a famous bicycle racer, Barney Oldfield, won a three-mile race at Grosse Point by more than a half mile. Again the publicity was "enormous" and the best advertising for Ford "thus far."[7]

By 1899, the year that Ransom E. Olds organized the Olds Motor Vehicle Company, eighty companies either were making or preparing to make automobiles of one kind or another. A number of them, including the Oldsmobile, the Locomobile, the Winton, the Duryea, the Haynes-Apperson, the Stanley Steam Car, and the American Electric Vehicle, advertised in trade magazines. Unlike other consumer products, automobile makers never utilized small single-column ads. Quarter, half, and full-page ads appeared in trade journals during the last few years of the nineteenth century and gradually made their appearance in popular magazines in the twentieth century. The rapid failure of automobile companies in the last years of the nineteenth century and early years of the twentieth not only made the public wary of placing orders which required deposits, it also led the public to a general suspicion about the stability of the entire industry. Since none of the early automobile companies produced for future sales or carried stocks of vehicles, each vehicle was produced and assembled to order. Many of the early advertisements for automobiles sought to convince the public that their firm was in business to stay, that they could actually deliver the automobile they advertised, and that it would perform as promised. For example, an 1896 ad of the Haynes-Apperson Company of Kokomo, Indiana, stressed the moderate price and reliability of prompt delivery of all orders. The ad featured a photograph of the automobile the company promised to deliver.[8]

Potential customers had a choice of steam, electric, or gasoline-powered vehicles. Dealers and makers, following the already well-established nineteenth-century pattern in advertising new products, assured the public that theirs was the "best," the "perfect," the "most dependable" make of the proper type. The Rider Electric Vehicle, for example, was simply "The perfect vehicle"; it enjoyed "absolute control of speed and direction," and customers were assured that both "minimum cost of operation and the highest degree of durability have been attained."[9] The American Electric Vehicle, which could be purchased from Montgomery Ward & Co., claimed to be able to fill orders immediately upon receipt and offered "perfection" in simplicity, design, and "artistic" style.[10] Although F. E. Stanley and his brother F. O. Stanley, who manufactured the famous "Stanley Steamer," did not engage in newspaper and magazine advertising, they and their steam-driven cars received a great deal of publicity from their performances in auto races. Steam cars were simple to drive, quiet, and fast. The Porter Company, a Boston firm which produced the Porter Stanhope, also a steam car, emphasized in their advertisements that their car was "The Perfect Automobile," "handsome and elegant," "conforms in its design to the modern horse carriages," and was "safe, simple, and durable." More important, perhaps, the Porter Stanhope was "absolutely non-explosive" and "free from all complications in its mechanism, so that an engineer is not necessary to its use."[11]

Producers of gasoline-powered vehicles utilized the same basic appeal in their early advertising. Automobile advertising until about 1905 reflected "the doubt which still existed in the public mind as to whether the automobile would run and whether it was safe."[12] Advertisements stressed the safety and dependability of the machine while seeking to build brand-name recognition. The Haynes-Apperson, "The only one that Always won," absolutely guaranteed no vibration in its "pleasure carriages." Ford's Model A was the "Boss of the road," while Packard "gets you there and gets you back." "Everyone" wanted a "Winton," and the Autocar could lift 275 times its weight, while the Oldsmobile simply advertised that it "goes."[13]

The first decade of the twentieth century witnessed remarkable growth and change in the automobile industry and in automobile advertising. The Riker Electric Vehicle, "The Perfect Automobile," ad in the May 26, 1900, issue of *Harper's Weekly*, appeared adjoining a similar size ad for the Crawford Bicycle, which for "real elegance and beauty" no other model could match. The bicycle ad was better illustrated and the copy certainly as appealing as the Riker ad. Two years later, readers of the *Overland Monthly* found advertisements for four automobile firms: the Oldsmobile, "in a class by itself—an everlasting runner" for $650 F.O.B.

Figure 7.1
Annual Sales and Registration of Passenger Automobiles and Population

Year	Popula-tion (1) 1,000,000	Annual Sales (2) (Factory) Passenger Car 1,000	Registration 1,000 (3)	Sales Ratio 1:2	Registration Ratio 1:3
1900	76.0	4.1	8.0	18536:1	9500:1
1905	83.8	24.2	77.4	3462.8:1	1082:1
1910	92.4	181.0	458.3	510:1	202:1
1915	100.5	895.9	2332.4	112:1	43:1
1920	106.5	1905.5	8131.5	56:1	13:1
1970	204.9	6546.8	108,407.3	31:1	1.9:1

Source: U.S. Department of Commerce, Bureau of the Census, Historical Statistics of the United States: Colonial Times to 1970 (Washington, D.C., 1975), II:716.

Detroit; The Locomobile Company of the Pacific which sold the Stanhope "B," one of their popular styles for $700 delivered in San Francisco; The Sunset Automobile Company, which built "anything—Stage Coach, Truck, Delivery Wagon, Touring Car, Runabout" for either steam or gasoline power and assured their customers that they had three years' experience; and the California Automobile Co., which built anything the customer wanted to order and offered monthly installment payment plans, or would sell "a few shares of stock in the company." In the same issue, an attractive ad for O'Brien & Sons offered customers "Carriages for Swelldom" (horse drawn) which were "Not Cheap but Unsurpassed for Quality, Style, and Finish."[14]

By 1904 over 120 different concerns made or assembled automobiles, including the Austin, Packard, Ford, Peerless, Pierce-Arrow, Rambler, White, Cadillac, Franklin, Oldsmobile, Winton, Studebaker, Buick, Maxwell, Columbia, and Haynes-Apperson. The following year over 24,000 passenger cars were built and sold and three times that number registered (see Figure 7.1).

As the vehicles became heavier and faster and incorporated more features, the average wholesale price increased from approximately $1,000 in 1900 to over $1,500 five years later.[15] Almost all automobiles still were produced on a custom-order basis, that is, a customer placed an order and the "factory" then made the vehicle to fill that specific order. To make prudent investments, to enjoy the economies of scale available in increased mechanization, and to gain a secure market for their product, automobile makers hoped to rapidly increase total demand. Once production increased at an accelerated pace, automobile manufacturers, present and prospective, could reasonably depend on a market capable of absorbing future production.

Between 1904 and 1910 the slow trickle of advertising in popular national magazines aimed at mass consumers became a flood. Presbrey estimated that by 1909 about a million dollars was spent advertising automobiles in the trade journals and only slightly less in popular magazines.[16] While the *Saturday Evening Post* led the national media in automobile advertising, magazines such as *Harper's Weekly, Literary Digest, Overland Monthly,* and *Ladies' Home Journal* also carried a large volume.[17] Early advertisements often included illustrations, almost always simple line drawings or half-tone reproductions of the unoccupied vehicle against a blank background. However, this rapidly changed to photographs of the vehicle being driven, usually with women passengers, rarely with women drivers. Occupants, when pictured, were always presented as upper or upper-middle class, and the early backgrounds usually depicted a rural, small-town, or country-club scene. Although the emphasis on comfort, luxury, and style increased toward the end of the first decade as the automobile became an accepted part of American life, most copy retained appeals to dependability, economy, simplicity, and ease of operation.

Ford's advertising quickly evolved into the simple direct "reason why" approach made famous by John Powers; however, the early Ford advertisements resembled the competition in the use of excessive claims. The 1903 advertisement for the Model A, the "Boss of the Road," reasonably promised prompt delivery, high quality at low cost, and easy handling. However, the copy also claimed, "It is positively the most perfect machine on the market, having overcome all draw-backs . . . is so simple that a boy of 15 can run it," and promised "IMMEDIATE DELIVERY."[18] "Don't experiment," a 1905 Ford ad advised, "Just buy a FORD." The copy argued that "experience is the key to automobile construction and *we have the key.*" Actually, the key was Henry Ford, who "has made a life work of the development of the Automobile."[19]

Claude Hopkins, who with the Lord & Thomas Agency directed advertising for Hudson, Willys, Overland, and Reo automobiles, always injected the builder, the designer or some other personality into his campaign. In addition, Hopkins argued that vague claims of being "the best" or the "most economical" simply caused customers to discount the rest of what the ad said. Far better, Hopkins suggested that ads be specific in claims but keep technical detail to a minimum, and keep the language simple and direct.[20]

Although Ford did not use Hopkins' firm to direct his advertising, the 1905 Ford ad embodied most of Hopkins' principles. The technical details were few and straightforward: "Model 'B' 4 cylinder, vertical, weight 1700 lbs., side entrance tonneau"; the claims specific: "light weight . . . ample power . . . and absolute simplicity"; and the auto was carefully identified with Henry Ford.[21]

As usual, not everyone agreed with Ford. In the same month that the Ford ad appeared, *Harper's Weekly* carried an entirely different type of advertisement for the Oldsmobile. The illustration showed two fashionably dressed women, one driving the car, the other outside, in front of an upper-class house. The copy claimed that "Oldsmobile has endeared itself to the feminine heart. . . . Its ease of control and freedom from getting out of order make every woman its friend." Quoting John Lothrop Motley as saying, "Give us the luxuries of life, and we will dispense with its necessaries," the ad went on to claim, "the *Oldsmobile* is both."[22] Four years later, in a full-page backcover of *Harper's Weekly*, a Pierce-Arrow advertisement frankly noted that "Without forgetting that, after all, a motor car is a piece of machinery, the Pierce-Arrow has never failed to offer its owner the highest luxury also."[23]

By 1909, Cadillac had decided that they would only produce larger and more expensive models, and that year the company announced that they would no longer market the smaller models. In advertising its comparatively low-priced automobiles between 1903 and 1909, Cadillac had stressed simple mechanism, a powerful engine, noiseless speed gears, and easy control. Occasionally, even Cadillac, when producing a wide range of vehicles, resorted to stunts to advertise the strength and power of the Cadillac:

A man drove a Cadillac up the steps of the Capitol in Washington. He paid for his fun, but it was worth the money to show the power of the Cadillac.[24]

The new advertising campaign for the higher-priced models claimed a high degree of perfection in durability, power, speed, dependability, and luxury. Cadillac became "the Standard of the World."[25]

By the end of the first decade of the twentieth century, there were nearly a half million automobiles registered in the United States, roughly one for every two hundred people in the country (see Figure 7.1). The industry was producing nearly 200,000 vehicles a year, and prices had declined to approximately the turn-of-the-century level. Clearly, the automobile was no longer to be considered a passing fad or an expensive plaything for the rich. As the size of the market increased, some manufacturers, such as Cadillac, Packard, and Pierce-Arrow, deliberately specialized in expensive luxury cars for the more affluent. Others produced a full line of cars with a wide range of prices and sought to differentiate their vehicles through advertising. Only a few, like Henry Ford, specialized in producing automobiles for mass consumption.

The "Perfect" electric automobile of the Riker Company and the other electric car manufacturers found stiff competition not only with each other, but particularly with the increasingly popular gasoline car. The early electric automobiles could rightfully claim the advantage in reliability and ease of operation. However, the continued improvement of the gasoline vehicles diminished and threatened to eliminate this differentiation. The major limitation of the electric cars, slow speed and the need to recharge the batteries on a frequent basis, eluded solution. Electric cars could go fast for a short period or slow for a longer period, but the limitations were about 20 miles per hour and 50 miles between recharging the batteries. Electric vehicle manufacturers, reasoning that these limitations would not bother women drivers, who seldom drove faster or for longer distances, aimed their advertising at women drivers and stressed the reliability and ease of operation. As early as 1905, the Pope Motor Car Company advertised the Waverley as a "Princely gift for your Wife."[26] A 1909 ad pronounced the Waverley "The Ideal Winter Vehicle for Busy Men and Society Women."[27] In one of the few automobile ads illustrated with a busy city street, crowded with both autos and horse-drawn carriages, the copy suggested that the Waverley was an ideal second car:

For use in the city and suburbs—where 99 per cent of the motoring is done—the simple, stylish Waverley Electric is more durable, more reliable, and gives more actual service at a lower cost per mile than any other vehicle, either horse-drawn or power-driven. Even the owners of gas cars are finding the Waverley a wise addition to their garage, for family use and winter service.

Maintained more easily and for much less than a team of horses, it has irresistible advantages in radius of travel, speed, safety, quietness, cleanliness, comfort, style, convenience and dependability for constant service, winter or summer. Women of refinement operate the Waverley with utmost ease, and need neither chauffeur, coachman nor escort.[28]

That same year, a quarter-page ad in *Ladies' Home Journal* depicted a woman driver picking up another lady in front of a large home, with the caption "The new Waverley makes the electric carriage one of the family conveniences which are simply indispensable."[29]

Manufacturers of gasoline-powered automobiles were not prepared to surrender the women's market to Waverley. Most advertisements pictured women in the vehicles and by the second decade of the twentieth century a number placed women in the driver's seat. In 1914 Paige countered the electric car claims of being best suited for women drivers with a full-page inside-cover ad in *Saturday Evening Post* with a caption which proclaimed: "Here is a Big, Roomy, Powerful Car that can be Driven Easily by a Woman."[30] Later that year the Willys-Overland Company, not to be outdone, advertised their Overland in a two-page spread in *Saturday Evening Post*. The illustration featured an Overland, with the

Don't experiment-Just buy a **FORD**

Experience is the Key to Automobile Construction and *we have the Key*

Henry Ford has made a life work of the development of the Automobile and presented to the world a car so perfected that the success of the Ford Motor Co. is without a parallel in the Automobile Industry.

The fundamental features of the first Ford Car were light weight (resulting in economy of maintenance), ample power (not too much and not too little, BUT ALWAYS POWER) and absolute simplicity, with the elimination of every unnecessary complication. These features still further developed are distinctive in Ford cars to-day. There have been no freaks, no failures, no experiments in Ford cars.

Send for detailed description of

Model "C" Tonneau Car, 1250 lbs., 2 cylinder opposed, price **$950.00.**
Model "F" Side Entrance Tonneau, weight 1400 lbs., 2 cylinder opposed, price **$1200.00.**
Model "B" 4 cylinder, vertical, weight 1700 lbs., side entrance tonneau, price **$2000.00.**
Delivery Car, weight 1350 lbs., 2 cylinder opposed, price **$950.00.**

Ford Motor Co., Detroit, Mich.

CANADIAN TRADE SUPPLIED BY THE FORD MOTOR CO. OF CANADA, LTD., WALKERVILLE, ONT.

Reprinted from *Harper's Weekly*, March 4, 1905.

Reprinted from *Overland Monthly*, July 1912.

Reprinted from *National Geographic*, November 1915.

The
PENALTY OF
LEADERSHIP

IN every field of human endeavor, he that is first must perpetually live in the white light of publicity. ¶Whether the leadership be vested in a man or in a manufactured product, emulation and envy are ever at work. ¶In art, in literature, in music, in industry, the reward and the punishment are always the same. ¶The reward is widespread recognition; the punishment, fierce denial and detraction. ¶When a man's work becomes a standard for the whole world, it also becomes a target for the shafts of the envious few. ¶If his work be merely mediocre, he will be left severely alone--if he achieve a masterpiece, it will set a million tongues a-wagging. ¶Jealousy does not protrude its forked tongue at the artist who produces a commonplace painting. ¶Whatsoever you write, or paint, or play, or sing, or build, no one will strive to surpass, or to slander you, unless your work be stamped with the seal of genius. ¶Long, long after a great work or a good work has been done, those who are disappointed or envious continue to cry out that it can not be done. ¶Spiteful little voices in the domain of art were raised against our own Whistler as a mountebank, long after the big world had acclaimed him its greatest artistic genius. ¶Multitudes flocked to Bayreuth to worship at the musical shrine of Wagner, while the little group of those whom he had dethroned and displaced argued angrily that he was no musician at all. ¶The little world continued to protest that Fulton could never build a steamboat, while the big world flocked to the river banks to see his boat steam by. ¶The leader is assailed because he is a leader, and the effort to equal him is merely added proof of that leadership. ¶Failing to equal or to excel, the follower seeks to depreciate and to destroy—but only confirms once more the superiority of that which he strives to supplant. ¶There is nothing new in this. ¶It is as old as the world and as old as the human passions—envy, fear, greed, ambition, and the desire to surpass. ¶And it all avails nothing. ¶If the leader truly leads, he remains—the leader. ¶Master-poet, master-painter, master-workman, each in his turn is assailed, and each holds his laurels through the ages. ¶That which is good or great makes itself known, no matter how loud the clamor of denial. ¶That which deserves to live—lives.

Cadillac Motor Car Co. Detroit. Mich.

Reprinted from *Saturday Evening Post*, January 2, 1915.

top down and seven very chicly dressed young women either riding in the car or admiring it. "Summer Days are Overland Days," the caption proclaimed, and the copy suggested that when summer "bakes you into a state of extreme and excessive perspiration, pessimism and discontent," escape to the "country club, woods, mountains, lake or river" in the Overland.[31] Paige continued to advertise as the family car, and two years later an ad for the Fairfield "Six-46" suggested, "take the 'Missus' along with you the next time you visit Automobile Row." The ad pictured the Fairfield "Six-46" with a woman driving and four children and two women passengers motoring on Michigan Avenue, Chicago, in front of the Chicago Art Institute and noted, "it is child's play to drive in the thickest city traffic."[32]

Men were, of course, always recognized by advertising agencies as the providers, and when it came to large purchases like an automobile, both men and women were encouraged to believe that "good" providers would, of course, buy the advertised product. The man provided the funds and made the final selection, but the woman, as superior judge of style and expert consumer, persuaded her provider to make the proper selection. Men who could not "properly" provide were made to feel guilty and their wives deprived. Automobile ads quickly fell into this pattern and became notorious for this type of appeal. No company exploited this type of appeal more fully than the Willys-Overland Company. A two-page ad in the *Saturday Evening Post* on the first page announced "This is the life" and pictured an obviously happy family in an Overland in front of a large, upper-class home, while the copy declared, "There are two ways to live nowadays. One way is the life that is daily chock-full of healthy activity, wholesome fun and lots of fresh air." On the facing page the caption read "—this is not" and pictured an obviously unhappy family waiting for the "stuffy, hot trolly car." "Here is the other side of the story, the other way some live," the copy argued, "the wrong way." "It's wrong. It's not fair to your children—your wife—or yourself," the ad advised men. "Get a car—an Overland—and over night all this is changed."[33] Another two-page ad that same year, this time obviously addressed to women, in *Ladies' Home Journal* pictured a woman and a man looking very dejected on one page, and the caption read, "She hasn't an Overland or Anything." On the following page, they appeared happily in an Overland (she's behind the wheel), and the caption read, "She has an Overland—an' everything."[34] Still another Overland ad pictured the "four great events" of a woman's life (i.e., marriage, first home, first baby, and first car) and read, "Happy the woman—and her name is legion—who by helpful suggestion persuades her provider against too small a car, or by loving restraint checks an over-generous husband who would otherwise make the mistake of too large a car."[35] Of course the Overland was just perfect. In many ways a 1920 Cadillac advertisement rendered the final judgment on the American woman as consumer and placed her squarely in her new role. Women, the ad declared, were "equipped with a sort of sixth sense" about "everything that contributes to social distinction."[36] Men, the ad went on to argue, must be educated in order to consume with discrimination, but women were born with the ability.

In 1911, the *Literary Digest*, heaping praise on the automobile industry, noted: "The strides made by our manufacturers in the decade are remarkable. The census of 1900 places the value of cars manufactured in this country at $4,748,000 in 1899, while the census of 1910 gave $249,202,000 as the amount for the year 1909. Wages paid increased in the time from $1,321,000 to $48,694,000."[37] Well might the editors of *Literary Digest* wax elegant over the development of the automobile industry—advertising revenues closely followed the industry's growth. By 1911 automobile advertising accounted for approximately one-eighth of all the advertising space in national magazines, more than the combined space used by all food products.[38]

Not only automobile advertising was proving very lucrative. A survey of thirty magazines by Crowell Publishing Company in 1914 indicated that advertising revenue from automobile accessories equalled that of the automobiles.[39] While the *Saturday Evening Post* quickly became the popular magazine of choice for auto advertising, quarter-page, half-page, full-page, and even double-page ads poured into magazines as diverse as *Harper's Weekly, Overland Monthly, Literary Digest, National Geographic, Ladies' Home Journal*, and a host of other popular and trade magazines. Presbrey estimated automobile advertising in trade journals at more than $1 million, with only slightly less in popular magazines. During the first six years of the second decade of the twentieth century, automobile production increased about 800 per cent and advertising expenditures for automobiles increased by approximately the same per cent.[40]

During the second decade of the twentieth century, automobile companies continued to use price, economy, and dependability in their advertising, but following a pattern made familiar in other industries, increasingly comfort, style, and status dominated the ads. For example, Hudson's ads claimed that their "54" would accelerate to 58 miles per hour from a standing start in 30 seconds and advertised speeds of up to 65 miles per hour.[41] The Packard promised faster pickup than its rivals and "Greater range of ability in high gear and more miles per gallon of gasoline."[42] The Oldsmobile simply promised acceleration "as fast as lightning."[43] The Franklin explained how their auto achieved speed, acceleration, and economy. The lightweight Franklin weighed 700 to 1,200 pounds less than its rivals. This advantage, plus a new engine, allowed more speed, faster pickup, and fuel economy. Supposedly, fuel expenses were cut in half, and because of the reduced weight the owner got an average of 10,746 miles from a set of tires. For those customers who wanted a heavier car, Franklin offered five chassis sizes and two-, four-, and six-cylinder motors at a price range from $1,650 to $5,000.[44] While the 1916 ads for Hudson promised high-quality workmanship, endurance, and style, the emphasis was on speed:

100 miles in 80 min., 21.4 sec., averaging 74.67 miles per hour for a 7 passenger touring car with driver and passenger.

75.69 miles in one hour with driver and passenger touring car.

Standing start to 50 miles an hour in 16.2 seconds.

One mile at the rate of 102.53 miles per hour.

1819 miles in 24 hours at average speed of 75.8 miles per hour.[45]

Hudson also claimed to hold the world hill-climbing record and claimed that the motors of many of the rival vehicles were unable to withstand the strain of climbing Pike's Peak. Of course the Hudson had no problem:

No hill-climb or mountain test in the world equals that imposed on motor cars that race to the summit of Pike's Peak. A Hudson Super-six Special made the best time of more than 20 contestants to the top of America's most famous mountain over the longest, steepest, highest travelable [sic] road in the world.[46]

A few companies like Cadillac, Paige, and Pierce-Arrow concentrated on producing large, powerful, and luxurious cars, but most companies produced a complete line and often emphasized the less expensive, more economical cars in their advertising campaigns. A few like Ford and Reo spent all their efforts on economy vehicles. In 1913 Reo announced that it was building only a single model, the Reo the Fifth, which would be R. E. Olds' "Farewell Car." Supposedly when Olds protested that he had no intention of retiring, Claude Hopkins, who was managing the advertising campaign, reminded him that Sarah Bernhardt had seven "farewell tours" and surely Olds was entitled to several farewell cars.[47] Reo the Fifth's basic cost was $1,095, with the top, windshield, lighting, and starting system optional. In announcing his "farewell car," Olds admitted that the basic price was slightly higher than some competitive models, but he argued, "I am building a car to run in five years as well as it runs when new." Customers would save money on costly repairs, and while the Reo was more expensive to build than his competitors' vehicles, Olds explained, "but I will save the extra by building a single model."[48] A year earlier, Franklin had advertised their four-cylinder Model "G" Runabout for $1,650 and the top of their line, the six-cylinder Model "H" limousine, for $5,000.[49] The Thomas B. Jeffery Company, which produced the Rambler, claimed in 1914 that the "Jeffery owner buys the quality of the finest cars at a moderate price." The ad warned customers that:

The man who pays four to six thousand for a motor car gets quality—represented by high-grade material, class, style, massive size, power, elegance, comfort, all those things. And his high first cost is followed by the terrific upkeep expense of a big heavy car.[50]

The Jeffery buyer, the ad claimed, got the same high quality at the modest price range of $1,550 to $3,700.[51]

Few automobile manufacturers carried the appeal to economy as far as the American Locomotive Company, builders of Alco motor cars, trucks, and taxicabs. A 1912 *Saturday Evening Post* advertisement addressed to businessmen asked, "What do your horses cost?" The copy claimed that while there were 30 million horses in the United States, with an estimated value of $3 billion, few horse owners, probably less than 1 per cent, knew how much keeping the horses cost. The solution? American Locomotive's new Transportation Cost Bureau, at no cost to the business, would "*blue print*" the existing system, supply accurate figures on how much "your horses are actually costing" and let the "figures tell their own unvarnished story." The Bureau would then "*chart*" a motor transportation system. Obviously, Alco stood ready to supply the vehicles needed to convert the firm's old horse-drawn transportation system to a modern, motorized, efficient system.[52]

"Up until about 1915," Frank Presbrey argued, "copy appeal in automobile advertising was the joy of touring combined with the mechanical perfectness of the car."[53] After 1915 Presbrey noted that a "note of smartness" crept into the copy and introduced "an additional and very powerful appeal that sold many more cars." The "grand air" which advertisements imparted to the ownership of automobiles provided what Presbrey called the "ultimate" appeal that was already recognized and often employed as "a most potent" appeal in advertisements for other products. In a statement remarkable for both its insightfulness and its deliberate obfuscation, Presbrey acknowledged that the social gratification and status associated with the ownership and consumption of a product, rather than the need for or the utility of the item, had become the most powerful appeal used in American advertising.

The ordinary family likes to have the luxuries the smart people have, and the influential younger generation especially loves the "right" thing. The note [of smartness] did not originate in automobile advertising particularly, but its skillful employment there has had a good deal to do with the tremendous growth of the industry—and with the growth of advertising since 1915. The achievements of this technique in automobile advertising have colored all advertising in which it can be applied. It has produced high results and given the advertising world a new conception of the tremendous appeal of "quiet elegance."[54]

A "note of smartness" did not creep into automobile advertising in the period after 1916; it was there from the beginning, and by the second decade of the century the use of social status represented a dominant theme in automobile advertisements.

The backgrounds used in car ads were almost invariably rural or suburban. Country clubs, not crowded city streets, figured prominently in the illustrations. Homes when depicted were seldom short of mansions, always with large, spacious lawns. From the very beginning in popular magazine advertisements, only chic women and handsomely dressed men, obviously people of wealth and status, drove or rode in cars. The entire tone of the ads made it clear that "smart," "successful," white upper-and middle-class people owned and drove whichever automobile was advertised.[55] As early as 1905, the Oldsmobile advertisements spoke of the "luxuries of life" to which one was obviously entitled if successful.[56] The 1909 Pierce-Arrow offered its owner the "highest luxury."[57] An advertisement for the Chalmers in 1912 pictured four smartly dressed men driving into a country club in the Chalmers, and one of them is saying "I'll get one just like this."[58] That same year a *Saturday Evening Post* ad showed a group stepping out of an Alco limousine; the women are in evening gowns and the men in formal dress and top hats. The copy exclaimed, "The charm in the Alco is the *culture in little things* . . .—a daintiness and good taste that catch the fancy."[59] A full-page and handsomely illustrated ad for the 1913 Rambler "Cross Country," which the copy claimed was "Distinguished in appearance and gratifying in comfort," reminded customers that the car was "an expression of the owner's good taste."[60]

After Cadillac ceased manufacturing lower-cost cars and concentrated their efforts on the larger, more costly models, their advertising deliberately cultivated a tone of luxury, distinctiveness, and status associated with owning "the standard for the world" in automobiles. A 1912 ad noted that the real value of owning a Cadillac "is not adequately expressed by its price."[61] Another ad that same year spent most of the copy describing the luxurious interior. The front seat of the limousine was upholstered in "hand buffed, dull finished, deep grained" black leather with a French roll across the front of the cushions. The top deck above the forward compartment was finely finished American black walnut, and the two revolving seats in the rear compartment were upholstered in the best quality blue broadcloth and trimmed with narrow lace.[62] Packard and the White Six, both luxury cars, emphasized the better-engineered "left-side drive," and Packard's slogan proclaimed "Ask the man who owns one."[63] The Winton Six advertised "an Intimately Private" car for both men and women. "Because our patrons require beautiful and distinctive cars," the ad promised, "we continue to give each purchaser precisely those colors and body style that most appeal to his individual taste . . . a PRIVATE CAR, an intimately personal possession."[64]

No matter how other automobile manufacturers sought to emulate Cadillac's status appeal, Cadillac remained the most successful in attaching prestige to its ownership. In 1915, for the introduction of a new V-8 motor, Theodore F. McManus, whose agency McManus, Inc., handled Cadillac advertising, wrote what is probably the best-known automobile ad ever to appear in the United States. Neither the name Cadillac nor a single characteristic of the automobile appeared in the text of the ad, which appeared in the *Saturday Evening Post* on January 2, 1915, under the title "THE PENALTY of LEADERSHIP."[65] "In every field of human endeavor, he that is first must perpetually live in the white light of publicity," McManus wrote, and "Whether the leadership be vested in a man or in a manufactured product, emulation and envy are ever at work."[66] Without mention of Cadillac, except in the trademark placed inconspicuously in the border of the advertisement, McManus' copy conveyed the ultimate status appeal for Cadillac. Essentially the same theme ran through Cadillac ads for the remainder of the decade. A year after McManus' masterpiece appeared, another full-page ad appeared in *Saturday Evening Post* with only a single simple statement: "THE BEST REASON IN THE WORLD FOR BUYING A CADILLAC IS WHAT EVERYONE THINKS, AND SAYS, AND *KNOWS* ABOUT CADILLAC." Even in the middle of World War I, Cadillac advertising retained a simple, clear statement of quality, prestige, and status. Cadillac, an ad near the end of 1918 noted, "Has been splendidly shown on an extended and dramatic scale, in the terrific wear and tear of war-service on the French front."[67] The real significance of the appeal of prestige and social status associated with the ownership of a Cadillac and other luxury automobiles lay not in any increased sales of luxury automobiles, for no matter how successful Cadillac and any other company captured the appeal of social status associated with ownership, the price of large, luxury automobiles remained out of reach for the mass market. The real significance proved to be the prestige and social status associated with driving any automobile.

The combined impact of the massive advertising campaigns by automobile manufacturers, and in particular the consistent use of the appeal of social status and acceptance attached to automobile ownership, no doubt helped popularize the auto, introduced it to the American consumer, and served to enhance the total demand for automobiles in the United States. The real revolution that the *Literary Digest* had waxed so eloquent and so enthusiastic over in 1911 had yet to occur, and its dramatic impact would be at the other end of the scale from the luxury automobiles like the Cadillac.

In 1906 Henry Ford told the editor of *Automobile* that "the greatest need today is a light, low-price car with an up-to-date engine of ample horsepower . . . it must be powerful enough for American roads and capable of carrying its passengers anywhere that a horse-drawn vehicle will go without the driver being afraid of ruining his car."[68] Ford was not alone in recognizing the enormous potential for a practical and affordable automobile. A few years after Ford's comments, *Harper's Weekly*, in a prophetic article, suggested that whoever produced "a car that will be entirely sufficient mechanically and whose price will be within the reach of millions who cannot yet afford automobiles, will not only grow rich but will be considered a public benefactor as well."[69] To this task Henry Ford set himself.

Perhaps more than any American manufacturer, Ford would capitalize on the seeming paradox in American society of consumers seeking to achieve status by the consumption of identical mass-produced items. Stuart Ewen, commenting on advertising for mass-produced items that promised "*You will be seen. You will be noticed. The symbols you display, your most valued possessions, will permit you to stand apart from the crowd. You will be noteworthy and honored. You will be someone,*" concluded that even though the same promise was being made through mass mailings, "This highly individuated notion of personal distinction—marked by the compulsory consumption of images—stands at the heart of the 'American Dream.' "[70] What mass production offered to Americans, especially those who as Ewen noted, "are now or who wish to become, part of the great American 'middle class,' " was a growing supply of "cheap *luxury* goods . . . the symbolic accoutrements of status."[71] In any hierarchy of goods which bestowed status, the automobile ranked very high.

In 1907, a year after Ford expressed his philosophy to the editor of *Automobile*, he finally gained effective control of the Ford Motor Company. The Ford Motor Company, organized in 1903, had been producing a line of medium-priced cars, including Models A, B, C, F, K, R, and N. The two-cylinder Model C sold for $950 in 1905, the two-cylinder Model F for $1,200, and the four-cylinder Model B cost $2,000. That same year, the average wholesale cost of American-made automobiles was about $1,600.[72] Apparently, some of the directors favored continuing the policy of producing a line of medium-priced vehicles and disagreed with Ford's plan to make further improvements in the Model N, which the Ford Company built in 1906. The Model N approached Ford's ideal of the "Universal Car" and was the direct ancestor of the famous Model T.[73] As David Hounshell pointed out, "When the Model T left the Ford Motor Company experimental room in 1908, it met all these [Ford's] mechanical demands." And more important, "Through an alignment of circumstances . . . Henry Ford and the Ford Motor Company put the car within the reach of those millions of Americans."[74] The introduction of assembly lines at the Ford Motor Company in 1913 marked the logical conclusion of the trend to interchangeable parts and mass production in American manufacturing technology. Production expanded from less than 200,000 in 1913 to more than 2 million a decade later. More important, unlike Singer with the sewing machine, or McCormick and the reaper, or even Pope and the bicycle, all of whom sold the most among expensive products in their respective areas, Ford set out to produce the least expensive car possible for a truly mass market. While Singer, McCormick, and Pope dominated their respective industries and markets, none of them enjoyed the reputation and dominance of Henry Ford in the automobile industry. Given Ford's open approbation of mass production and marketing and openness in sharing technology, it was not surprising that manufacturers of products other than automobiles rapidly followed in Ford's technological footsteps.[75]

Surprisingly, perhaps, for a revolutionary who championed mass production and consumption in the broadest sense and who sought to make a car for every American, Ford's advertising campaigns were quite conservative. Yet, in a very real sense Ford's definition of advertising was much broader and still more focused than most of his competition. From the beginning Ford paid as much attention to free publicity as to paid advertisements. While his paid ads appealed to the average middle-class customer, his publicity was often flamboyant. Ford advertisements always emphasized the car as a practical means of transportation at the same time that Ford competed vigorously in automobile races. While other companies advertised their car's speed, Ford argued:

Our purpose is to construct and market an automobile specially designed for everyday wear and tear—business, professional, and family use; an automobile which will attain to a sufficient speed to satisfy the average person without acquiring any of those breakneck velocities which are so universally condemned [and advertised by the competition].[76]

Publicity and name recognition, while differing from paid advertising, played a major role in selling Ford automobiles. The great public attention Ford had received in winning the Grosse Point Race convinced him of the value of publicity, and unlike his paid advertising, the publicity, of which Ford himself was often at the center of attention, was far from conservative.

Undoubtedly the most and in many ways the best publicity Ford received came from the protracted legal battle over the Selden Patents. In 1879, George B. Selden, a New York attorney, applied for a patent on a projected gasoline vehicle, although he had never built a practical car. After repeated rejections and re-applications, Selden received a patent in 1895 and promptly declared his exclusive right to make or to license the manufacture of gasoline automobiles. Most of the early companies submitted, obtained a license, and then formed the Association of Licensed Automobile Manufacturers. The Association, which included among its twenty-six members Cadillac, Pope, Winton, Franklin, Oldsmobile, Haynes-Apperson, Pierce-Locobile, and Packard, together with Selden, advertised in 1903 that "No other manufacturers or importers are authorized to make or sell gasoline automobiles, and any person making, selling, or using such machines made or sold by any unlicensed manufacturers or importers will be liable to prosecution for infringement."[77] While Selden may have been sincere in attempting to protect his patent, the Association members seemed primarily interested in discouraging consumers from buying the automobiles of non-Association members. The tactics resembled early patent-medicine advertisements warning against patent infringements. The major target was no doubt the Ford Motor Company, which promptly responded with an ad which denied the validity of the Selden patent and guaranteed protection for dealers, agents, and users of Ford cars:

We are pioneers of the GASOLINE AUTOMOBILE. Our Mr. Ford made the first Gasoline Automobile in Detroit and the third in the United States. His machine made in 1893 (two years previous to the granting of the Selden patent November 5, 1895) is still in use.[78]

In the eight-year protracted battle with the Association and Selden, Ford received enormous free publicity and emerged as a kind of folk hero.

"Henry Ford's idea is to build a high-grade, practical automobile, one that will do any reasonable service, that can be maintained at a reasonable expense, and at as nearly $450 as it is possible to make it," stated one of the Ford advertisements in the middle of the Selden struggle, "thus raising the automobile out of the list of luxuries, and bringing it to the point where the average American citizen may own and enjoy his automobile."[79] The case was widely reported in the popular press and cleverly supplemented by Ford's paid advertisements. Using slogans such as "Nobody Mortgages his House to Buy a Ford" and depicting Ford as a "trust-buster" and a friend of the common man, Ford appeared as a champion of the people. Countless jokes about Ford and his "Tin Lizzie," the Model T, circulated. Ford relished the jokes; he collected them and even promoted them. Rumors persisted that Leroy Pelletier, Ford's advertising manager and an old circus press agent, even wrote some of them. By 1911, when Ford won the Selden case on appeal, Henry Ford could well declare "Our best advertising, is free advertising."[80] Ford, who would dominate the automobile industry for the next decade, emerged from the Selden fight as a hero of the people, fighting their battles against a monopoly that would make car prices higher and perhaps even deny the average man an automobile.

On January 5, 1914, less than a year after the assembly-line mass-production system went into operation, Ford announced that the company would henceforth pay a minimum of $5 for an eight-hour day. The announcement made sensational copy; newspapers and popular magazines were filled with articles attacking, praising, and analyzing the five-dollar day. Various motives have been ascribed to Ford's decision. He was denounced as a Utopian fanatic and praised as an enlightened humane capitalist. A few cynics even argued that Ford only operated from self-interest. True, labor turn-over on the assembly line amounted to nearly 400 per cent in the short time it had been in operation. Actually, all were probably at

Figure 7.2
Ford Model "T" Sales Compared to Total U.S. Automobile Sales, 1908–1916

Year	Total Sales Model T	Total Sales (Passenger) Autos	Model T %	Model T Price	Average U.S. Auto Wholesale Values
1908	$ 5,986	$ 63,500	9 %	$ 850	$ 1,280
1909	12,292	123,900	10	950	1,283
1910	19,293	181,000	10.7	780	1,188
1911	40,402	199,300	20	690	1,128
1912	78,611	356,000	22	600	940
1913	182,809	461,500	39.6	550	865
1914	260,720	548,100	47.6	490	766
1915	355,276	895,900	39.6	440	642
1916	577,036	1,525,000	37.8	360	603

Sources: U.S. Department of Commerce, Bureau of the Census, *Historical Statistics of the United State: Colonial Times to 1970* (Washington, D.C., 1975), II:716. And adapted from David Hounshell, *From the American System to Mass Production, 1800-1932* (Baltimore: The Johns Hopkins University Press, 1984), p. 224. Reprinted by permission.

least partly correct, as Hounshell noted, "[James] Couzens got his free advertising, Ford his hero-worship, 'acceptable' workers extraordinarily high earnings. . . . The five-dollar day assured the company that the essential human appendages to this machine would always be present."[81] Ford himself became the center of attention; his life, his accomplishments, his eccentricities, and his pronouncements, as well as his factories and cars, made headlines. In James Wood's words, "The advertising volume of the move was inestimable."[82]

A year later, in 1915, in what experts called a "master stroke of advertising," Ford announced that if the Ford Motor Company produced and sold 300,000 cars that year, he would rebate (this probably was the first rebate in the automobile industry—they would become common) $40 to $60 to each buyer. For a few thousand dollars to buy newspaper space for the announcement, Ford received hundreds of thousands of dollars in free advertising. In addition, every Ford dealer now had a stake in advertising the rebate. In 1914, Ford had sold more than a quarter million Model T cars, roughly 47 per cent of the total passenger cars sold in the United States that year. The average automobile produced in the United States in

1915 had a wholesale value of approximately $640; the Ford Model T sold for $200 less (see Figure 7.2). Ford sold over 355,000 Model Ts in 1915, and amidst splendid national publicity gleefully rebated the money he had promised.

As flamboyant as Ford's performance, personality, and public actions often were, the advertisements were direct, simple, and to the point. For example, a *Saturday Evening Post* ad for the Model T stressed the fact that the magneto was built into the motor and added, "When Henry Ford designed the Model T magneto he practically eliminated ignition problems, and about 90 per cent of the annoyances which beset other motor cars."[83] The copy promised economy of up-keep and "best of all, Ford Service for Ford Owners." In 1913, the year Ford introduced the assembly line, an ad advised prospective buyers:

FORD ... you get yours if you place an early order. ... In spite of the greatly enlarged production, late buyers are almost certain to be disappointed. Get yours today. Everybody's driving a Ford, more than 200,000 in service.[84]

Two years later, when Ford's advertisement for the Model T simply showed a picture of the "Tin Lizzie" touring car model with the caption "BUY IT BECAUSE IT IS A BETTER CAR," most Americans believed him. The following year, the last full year before the United States entered World War I, Ford produced and sold over a half million automobiles, nearly a 10,000 per cent increase in the eight short years since the Model T was introduced.

With America's entry into World War I, the automobile industry cut back its production and decreased its advertising. Automobile factories converted to wartime production of guns, shells, tanks, and military vehicles. Car sales were cut in half and the demand for cars often exceeded the available supply.

Americans did not end their short, but intense, love affair with the automobile. Indeed, so successfully had advertising sold the car as a part of the "good life" that the automobile became increasingly incorporated into ads for other products. As early as 1915, an ad for Mogul Egyptian Cigarettes featured a couple on a moonlight automobile drive with the caption, "Just like being in Cairo."[85] The use of automobiles in cigarette advertising, especially convertibles, proved to be a trend which would accelerate in the following decade. Ford and other car manufacturers did not stop advertising; rather, as Presbrey suggested, they changed their copy to selling "goodwill," explaining why they were unable to meet demand, urging Americans to win the war, which they blamed on the Kaiser, and wooing consumer loyalty.

With the end of the war, the automobile industry immediately started the conversion to peacetime production and resumed advertising. A typical ad, by Pierce-Arrow, noted: "We are ready for peace, going full speed ahead, with the factory never busier. We will keep it going." From a low of 943,436 automobiles in 1918, production increased to nearly 2 million vehicles in 1920.

The success of the Ford Motor Company illustrated both the possibilities of mass production and of producing for mass markets. The profits available for those manufacturers who succeeded in mass producing decreasing-cost consumer goods, and who through advertising assured themselves of future markets for these goods, proved irresistible to the American business community. The question Reginald McIntosh Cleveland asked in *World's Work*, only a year after Ford started mass production, "How many automobiles can America buy?" was partly answered by the introduction of annual "new models" and by the intensity of the advertising using the social status and prestige associated with ownership in the decade of the twenties.[86]

In an unusually modest vein, Frank Presbrey admitted that "Advertising did not win" World War I. However, he was quick to claim that it did more than its bit in selling the war, in winning public support for the war, and in convincing Americans to buy bonds, to tolerate shortages, and even to enlist in the armed services. Having earlier demonstrated the ability to induce demand and to sell products, advertising during the war demonstrated the ability to sell goodwill, to win support for public efforts, to mobilize loyalty and patriotism, and to incite hatred of the enemy. The influence was reciprocated, and for the first time in our history, public events dominated advertising as they had at no other previous time. Advertising for almost every product included the wartime theme. In the early years of the war, the volume of advertising for consumer goods declined since businesses did not feel a need to create demand for products they could no longer supply to the civilian population. In fact, so severely did advertising decline that by the middle of the war businessmen were being urged by government officials not to cease advertising and thereby risk the loss of the potential peacetime markets and lose the goodwill that had been built-up through earlier campaigns. Most manufacturers needed little urging; they knew, long before any politician told them, that "the business of America is business," and that business involved selling. While the volume of advertising slackened for a very short period after the United States entered the war, it quickly resumed with an emphasis on "goodwill" and institutional advertising.[87]

The success of advertising in winning support for the war and the almost astonishing success of goodwill and institutional advertising convinced advertising executives more than any other group of the power of their profession. Already self-conscious, and well aware of the prewar criticisms and attacks on their profession, advertising agencies launched their own goodwill and institutional campaigns. As Daniel Pope noted, "Advertising men of the World War I era were very much aware that they had come a long way in a generation or less."[88] They did not need Presbrey to tell them that, with the selling of the automobile and the successes of World War I, "advertising came of age."

Given the massive advertising budgets of the 1920s, and with salaries for ad executives often higher than in other businesses, it was little wonder that advertising professionals began to believe their own rhetoric. By 1928, R. H. Grant, vice-president of Chevrolet Motor Company, felt forced while speaking to the International Advertising Association to remind his audience that automobile manufacturers, as well as advertising agencies, had some small role in the success of the automobile industry. Only a few years earlier, Bruce Barton's *The Man Nobody Knows* had carried the advertising profession's self-flattery to its illogical extreme by making Jesus Christ the world's greatest sales and advertising man who "picked up twelve men from the bottom ranks of business," and sold the world Christianity.[89]

Regardless of the image the advertising profession projected of their newly discovered status and influence, the profession never developed a clear sense of the ethical limits of advertising. Apparently, neither advertising executives nor the firms that employed them ever questioned the tactics used to sell products. Nowhere is this failure more apparent than in the shameless use of guilt to sell products to women, that is, if you do not use this, you are depriving your family, your children, your spouse. Choosing to ignore the realities of a major movement of women out of the household and into the work force, advertisements continued to drive home the message that the woman's proper place was in the home. At the same time that advertisers were busy urging women to buy mass-produced items that had traditionally been produced in the home, and thereby transforming women from producers to consumers, the appeal used in advertising copy offered women no substitute for their traditional role, except consumption for the sake of social status. Not content with their own failure to exercise ethical limits in advertising appeal, advertising executives used unbridled economic power to silence criticism.

It is a temptation, which I think must be resisted, to accept at face value the self-aggrandizing claims of the advertising industry. However alluring the prospect, to ascribe to advertising all the power the industry claims when talking to business clients and then denies in the face of public criticism flies in the face of the weight of historical evidence. Actually, the power of advertising, while certainly formidable, has proven much more limited than either its practitioners or its critics care to admit. Time and time again, advertising has proven powerless to instigate, to sustain, or to reverse trends in public opinion or fashions of consumption.

What advertising did, and does, was exploit those already well-ingrained characteristics of American society. In connecting consumption to the achievement of social acceptance and status, given the modern reality of decreasing cost industries and mass production, advertising simply put the old wine of materialism and conformity into new bottles seemingly available to everyone. To understand the impact of advertising on American society, we also need to address the potential and the problems of mass production.

In a long and provocative article for *Fortune* magazine in 1967, Daniel Boorstin, a distinguished historian and later Librarian of Congress, argued that the great lasting achievement of advertising was the creation of new communities—Consumption Communities:

A Consumption Community consists of people who have a feeling of shared well-being, shared risks, common interests, and common concerns that come from consuming the same kinds of objects. . . . [These] Consumption Communities could not come into being until there were large numbers of objects being made that were, from the consumer's point of view, indistinguishable from one and other. . . . The making of large numbers of similar objects gradually extended to all items of consumption. . . . And the supreme achievement of price mass production was, of course, the automobile, which soon became the omnipresent symbol of American Consumption Communities. By the third decade of the century, the house that a man lived in, together with antiques and certain art works (and the land he lived on), was the only object that had not become fungible—readily replaced in the market by others that were indistinguishable.[90]

Tying together, in an admiring portrait, both advertising and mass production, Boorstin concluded that it was the new Consumption Communities, advertising's great creation, that allowed America to assimilate the millions of immigrants who came to America after the Civil War. According to Boorstin, the sense of community in America no longer stems from common ideas, values, beliefs, and traditions but from the "countless gossamer webs [of consumption] tying together the trivia of our lives every day."[91] However, Boorstin's claims for the accomplishments of his "Consumption Communities" ring as hollow as the ad man's pitch! Surely there is more to the sense of a shared community than smoking the same cigarettes, eating the same cereals, and driving the same automobiles.

Still, however much we may lament it, one must concede that by the end of World War I, advertising had sold the concept of consumption as the means to achieve social status. The sale may well have been to willing, even eager, customers, but it was complete. In separating consumption from the need for a product, advertising helped to hasten both the adoption and acceptance of mass production. In a period of less than two decades, local and even individual tastes, developed over generations for a wide variety of consumer goods, were homogenized for the need of selling mass produced uniform goods. If Ford represented the triumph of mass production to his admirers, he represented the terror of uniformity and conformity to his critics. Moreover, the toll that mass production extracted from workers was matched to the loss from the uniformity of mass production. All too often, the price of decreasing costs associated with mass marketing was a frightening loss of the rich mosaic of American culture.

Even the promised social status and acceptance evaded American consumers. After all, what distinction comes from the consumption of products produced and consumed on a mass basis? Despite Boorstin's claims, the consumers of mass-produced items do not join a community, only a crowd.

Historically, advertising has proven powerless to initiate or to prevent major shifts in the acceptance of and the demand for products or fashions or to produce shifts in public behavior. The recent and largely successful campaign against smoking, on the other hand, does provide a graphic illustration of advertising's potential. When accompanied by a campaign of education and public awareness, advertising can indeed play a fundamental role in shaping public perceptions. Advertising can succeed in this role, however, only if the campaign "stays ever-lastingly after it." Social planners, politicians, reformers, and we as a society need to be ever mindful of the limitations as well as the potentials of advertising as an agent for social change. Surely, we as a society, at long last recognize that a century of endless and mindless pursuit of consumption in a quest for social status has led us to an environmental abyss from which we must draw back. We need desperately to turn our attention from consumption to the myriad of social problems that confront us. Advertising has the potential to play a powerful role in redefining social norms, and if we turn our attention and our energies to social problems that confront us and that threaten the very fabric of American society, then advertising can play a powerful role in defining a better society.

NOTES

PREFACE

1. Marshall McLuhan, *Understanding Media: The Extensions of Man.* (New York, 1964), 232.

2. James D. Norris, "Advertising and the Transformation of American Society, 1865–1920," *Year Book of the American Philosophical Society, 1970,* 475–476.

3. Stuart Ewen, *Captains of Consciousness: Advertising and the Social Roots of the Consumer Culture* (New York, 1976) and *All Consuming Images: The Politics of Style in Contemporary Culture* (New York, 1988); Richard W. Fox and T. J. Jackson Lears, ed., *The Culture of Consumption: Critical Essays in American History, 1880–1980* (New York, 1983); Daniel Horowitz, *The Morality of Spending: Attitudes Toward the Consumer Society in America, 1875–1940* (Baltimore, 1985); and Roland Marchand, *Advertising and the American Dream: Making Way for Modernity, 1920–1940* (Berkeley, 1985).

4. Martin P. Mayer, *Madison Avenue, U.S.A.* (New York, 1958), 310. Emphasis added.

5. Neil H. Borden, *The Economic Effects of Advertising* (Chicago, 1942), 846–871.

6. Richard Christiansen, "The Commercial View of a Serene America," St. Louis *Post–Dispatch*, July 21, 1972. Courtesy of Chicago Daily News/1972.

CHAPTER 1

1. U.S. Department of Commerce, Bureau of the Census, *Historical Statistics of the United States: Colonial Times to 1970*, Part II (Washington, D.C., 1975), 728–731.

2. Ibid.; Ralph Andreano, ed., *The Economic Impact of the Civil War* (Cambridge, Massachusetts, 1962), 188–190; and Jeffrey Williamson, *American Growth and the Balance of Payments, 1820–1913: A Study of the Long Swing* (Chapel Hill, N.C., 1964), 6–7.

3. Ray A. Billington, *Westward Expansion: A History of the American Frontier*

(Fourth Edition, New York, 1974), 561–562; and Harold G. Vatter, *The Drive to Industrial Maturity: The U.S. Economy, 1860–1914* (Westport, Connecticut, 1975), 119–120.

4. Vatter, *Industrial Maturity*, 118–119. Vatter's argument that a rapidly expanding domestic supply relieved the U.S. economy of the need to divert capital to import foodstuffs has a great deal of merit.

5. Lance E. Davis, et al., *American Economic Growth: An Economist's History of the United States* (New York, 1972), 128. This is an excellent study of the process of economic growth in the United States employing many of the methods and findings of the "new economic history" and should not be confused with the standard textbooks in the area.

6. Robert Higgs, *The Transformation of the American Economy, 1865–1914: An Essay in Interpretation* (New York, 1971), 22. This slim volume approaches the development of the American economy in unusual and provocative ways.

7. Ibid., 22–24; and Simon Kuznets and Ernest Rubin, *Immigration and the Foreign Born* (New York: National Bureau of Economic Research, 1954).

8. Lee C. Soltow, "Evidence on Income Inequality in the United States, 1866–1965," *Journal of Economic History* 19 (June, 1969), 279.

9. George G. S. Murphy and Arnold Zellner, "Sequential Growth, the Labor-Safety-Valve Doctrine, and the Development of American Unionism," *Journal of Economic History*, 19 (September, 1959), 402–419. This thesis clearly would not apply to the agricultural sector of the economy.

10. Davis, *American Economic Growth*, 61.

11. Simon Kuznets, "Proportion of Capital Formation to National Products," *American Economic Review*, 42 (May, 1952), 507–526.

12. Lewis E. Atherton, *Main Street on the Middle Border* (Bloomington, Indiana, 1954), 50–51 and 1567–1568. For an analysis of the activities, role, and significance of local merchants see also: Lewis E. Atherton, *The Pioneer Merchant in Mid–America* (Columbia, Missouri, 1939); the same author's, *The Southern Country Store, 1800–1860* (Baton Rouge, Louisiana, 1949); and Thomas D. Clark, *Petticoats and Plows: The Southern Country Store* (Indianapolis, Indiana, 1944).

13. Atherton, *Main Street*, 46–50.

14. Ibid., 222.

15. Neil Borden, *The Economic Effects of Advertising* (Chicago, 1942), 144.

16. James H. Young, *The Toadstool Millionaires: A Social History of Patent Medicines in America Before Federal Regulation* (Princeton, New Jersey, 1961), 42–43.

17. Ibid., 43.

18. *Southern Planter*, January 1860, advertising sheet, 14–15.

19. *Southern Planter*, March 1867, advertising sheet, 2–3.

20. Frank Presbrey, *The History and Development of Advertising* (Garden City, New York, 1929), 285–287; and Boris Emmett and John E. Jeuck, *Catalogues and Counters: A History of Sears, Roebuck and Company* (Chicago, 1950), 19.

21. Presbrey, *The History and Development of Advertising*, 287–288.

22. Emmett and Jeuck, *Catalogues and Counters*, 112.

23. The evidence for the shift in the total demand curve is overwhelming. One need only look at the increasing production of countless items which not only rose, but rose on a per capita basis, a condition not necessary for a shift in total demand.

James P. Wood, *The Story of Advertising* (New York, 1958), 185–187; Herman E. Koos, *American Economic Development: The Progress of a Business Civilization* (Englewood Cliffs, New Jersey, 1974), 388–389. See also Susan P. Benson, *Counter Cultures: Saleswomen, Managers, and Customers in American Department Stores, 1890–1940* (Urbana, Illinois, 1986), 1–18. Even though Benson's work deals with a slightly later period, it is an excellent study and provides the best understanding available of the exact nature of department stores.

24. Presbrey, *The History and Development of Advertising*, 247.

25. Wood, *Story of Advertising*, 186–187.

26. "Advertisement" in the first issue of the *Farm Journal*, reproduced in Wood, *Story of Advertising*, 188.

27. Presbrey, *The History and Development of Advertising*, 303; and Daniel Pope, *The Making of Modern Advertising* (New York, 1983), 134. Some of John E. Powers' great influence on the development of modern advertising style will be discussed later.

28. Benson, *Counter Cultures*, 18.

29. Sidney A. Sherman, "Advertising in the United States," *Journal of the American Statistical Association* 7 (December 1900), 9–10.

30. *Harper's Weekly*, September 1, 1866.

31. Wood, *Story of Advertising*, 192–193.

32. See for example *Harper's Weekly*, September 3, 1870; and *Peterson's Ladies' National Magazine* (1870), 57–58.

33. Presbrey, *History and Development of Advertising*, 394.

34. Ibid., 394–395; and Donald S. Tull, "A Re–examination of the Causes of the Decline in Sales of Sapolio," *Journal of Business*, 28 (January 1955), 128–129. The rise and decline of Sapolio has, as Tull suggests, become almost a legend. No discussion of advertising could be considered complete without a discussion of Sapolio as an illustration of what happens when firms that depend upon advertising to differentiate their product reduce their advertising expenditures. Tull provides a more complex and satisfactory explanation which suggests limits on the ability of advertising to create and sustain demand. In the twentieth century, Sapolio would drastically shift the appeal of their advertising away from practicality, use, and purity. See below, Chapter 3.

35. Tull, "A Re–examination," *Journal of Business*, 28:128–129. As Tull points out, the traditional explanation of Sapolio's decline has been that it decreased its advertising, and he convincingly demonstrates that this is simply not true. Consumer preference had more to do with Sapolio's demise than any other factor (see below, Chapter 3).

36. Andrew B. Jack, "The Channels of Distribution for an Innovation: The Sewing Machine Industry in America, 1860–1865," *Explorations in Entrepreneurial History*, 9 (February 1957), 117–118.

37. Ibid., 134. See also [Patrick] Glen Porter and Harold Livesay, *Merchants and Manufacturers: Studies in the Changing Structure of Nineteenth-Century Marketing* (Baltimore, 1971), 194.

38. Ibid., 114.

39. Ibid., 134.

40. David Hounshell, *From the American System to Mass Production, 1800–*

1932: The Development of Manufacturing Technology in the United States (Baltimore, 1984), 87.

41. Jack, "Channels of Distribution," 9:134.

42. *Harper's Weekly*, May 14, 1870. Emphasis added.

43. *Harper's Weekly*, November 3, 1866.

44. See for example *Harper's Weekly*, May 14 and October 22, 1870, and March 16, 1872; and *Peterson's Ladies' National Magazine* (1871), 60.

45. Powers' advertisement is reproduced in Presbrey, *History and Development of Advertising*, 305. The Willcox and Gibbs machine was manufactured by J. R. Brown & Sharp of Providence, Rhode Island. While the machine was of superior quality, the production never reached the level of Singer. However, Brown & Sharp pioneered in the development of machine tools and gauges necessary for producing interchangeable parts for sewing machine manufacture and supplied Singer with equipment. See Hounshell's excellent study *From the American System to Mass Production*, 75–89.

46. *Southern Planter*, February 1855 and March 1860.

47. *American Farmer*, January 1868.

48. *Southern Planter and Farmer*, April 1870.

49. *American Farmer*, June 1881.

50. Hounshell, *From the American System to Mass Production*, 153–187.

51. *Harper's Weekly*, March 16, 1872.

52. Sherman, "Advertising," 7: insert.

CHAPTER 2

1. Frank L. Mott, *History of American Magazines, 1865–1885*, II (Cambridge, Massachusetts, 1939), 4. Mott's classic study is by far the best source of information on the history of magazines, and all the authors writing since have drawn heavily on his work.

2. Frank Presbrey, *The History and Development of Advertising* (Garden City, NY, 1929), 210, 231.

3. Ibid., 210.

4. Ibid., 281.

5. Daniel Pope, *The Making of Modern Advertising* (New York, 1983), 118. For business history, Pope's work, a revision of his 1973 dissertation, draws extensively on secondary sources and in particular on *Printers' Ink* and *Advertising Age*, as do his predecessors. This observation is not intended as a criticism of Pope's work; on the contrary, it is simply a recognition that given the available sources, Pope did the best one could expect. However, a really analytical business history from original sources must wait until major advertising firms make their papers available to scholars.

6. Presbrey, *History and Development of Advertising*, 294–296.

7. Ibid., 455. Actually, the efforts of the life insurance companies may have been very well directed; Daniel Horowitz, *The Morality of Spending: Attitudes Toward the Consumer Society in America, 1875–1940* (Baltimore, 1985), 14–27, has documented the tendency of even lower-class working families to budget modest sums for life insurance.

8. Presbrey, *History and Development of Advertising*, 281.

9. Ibid., 460.

10. Ibid., 460–461. After extensive sampling of the *American Farmer* and the *Southern Planter*, and less extensive sampling of the *Prairie Farmer* for the period, I arrived at the same conclusion as Presbrey. More important, even though Presbrey never mentions it, is the difference in appeal which becomes more obvious as one approaches the 1880s.

11. Mott, *History of American Magazines*, II:56–57.

12. James P. Wood, *The Story of Advertising* (New York, 1958), 193.

13. Mott, *History of American Magazines*, II:224–226.

14. Ibid., II:17–18.

15. Wood, *The Story of Advertising*, 199. Emphasis added.

16. Theodore Peterson, *Magazines in the Twentieth Century* (Urbana, 1964), 2–3; Presbrey, *History and Development of Advertising*, 464–465; and Wood, *The Story of Advertising*, 193–196.

17. Wood, *The Story of Advertising*, 193–196.

18. Quoted in Presbrey, *History and Development of Advertising*, 468.

19. Peterson, *Magazines in the Twentieth Century*, 32; and Presbrey, *History and Development of Advertising*, 466–467.

20. Sidney A. Sherman, "Advertising in the United States," *Journal of the American Statistical Association*, 7 (1900), insert. Sherman claimed that for the period 1874 to 1880 *Harper's Weekly* carried no advertisements. In spite of my efforts, I am unable to confirm or deny Sherman's claim. Advertisements were most often bound at the rear, or at the very front and the rear of the magazine, and librarians, apparently to save space and binding costs, frequently, and to their everlasting damnation, removed the advertisements before the magazines were bound.

21. Sherman, "Advertising in the United States," 7, insert; Wood, *Story of Advertising*, 201; and *Harper's Weekly*, September 18, 1886, and December 7, 1889.

22. *Harper's Weekly*, December 7, 1889.

23. See, for example, *Harper's Weekly*, September 18, 1886, and December 7, 1889.

24. Peterson, *Magazines in the Twentieth Century*, 2–3.

25. Ibid., 3–4.

26. Ibid., 5.

27. Ibid., 5–6; Presbrey, *The History and Development of Advertising*, 356–359; and Warner Miller, "American Paper Mills," in Chauncey M. Depew, ed., *One Hundred Years of American Commerce, 1795–1895*, II (New York, 1895), 302–307.

28. Peterson, *Magazines in the Twentieth Century*, 5–6.

29. Wood, *The Story of Advertising*, 202.

30. Ibid., 211–212; Peterson, *Magazines in the Twentieth Century*, 11–12.

31. James P. Wood, *Magazines in the United States: Their Social and Economic Effect* (New York, 1949), 112–113. It is little wonder that in marketing the new product "Kotex," the advertising agency first sought to (and did) convince *Ladies' Home Journal* to carry the ads. The agency realized that if the *Journal* accepted the ads, other magazines would follow the lead. See Anne M. Spurgeon, "Marketing the Unmentionable: Wallace Meyer and the Introduction of Kotex," *The Maryland Historian* 19 (Spring/Summer, 1988), 17–30.

32. Wood, *Magazines in the United States*, 112.

33. Wood, *The Story of Advertising*, 211.

34. Peterson, *Magazines in the Twentieth Century*, 12–13; Wood, *The Story of Advertising*, 214–215.

35. Peterson, *Magazines in the Twentieth Century*, 13.

36. Wood, *The Story of Advertising*, 204–205; and Peterson, *Magazines in the Twentieth Century*, 8–9.

37. *Munsey's Magazine*, September 1893.

38. Peterson, *Magazines in the Twentieth Century*, 7–10.

39. Wood, *Magazines in the United States*, 104.

40. Peterson, *Magazines in the Twentieth Century*, 8.

41. Wood, *The Story of Advertising*, 205; and Peterson, *Magazines in the Twentieth Century*, 10–11.

42. *McClure's Magazine*, July, 1894.

43. Wood, *The Story of Advertising*, 207–208.

44. Wood, *Magazines in the United States*, 185.

45. Peterson, *Magazines in the Twentieth Century*, 10–11.

46. Quoted in Wood, *Magazines in the United States*, 185.

47. Sherman, "Advertising in the United States," 7, insert; and Wood, *Magazines in the United States*, 124–125. When the *Harper's Bazar* was purchased by Hearst Magazines, Inc. in 1913, the spelling was changed to *Bazaar*. *Vogue* purchased and absorbed *Vanity Fair* in 1936, and the masthead read "*Vogue*, incorporating *Vanity Fair*."

48. Pope, *The Making of Modern Advertising*, 25–27. Partly because he too was concerned with advertising directed at national markets and partly because of the force of his data and argument, I am inclined to accept Pope's estimates as the most accurate available; however, one needs to keep in mind that Sherman estimated a total outlay for all advertising at $500 million in 1900.

49. Sherman, "Advertising," 7:27; and Peterson, *Magazines in the Twentieth Century*, 9–10.

50. Peterson, *Magazines in the Twentieth Century*, 226–227; Pope, *The Making of Modern Advertising*, 169–172.

51. Pope, *The Making of Modern Advertising*, 172. In spite of the claims of advertising agencies, the fact remains that success has come very slowly for the ABC. At no time have more than 10 per cent of the magazines published in this country belonged. See Peterson, *Magazines in the Twentieth Century*, 227.

52. Sherman, "Advertising," 7:28.

53. Ibid., 7:25.

54. Wood, *The Story of Advertising*, 205–206.

55. Quoted in Pope, *The Making of Modern Advertising*, 133, 134.

56. Ibid., 138.

57. Quoted in Pope, *The Making of Modern Advertising*, 142. Pope's treatment of the transformation of advertising agencies is excellent, and I see no reason to repeat it here. Readers should also consult Ralph M. Hower, *The History of an Advertising Agency: N. W. Ayer & Son at Work, 1869–1949* (Cambridge, Massachusetts, 1949), for a thorough but uncritical history of an agency. Presbrey, *The History and Development of Advertising*, and Wood, *The Story of Advertising*, both contain a great deal of information about agencies, as does A. D. Lasker,

The Lasker Story as He Told It (Chicago, 1953). Until advertising agencies make their papers available to scholars, Pope's work will probably be the closest to a satisfactory business history that we can expect.

58. Pope, *The Making of Modern Advertising*, 134–181. In a more recent article on James Rorty, Daniel Pope has expanded his work on the role of copywriters and advertising agents. With the translation to professional copywriters, a pattern becomes obvious. The ads became important sources of how professionals approached selling. Not only what appeals they thought would sell, but what appeals they used consistently. See Daniel Pope, "His Master's Voice: James Rorty and the Critique of Advertising," *The Maryland Historian* 19 (Spring/Summer, 1988), 5–15.

59. Sherman, "Advertising," 7:24–25.

60. Pope, *The Making of Modern Advertising*, 237; Ernest L. Boyd, "A Critical Study of the Doctrines of Persuasion in Speech and Advertising" (unpublished Ph.D. dissertation, Northwestern University, 1954), 26–27; John E. Hollitz, "The Challenge of Abundance: Reactions to the Development of a Consumer Economy, 1890–1920" (unpublished Ph.D. dissertation, University of Wisconsin–Madison, 1981), 42–43. For an excellent analysis of the basic psychology employed in advertisements, see Merle Curti, "The Changing Concept of 'Human Nature' in the Literature of American Advertising," *Business History Review*, 4 (Winter, 1967), 335–357.

61. Quoted in Wood, *The Story of Advertising*, 228.

62. Wood, *Magazines in the United States*, 230; and same author, *The Story of Advertising*, 208; and *McClure's Magazine*, June, 1901.

CHAPTER 3

1. Frank Presbrey, *The History and Development of Advertising* (Garden City, New York, 1929), 338–339.

2. Ibid., 339.

3. Ibid., 338–339. For information on the history of cleanliness see: Rene J. Dubos, *Mirage of Health* (New York, 1959) [a worldwide perspective]; Lawrence Wright, *Clean and Decent: The Fascinating History of the Bathroom and the Water Closet* (New York, 1960); David Glassburg, "The Public Bath Movement in America," *American Studies* 20 (Fall 1970):5–20; Judith W. Leavitt and Ronald Numbers, eds., *Sickness and Health in America: Readings in the History of Medicine and Public Health* (Madison, Wisc. 1978); Fred E. H. Shroeder, "Feminine Hygiene, Fashion and the Emancipation of Women," *American Studies*, 17 (1976):101–109; Marilyn Thorton Williams, "New York's Public Baths: A Case in Urban Progressive Reform," *Journal of Urban History* 7 (1980):49–81; Richard L. Bushman and Claudia L. Bushman, "The Early History of Cleanliness in America," *Journal of American History*, 74 (March 1988):1213–1238; see also: Alfred Lief, *"It Floats," The Story of Procter and Gamble* (New York, 1958), and Oscar Schisgall, *Eyes on Tomorrow: The Evolution of Procter and Gamble* (Chicago, 1981).

4. Ralph M. Hower, *The History of an Advertising Agency: N. W. Ayer & Son at Work, 1869–1939* (Cambridge, Massachusetts, 1939), 92–93.

5. Ibid., 210–215. Hower's calculations are made from the amount of money N. W. Ayer & Son spent for advertising space; however, the agency received its

compensation as a commission of space sold. While patent medicine disappeared as a category of commodity groups, the present drug and toilet products almost certainly includes some patent medicines.

6. Daniel Pope, *The Making of Modern Advertising* (New York, 1983), 184–226.

7. Sidney A. Sherman, "Advertising in the United States," *Journal of the American Statistical Association*, 7 (December, 1900): 17–18; and Presbrey, *The History and Development of Advertising*, 361–362.

8. Presbrey, *The History and Development of Advertising*, 362–364.

9. Samuel Colgate, "American Soap Factories," in Chauncey M. Depew, ed., *One Hundred Years of American Commerce, 1795–1895*, II (New York, 1895), 425; U.S. Department of Commerce, Bureau of the Census, *Thirteenth Census of the United States, Abstract* (Washington, D.C., 1923), 501. Soap and candle production was reported as one figure in the nineteenth century; however, later separate figures indicate that candles represented a small portion of the figure which declined throughout the century.

10. Indeed, Colgate complained that the demand for "cheap" soap had resulted in "filling" or "crutching," which was the introduction of substances such as water, talc, clay, or chalk designed to increase the weight and bulk of the soap. Colgate referred to the substances as "adulterants," which perhaps explains some of the early emphasis on purity, such as Ivory's 99 and 44/100 per cent pure. Colgate, "American Soap Factories," 424–425.

11. Richard L. Bushman and Claudia L. Bushman, "The Early History of Cleanliness in America," *Journal of American History*, 74 (March 1988), 1231. This is an excellent article which incorporates almost all of the recent literature on cleanliness and the cleanliness movement in America and which draws on advertisements to illustrate the change in consumer habits occasioned by the cleanliness movement. At the same time, the authors document the growing demand for personal soap.

12. James P. Wood, *Story of Advertising* (New York, 1958), 47–48.

13. Colgate noted that Babbitt had introduced the "first pressed cakes of laundry–soap in this country" and listed Babbitt along with N. K. Fairbanks & Company, James S. Kirk & Company, D. S. Brown & Company, Procter and Gamble, and Colgate & Company as the leaders of the soap industry and "the great firms engaged in the business." Colgate, "American Soap Factories," 426.

14. *Harper's Weekly*, November 20, 1880. For several years Babbitt's would continue to feature these small, doll–like figures in their advertisements, and the ads, apparently to save money, were printed sideways on the page as in Figure 3.3.

15. Presbrey, *The History and Development of Advertising*, 396–397; and *Harper's Weekly*, November 20, 1880. Presbrey noted that by 1928 Procter & Gamble had an advertising budget of approximately $3 million.

16. "Ivory Soap advertisement, 1881," reprinted in Julian L. Watkins, *The 100 Greatest Advertisements: Who Wrote Them and What They Did* (New York, 1959), 6.

17. See, for example, *Outlook*, October 18, 1902.

18. *Outlook*, August 4, 1900; and *Literary Digest*, May 26, 1906.

19. *Ladies' Home Journal*, June 1889.

20. Presbrey, *The History and Development of Advertising*, 396.

21. Ibid., 395–396; *Overland Monthly*, 1904; *Harper's Weekly*, September 18, 1886; *Outlook*, May 19, 1900.

22. *Ladies' Home Journal*, May 1889. Full back–cover advertisement.

23. Cuticura carried ads in almost every issue of *Ladies' Home Journal*, from 1891 to 1914, with essentially the same medical appeal.

24. *Harper's Weekly*, 1902.

25. *Outlook*, September 6, 1904.

26. *Outlook*, October 18, 1902.

27. Edgar R. Jones, *Those Were the Good Old Days: A Happy Look at American Advertising, 1880–1930* (New York, 1939), (ad for Packer's Tar Soap, 1900).

28. "The Amazing Genesis of Soap Advertising," *Advertising Weekly*, May 1, 1926.

29. Bushman and Bushman, "History of Cleanliness," 1238.

30. *Ladies' Home Journal*, September 1920.

31. See, for example, the Cashmere Bouquet advertisement in *Harper's Weekly*, September 18, 1886. In *Harper's*, Cashmere Bouquet ads almost always appeared immediately below the Pears' Soap ads in quarter–page size.

32. *Harper's Weekly*, May 13, 1876.

33. Quoted in Presbrey, *The History and Development of Advertising*, 403.

34. *Outlook*, September 1901.

35. *Outlook*, May 30, 1903.

36. *Literary Digest*, June 8, 1907.

37. See, for example, *Frank Leslie's Illustrated Weekly*, January 18, 1890. The caption claimed that Williams Shaving Soap produced a lather which was "a marvel of richness, delicacy, and sweetness."

38. Presbrey, *The History and Development of Advertising*, 399–400. Although the prohibition against facial hair seemed to have been absolute in advertising directed primarily to women, those ads directed primarily to men, for example, the trademark for Mennen's Borated Talcum Powder, often featured men with handlebar mustaches. See *Literary Digest*, June 29, 1907.

39. *Ladies' Home Journal*, May 1919. The ad proved offensive to a large number of people; supposedly 200 subscriptions to the *Journal* were cancelled in one day, and the J. Walter Thompson Agency was urged to withdraw the ad. See *American Druggist*, October 1933.

40. *Harper's Bazar*, January 21, 1885.

41. *Harper's Bazar*, February 8, 1890.

42. *Harper's Bazar*, May 10, 1890.

43. *Harper's Bazar*, November 1896 and June 1900.

44. *Ladies' Home Journal*, May 1905.

45. See, for example, *Ladies' Home Journal*, February 1905.

46. See *Harper's Bazar*, January, February, March, and May 1915.

47. *Ladies' Home Journal*, June 1914 and February 1917.

48. *Ladies' Home Journal*, May 1914.

49. *Ladies' Home Journal*, March 1920.

50. Stuart Ewen, *Captains of Consciousness: Advertising and the Social Roots of the Consumer Culture* (New York, 1976), 47.

51. *Harpers' Weekly*, September 3, 1870.

52. Presbrey, *The History and Development of Advertising*, 378–379.

53. Ibid., 378.

54. *Overland Monthly*, December 1888.

55. Donald S. Tull, "A Re–examination of the Causes of the Decline in Sales of Sapolio," *Journal of Business* 28 (January, 1955), 132.

56. Ibid., 129–133.

57. U.S. Department of Commerce, Bureau of the Census, *Historical Statistics of the United States: Colonial Times to 1970*, Part I (Washington, D.C., 1975), 699. The amounts are expressed in current producers' prices, and implicit price indexes for major consumer groups.

58. Betty Friedan, *The Feminine Mystique* (New York, 1963).

CHAPTER 4

1. Quoted in Daniel Pope, *The Making of Modern Advertising* (New York, 1983), 240–241.

2. Ibid., 233–241. Pope's analysis of the changing "Messages of Persuasion" is excellent and I have relied heavily upon it.

3. U.S. Department of Commerce, Bureau of the Census, *Historical Statistics of the United States: Colonial Times to 1970*, Part II (Washington, D.C., 1975), 697–699.

4. Presbrey, *The History and Development of Advertising*, 405. My argument with Presbrey is not about classifying pianos, organs, and phonographs as luxury items; clearly they indeed are. Rather, the category should have included a much larger variety of goods. More importantly, Presbrey never suggests that these luxury items were advertised differently than other goods.

5. See, for example, *Harper's Weekly*, October 22, 1870. For scholarly treatments of the piano industry consult: Ernest Closson's very brief *History of the Piano* (New York City: 1974 [a Delano Ames translation of the 1947 edition]); Van Allen Bradley, *Music for Millions: The Kimbal Piano and Organ Story* (Chicago, 1957); Theodore E. Steinway, *People and Pianos* (New York, 1953); Alfred Dodge, *Development of the Piano Industry Since the Centennial Exhibition at Philadelphia, 1876* (Covina, California, 1980 [a reprint of the 1913 edition]); and especially Craig H. Roell, *The Piano in America, 1890–1940* (Chapel Hill, N.C., 1989).

6. See for example *Peterson's Ladies' National Magazine*, November 1880.

7. *Harper's Weekly*, October 22, 1870; and October 12, 1872.

8. *Peterson's Ladies' National Magazine*, December 1880.

9. Ibid.

10. *Godey's Ladies Book*, January 1889.

11. *Overland Monthly*, 55:1909.

12. William Steinway, "American Musical Instruments," in Chauncey M. Depew, ed., *One Hundred Years of American Commerce, 1795–1895*, II (New York, 1895), 512–513. Steinway's "careful and conservative estimate" was that some 200 firms were engaged in making pianofortes, with an estimated capital of over $40 million and employing about 40,000 "skilled artisans." Lesser numbers were engaged in making reed-organs, and recently American firms had started producing harps, violins, guitars, flutes, brass wind-instruments, and indeed "all classes and kinds of musical instruments." While carefully distinguishing between increased economy of scale involved in large-scale production and "mass-production," David

A. Hounshell, *From the American System to Mass Production, 1800–1932: The Development of Manufacturing Technology in the United States* (Baltimore, 1984), 67–123 and 189–215, makes a very convincing case for the significant economies of scale developed in both bicycle and sewing machine production.

13. Edward Howard, "American Watches and Clocks," in Chauncey M. Depew, ed., *One Hundred Years of American Commerce, 1795–1895*, II (New York, 1895), 541. Hounshell convincingly demonstrates that the parts produced at the time Howard wrote were not perfectly interchangeable; nevertheless the watch and clock industry was a decreasing cost industry and more important an early advocate of aggressive marketing. Hounshell, *From the American System to Mass Production*, 60.

14. Howard, "American Watches and Clocks," 543.

15. Hounshell, *From the American System to Mass Production*, 60; and [Patrick] Glen Porter and Harold C. Livesay, "Oligopoly in Small Manufacturing Industries," *Explorations in Economic History*, 7 (Spring, 1970), 371–375, pointed out that oligopoly proved common in small industries that involved "skilled craftsmanship in production" and concluded that "the cluster of industries producing time pieces and related goods, including watches, clocks, parts for watches and clocks, and watch cases were among the most consistent oligopolistic businesses in the latter half of the last century." The same observation could have been made about musical instrument businesses.

16. *Harper's Weekly*, January 29, 1870.

17. Presbrey, *The History and Development of Advertising*, 405.

18. *Overland Monthly*, 69:1915.

19. *Harper's Weekly*, April 19, 1884; *Peterson's Ladies' National Magazine*, December 1882, and April 1881.

20. *Harper's Weekly*, July 8, 1882, and May 8, 1886.

21. See, for example, *Frank Leslie's Illustrated Weekly*, February 1895; see also the *Harper's Weekly* for December 1888.

22. Hounshell, *From the American System to Mass Production*, 189. Hounshell's description of the development of the bicycle industry, the innovations in production, and the advantages of large-scale production is excellent.

23. Presbrey, *The History and Development of Advertising*, 410–411. Emphasis added.

24. Albert A. Pope, "The Bicycle Industry," in Chauncey M. Depew, ed., *One Hundred Years of American Commerce, 1795–1895*, II (New York, 1895), 550.

25. Pope, "The Bicycle Industry," 551.

26. Hounshell, *From the American System to Mass Production*, 197–199.

27. Pope, "The Bicycle Industry," 551.

28. U.S. Department of Commerce, Bureau of the Census, *Thirteenth Census of the United States: Taken in the Year 1910* (Washington, D.C., 1913), 505.

29. Hounshell, *From the American System to Mass Production*, 193.

30. Quoted in Ibid., 214.

31. *Overland Monthly*, 12:1888.

32. *Harper's Weekly*, May 4, 1889.

33. Presbrey, *The History and Development of Advertising*, 401–402.

34. James R. McGovern, "The American Woman's Pre–World War I Freedom in Manners and Morals," *Journal of American History*, 55 (September 1968), 320.

35. Ibid.

36. See, in particular, the Gold Dust Washing Powder ads in *Ladies' Home Journal*, in any issue, 1910.

37. *Ladies' Home Journal*, December 1888.

38. *Ladies' Home Journal*, April 1914.

39. Quoted in McGovern, "The American Woman's Pre–World War I Freedom in Manners and Morals," 321.

40. Ibid., 321.

41. Ibid., 320.

42. Ruth S. Cowan, "The 'Industrial Revolution' in the Home: Household Technology and Social Change in the 20th Century," *Technology and Culture*, 17 (January 1976), 14–15. Cowan points out that prior to World War I, illustrations of women doing household work were most often servants, and by the end of the 1920s the jobs were being done by the housewives. In addition, the number of persons employed as household servants declined from 1.85 million in 1910 to 1.41 million in 1920, while the number of households increased over 4 million. Electrical appliances for household use depended, of course, on the electrification of homes. As late as 1917, less than one–quarter of the dwellings in the United States had electricity; only three years later, this had doubled, and by the end of the decade of the 1920s, over four–fifths of the rural non-farm and urban dwellings had electricity.

43. See also Ruth S. Cowan's excellent study, *More Work for Mother: The Ironies of Household Technology from the Open Hearth to the Microwave* (New York, 1983).

44. Ibid., 94.

45. *Harper's Bazar*, June 27, 1885.

46. *Harper's Bazar*, January 31, 1885.

47. *Harper's Bazar*, May 1905.

48. *Harper's Bazar*, January 1900.

49. *Harper's Bazar*, April 1905.

50. *Harper's Bazar*, January 1920.

51. *Literary Digest*, April 2, 1910.

52. *Literary Digest*, April 2, 1910. In truth, the White Frost icebox was singularly unattractive and soon disappeared.

53. *Literary Digest*, May 1, 1909.

54. *Literary Digest*, April 24, 1909.

55. *Literary Digest*, April 3, 1915.

56. *Literary Digest*, July 24, 1920.

57. *Literary Digest*, June 26, 1920.

58. *Harper's Bazar*, January, April, August, October, and December, 1920.

59. *Harper's Bazar*, January 27, 1888; July 12, 1890; and April 1905.

60. *Harper's Bazar*, April 1910 and *Bazaar*, May 1915.

61. St. Louis *Post–Dispatch*, March 14, November 22, and November 2, 1905.

62. St. Louis *Post–Dispatch*, June 14, 1905.

63. *Literary Digest*, June 11, 1910; and April 6, 1910.

64. Cowan, "The 'Industrial Revolution' in the Home," 17:16. Cowan cites A. Michael McMahon's paper, "An American Courtship: Psychology and Advertising Theory in the Progressive Era," *American Studies*, 13 (Fall, 1972), 5–18, and notes

his suggestion that the guilt element in advertising may have resulted from new techniques developed by the advertising industry, rather than from an attitudinal change on the part of the audience.

65. Cowan, "The 'Industrial Revolution' in the Home," 17:16.

66. *Ladies' Home Journal*, March 1900.

67. *Ladies' Home Journal*, March 1910.

68. *Ladies' Home Journal*, March 1920.

69. *Ladies' Home Journal*, July 10, 1910.

70. Stuart Ewen, *Captains of Consciousness: Advertising and the Social Roots of the Consumer Culture* (New York, 1976), 164.

CHAPTER 5

1. Harold Barger, *Distribution's Place in the American Economy since 1869*, National Bureau of Economic Research No. 58 (New York, 1955), 6. Because estimates of output and distribution, as well as value-added data, are best calculated from various census bureau studies and because the basis of comparison varied greatly over time and between the various data sets, the compilation and calculation of long-term data sets is both highly technical and can be extremely time consuming. Fortunately, much of this task has been accomplished already. Like any historian approaching the problem, I have relied extensively on the excellent publications of the National Bureau of Economic Research.

2. Ibid., x–xi and 44. Emphasis added.

3. Ibid., 9–31.

4. Warner's Corsets advertised extensively in popular magazines throughout the latter part of the nineteenth and early twentieth century. See, for example, *Outlook*, November 2, 1901.

5. Frank Presbrey, *The History and Development of Advertising* (New York, 1929), 361–362.

6. Daniel Pope, *The Making of Modern Advertising* (New York, 1983), 46.

7. Ibid., 47.

8. Ibid., 48.

9. Ruth S. Cowan, *More Work for Mother: The Ironies of Household Technology from the Open Hearth to the Microwave* (New York, 1983), 74.

10. Sidney A. Sherman, "Advertising in the United States," *Journal of the American Statistical Association*, 7 (December, 1900), 19 and Insert. Care must be exercised in accepting all ads classified as clothing; on occasion, cloth, hooks and eyes, and other sewing materials were classified as clothing.

11. Frank Presbrey, *The History and Development of Advertising* (New York, 1929), 361–363.

12. Paul H. Nystrom, *Economics of Fashion* (New York, 1928), 132–139. For informative studies on fashion and clothing manufacture consult: Agnes B. Young, *Recurring Cycles of Fashion, 1760–1937* (New York, 1937); Joel Seidmen, *The Needle Trades* (New York, 1942); Jessica Daves, *Ready–made Miracle: The Story of Fashion for the Millions* (New York, 1967); Claudia B. Kidwell and Margaret C. Christman, *Suiting Everyone: The Democratization of Clothing in America* (Washington, D.C., 1974); Marilyn J. Horn, *The Second Skin: An Interdisciplinary Study of Clothing*, Second Edition (Boston, 1975); Sandra Ley, *Fashion for Every-*

one: The Story of Ready to Wear, 1870's–1970's (New York, 1975); Margaret Walsh, "The Democratization of Fashion: The Emergence of the Dress Pattern Industry," *Journal of American History* 66 (September 1979):299–313; Stuart Ewen and Elizabeth Ewen, *Channels of Desire: Mass Images and the Shaping of American Consciousness* (New York, 1982); and Roland Barthes, trans. by Matthew Ward, *The Fashion System* (New York, 1983).

13. *Saturday Evening Post*, October 12, 1912. Emphasis added.

14. *Saturday Evening Post*, October 24, 1914.

15. St. Louis *Post–Dispatch*, March 6, 1880.

16. St. Louis *Post–Dispatch*, November 1920.

17. *Ladies' Home Journal*, December 1888.

18. *Ladies' Home Journal*, April 1896.

19. *Harper's Bazar*, February and March 1905. Emphasis added.

20. *Ladies' Home Journal*, March 1909.

21. *Ladies' Home Journal*, October 1905. Emphasis added.

22. *Ladies' Home Journal*, March 1910.

23. *Harper's Bazar*, January 1915.

24. *Harper's Bazar*, March 1920.

25. *Ladies' Home Journal*, September 1917.

26. *Ladies' Home Journal*, November 26, 1900.

27. Nystrom, *Economics of Fashion*, 13. Nystrom cites a large number of unsuccessful attempts by advertisers to create or prolong styles.

28. Cowan, *More Work for Mother*, 75.

29. *Ladies' Home Journal*, March 1917.

30. *Ladies' Home Journal*, March 1920.

31. Presbrey, *The History and Development of Advertising*, 393.

32. Ibid., 392; and *Literary Digest*, October 19, 1907.

33. Presbrey, *The History and Development of Advertising*, 408.

34. An 1894 advertisement reprinted in Ralph M. Hower, *The History of an Advertising Agency: N. W. Ayer & Son at Work, 1869–1949* (Cambridge, Massachusetts, 1949), 299.

35. *Literary Digest*, October 4, 1913.

36. *Ladies' Home Journal*, May 1908.

37. *Literary Digest*, June 5, 1915.

38. *Literary Digest*, May 27, 1905.

39. *Ladies' Home Journal*, October 1917. Emphasis added.

40. *Literary Digest*, January 14, 1911.

41. *Literary Digest*, April 9, 1910.

42. *Literary Digest*, April 16, 1910.

43. *Literary Digest*, October 5, 1907.

44. *Literary Digest*, April 2, 1910.

45. *Literary Digest*, February 4, 1911, and April 1, 1905.

46. *Literary Digest*, January 7 and 14, 1911.

47. *Literary Digest*, April 2, 1910.

48. Presbrey, *The History and Development of Advertising*, 422.

49. *Literary Digest*, April 2, 1910.

50. *Ladies' Home Journal*, March 1920.

51. *Literary Digest*, May 1, 1915, and June 12, 1915.

52. *Ladies' Home Journal*, March 1909.

53. *Ladies' Home Journal*, March 1910.

54. *Saturday Evening Post*, July 1 and July 15, 1916.

55. *Ladies' Home Journal*, July 1917.

56. For information regarding the soft drink industry see: E. J. Kahn, *The Big Drink* (New York, 1960); John J. Riley, *A History of the American Soft Drink Industry* (New York, 1972); and Pat Watters, *Coca–Cola: An Illustrated Biography* (Garden City, New York, 1978).

57. See, for example, *Harper's Weekly*, April 19, 1884; *The Independent*, September 18, October 2, and October 16, 1890; and *McClure's*, March 1900.

58. *McClure's*, May 1909.

59. *McClure's*, October 1898.

60. *McClure's*, June 1903.

61. Frank Presbrey, *The History and Development of Advertising* (New York, 1929), 420.

62. James W. Tufts, "Soda–Fountains," in Chauncey M. Depew, ed., *One Hundred Years of American Commerce, 1795–1895*, II (New York, 1895), 471–474.

63. Ibid., 472.

64. Ibid., 473.

65. Presbrey, *The History and Development of Advertising*, 421.

66. *Frank Leslie's Illustrated Weekly*, June 6, 1895.

67. *Harper's Weekly*, June 26, 1909.

68. Presbrey, *The History and Development of Advertising*, 421.

69. Ibid., 421.

70. *Saturday Evening Post*, March 15, 1915.

71. See, for example, *Saturday Evening Post*, May 20, 1916, and February 10, 1917.

72. James E. Pepper, "American Distilleries," in Chauncey M. Depew, ed., *One Hundred Years of American Commerce, 1795–1895*, II (New York, 1895), 411.

73. Ibid., 412.

74. *Harper's Weekly*, August 14, 1897. Emphasis added.

75. *Harper's Weekly*, August 7, 1897.

76. *Harper's Weekly*, January 24, 1903.

77. *Harper's Weekly*, April 20, 1901.

78. *Harper's Weekly*, October 28, 1905.

79. *Harper's Weekly*, March 4, 1905.

80. *Harper's Weekly*, March 6, 1909. It is a strange paradox that drinking alcoholic beverages would become much more closely associated with social status after prohibition than before.

81. Fred Pabst, "The Brewing Industry," in Chauncey M. Depew, ed., *One Hundred Years of American Commerce, 1795–1895*, II (New York, 1895) 417. Certainly most modern Americans would agree that beer is, indeed, the national beverage of the United States and is probably the most heavily advertised product in the market. Modern beer advertising illustrates the power of advertising to equate consumption of a product with social acceptability and social status and thereby increase total demand for the product. Perhaps for more than any product other than cigarettes, every beer ad is designed not only to win brand recognition and loyalty, but to also increase the total demand.

82. *Harper's Weekly*, February 9, 1895.

83. *Harper's Weekly*, June 26, 1897.

84. Ibid.

85. *Harper's Weekly*, July 4, 1903.

86. *Harper's Weekly*, March 4, 1905.

87. *Harper's Weekly*, February 22, 1909.

88. Thomas C. Cochran, *The Pabst Brewing Company* (New York, 1948), 199.

89. Pope, *The Making of Modern Advertising*, 82. Modern beer advertising campaigns have succeeded in changing taverns into local social clubs. Beer drinkers are never depicted in solitary but always in a social situation, and the consumption of beer has become a social exercise.

CHAPTER 6

1. Neil H. Borden, *The Economic Effects of Advertising* (Chicago, 1942), 214–219. Borden included two chapters on the effect of advertising on tobacco products because of the heavy advertising over a long period, the large amount of data available, and because the "economic effects of this advertising have been the subject of sharp controversy." In terms of consumption of tobacco, it was not until 1919 that more tobacco was consumed in cigarette smoking than in chewing tobacco. The next year, 1920, cigarettes passed cigars in pounds of tobacco consumed per capita, and six years later surpassed smoking (pipe and roll–your–own cigarettes) tobacco. Consumption of snuff remained relatively constant at about .3 pounds per person for the first three decades of the twentieth century.

2. Ibid., 227.

3. Ibid., 223.

4. Patrick G. Porter, "Origins of the American Tobacco Company," *Business History Review*, 43 (Spring, 1969), 59–76. Porter points out that the American Tobacco Company controlled about 80 per cent of the domestic production of these tobacco items.

5. Ibid., 69–70.

6. Ibid., 70–71. For biographical information on James Duke consult: John W. Jenkins, *James B. Duke, Master Builder* (New York, 1927) and John K. Winkler, *Tobacco Tycoon, The Story of James Buchanan Duke* (New York, 1942); for the tobacco and cigarette industry see: Reavis Cox, *Competition in the American Tobacco Industry* (New York, 1933); J. C. Robert, *The Story of Tobacco in America* (New York, 1949); Nannie M. Tilley, *The Bright–Tobacco Industry* (Chapel Hill, 1948); Nannie M. Tilley, *The R. J. Reynolds Tobacco Company* (Chapel Hill, 1985); and Patrick Reynolds and Tom Shachtman, *The Gilded Leaf: Triumph, Tragedy, and Tobacco* (Boston, 1989).

7. Porter, "Origins of the American Tobacco Company," 74–76.

8. Ibid., 72–76; and Sidney A. Sherman, "Advertising in the United States," *Journal of the American Statistical Association* (December, 1900), 7:134.

9. Pope, *The Making of Modern Advertising*, 52–53.

10. Wood, *The Story of Advertising*, 374. A discreetly placed fence rail, with the words "Smoking Tobacco," removed most of the physical evidence of the bull featured in the famous "Bull" Durham "bullishness" trademark.

11. *Harper's Weekly*, January 6, 1900; July 6, 1901; and January 10, 1903. *Harper's Weekly*, perhaps because it catered to an upper and middle–class readership, carried more tobacco advertisements than any other popular magazine up to World War I.

12. *Harper's Weekly*, May 20, 1899.

13. *Saturday Evening Post*, March 23, 1912.

14. *Saturday Evening Post*, May 6, 1916.

15. *Saturday Evening Post*, May 18, 1918.

16. Unlike cigarettes, which machine rolling made a decreasing cost industry, cigars remained hand-rolled. Only in recent years would inexpensive machine-rolled cigars made from reconstituted tobacco be successfully marketed in the United States. However, there is still great prejudice against machine-rolled cigars, and almost all high-quality cigars are hand-rolled.

17. Pope, *The Making of Modern Advertising*, 53.

18. *Harper's Weekly*, May 19, 1900.

19. Ibid.

20. *Harper's Weekly*, September 21, 1901.

21. *Harper's Weekly*, January 7, 1905.

22. Ibid., February 18, 1905.

23. Ibid., March 20, 1909.

24. *Saturday Evening Post*, August 15, 1914.

25. Ibid., March 13, 1915.

26. *Saturday Evening Post*, May 4, 1918.

27. Ibid., May 4, 1918.

28. Borden, *The Economic Effects of Advertising*, 208–212.

29. Ibid., 216. In 1970 the production of cigarettes in the United States stood at only slightly less than 2,500 cigarettes for every man, woman, and child in the country.

30. Ibid., 216–219.

31. Wood, *The Story of Advertising*, 171.

32. Borden, *The Economic Effects of Advertising*, 223–225. In explaining the very low consumption of cigarettes by women, less than 5 per cent of the total market in 1925, Borden quoted George Washington Hill, president of the American Tobacco Company, in court testimony in 1938 as saying, "We never dared to talk about women smoking cigarettes, until what is known in the trade as the Lucky Strike campaign [Lucky Strike, to a cry of outrage, launched the first cigarette advertising campaign directed to women and featuring women smokers in the ads in 1927]. We had a series of testimonials of opera singers, and among others was Madame Schumann–Heink. She was the first woman that ever publicly came out and testified that she smoked cigarettes, and she had a rather unpleasant experience. She was in the West and she had some dates with women's colleges to sing out there, and as soon as she published this she began to get cancellations on some of those dates, and she quit. But that was the start of the breaking down of the prejudice, and from that time on, of course, all cigarette manufacturers have developed all the romance they could use, using women's testimonials and women in romantic situations."

33. Quoted in Wood, *The Story of Advertising*, 372.

34. Ibid.

35. Borden, *The Economic Effects of Advertising*, 223. The author well remembers playing summer town-team baseball as a high school student in the late 1940s when the use of chewing tobacco or snuff by practically the entire team was tolerated as acceptable adolescent behavior, but the use of cigarettes was severely disciplined.

36. Ralph M. Hower, *The History of an Advertising Agency: N. W. Ayer & Son at Work, 1869–1949* (Cambridge, Massachusetts, 1949), 588–591.

37. Henry N. McKinney, partner, N. W. Ayer & Son, to Ohio Editorial Association, January 7, 1904, quoted in Ibid., 580–581.

38. Hower, *History of an Advertising Agency*, 581. Hower's remarks take on an even greater significance when one realizes that cigarette companies, like many low-cost convenience-item producers, tended to emphasize daily newspapers over national magazines in their advertising budgets. See Presbrey, *The History and Development of Advertising*, 594–595.

39. Wood, *The Story of Advertising*, 373; and *How It Was in Advertising: 1776–1976*, compiled by the editors of *Advertising Age* (Chicago, 1976), 35.

40. *The Independent*, September 13, 1919.

41. Wood, *The Story of Advertising*, 373.

42. Ibid., 374.

43. *Saturday Evening Post*, February 17, 1912.

44. Wood, *The Story of Advertising*, 375.

45. *Harper's Weekly*, September 18, 1915.

46. *Harper's Weekly*, September 24, 1915.

47. Borden, *The Economic Effects of Advertising*, 215. Actually, the year prior to the American Tobacco campaign, a Chesterfield poster featured a man and a woman seated on a moonlit river bank, the man lighting a cigarette and the woman asking him to "blow some my way."

48. Ibid., 215; and Wood, *The Story of Advertising*, 375.

49. Stephen Fox, *The Mirror Makers: A History of American Advertising and Its Creators* (New York, 1984), 114.

50. Borden, *The Economic Effects of Advertising*, 222.

CHAPTER 7

1. Frank Presbrey, *The History and Development of Advertising* (Garden City, New York, 1929), 556.

2. Roland Marchand, *Advertising and the American Dream: Making Way for Modernity, 1920–1940* (Berkeley, 1985), 156–165. Marchand's analysis of advertising and the consumption ethic in American society deserves reading by anyone interested in the influence of advertising. While we differ in emphasis and concern, I am convinced that many of the trends which Marchand analyzes were already evident before the decade of the 1920s started.

3. David A. Hounshell, *From the American System to Mass Production, 1800–1932: The Development of Manufacturing Technology in the United States* (Baltimore, 1984), 217–261.

4. Presbrey, *The History and Development of Advertising*, 557.

5. James P. Wood, *The Story of Advertising* (New York, 1958), 297–298.

6. Ibid., 299–300.

7. Ibid., 311–312.

8. Presbrey, *The History and Development of Advertising*, 558. For studies on the automobile industry consult: Merrill Denison, *The Power to Go* (Garden City, New York, 1956); Alfred D. Chandler, Jr., comp. and ed., *Giant Enterprise: Ford, General Motors, and the Automobile Industry* (New York, 1964); Ralph Cecil Epstein, *The Automobile Industry* (New York, 1928 [reprint 1972]); John B. Rae, *The Road and the Car in American Life* (Cambridge, Mass., 1971); James J. Flink, *The Car Culture* (Cambridge, Mass., 1975); James J. Flink, *America Adopts the Automobile, 1895–1910* (Cambridge, Mass., 1970); and James J. Flink, *The Automobile Age* (Cambridge, Mass., 1988).

9. *Harper's Weekly*, February 17, 1900.

10. Philip Van Doren Stern, *A Pictorial History of the Automobile as Seen in Motor Magazine, 1903–1953* (New York, 1953), 148.

11. Quoted in Wood, *The Story of Advertising*, 304–305.

12. Presbrey, *The History and Development of Advertising*, 558.

13. Wood, *The Story of Advertising*, 304–305; and Presbrey, *The History and Development of Advertising*, 558–559.

14. *Overland Monthly* 40:ix–xix (1902).

15. U.S. Department of Commerce, Bureau of the Census, *Historical Statistics of the United States: Colonial Times to 1970*, II (Washington, D.C., 1975), 716.

16. Presbrey, *The History and Development of Advertising*, 559. For studies of the Ford Motor Company see: Sidney Fine, *The Automobile Under the Blue Eagle* (Ann Arbor, 1963); Robert Lacey, *Ford, the Man and the Machine* (Boston, 1986); and Stephen Meyer III, *The Five Dollar Day: Labor Management and Social Control* (Albany, 1981).

17. Wood, *The Story of Advertising*, 304.

18. *Saturday Evening Post*, 1903 advertisement of the Model A Ford reproduced in Wood, *The Story of Advertising*, 313.

19. *Harper's Weekly*, March 4, 1905. For further information on Henry Ford consult: Allen Nevins and Frank E. Hill's seminal work *Ford*, 3 vols. (New York, 1954). See also: John B. Rae, ed., *Henry Ford* (Englewood Cliffs, New Jersey, 1969); David Lanier Lewis, *The Public Image of Henry Ford* (Cambridge, Mass., 1970); and James Brough, *The Ford Dynasty* (Garden City, New York, 1977).

20. Claude C. Hopkins, *My Life in Advertising: Scientific Advertising* (Chicago, 1966), 112–125.

21. *Harper's Weekly*, March 4, 1905.

22. *Harper's Weekly*, March 25, 1905.

23. *Harper's Weekly*, January 2, 1909.

24. Stern, *Pictorial History*, 138.

25. Ibid., 150.

26. Ibid., 126.

27. *Harper's Weekly*, January 2, 1909.

28. Ibid.

29. *Ladies' Home Journal*, March 1909.

30. *Saturday Evening Post*, March 14, 1914.

31. *Saturday Evening Post*, July 18, 1914.

32. *Saturday Evening Post*, May 6, 1916.

33. *Saturday Evening Post*, March 10, 1917.

34. *Ladies' Home Journal*, July 1917.

35. *Ladies' Home Journal*, November 1917.

36. *Ladies' Home Journal*, September 1920.

37. *Literary Digest*, September 11, 1912.

38. Wood, *The Story of Advertising*, 307.

39. Presbrey, *The History and Development of Advertising*, 560.

40. Ibid., 559–560.

41. *Literary Digest*, September 14, 1912.

42. *Literary Digest*, July 10, 1915.

43. *Literary Digest*, July 3, 1915.

44. *Literary Digest*, June 7, 1913.

45. *Literary Digest*, August 26, 1916.

46. *Literary Digest*, September 23, 1916.

47. Hopkins, *My Life in Advertising*, 122.

48. *National Geographic Magazine*, June 1913.

49. *Literary Digest*, September 14, 1912.

50. *Literary Digest*, January 31, 1914.

51. Ibid.

52. *Saturday Evening Post*, January 1912.

53. Presbrey, *The History and Development of Advertising*, 560.

54. Ibid., 561.

55. In hundreds of advertisements in popular magazines from 1865 to 1920 which I examined, no Black person was ever depicted as the consumer. When Blacks appeared it was either as a servant or as a personality such as the Cream Of Wheat cook or Aunt Jemima. Moreover, I failed to find any national-brand advertisements directed to Black consumers.

56. *Harper's Weekly*, March 25, 1905.

57. *Harper's Weekly*, January 2, 1909.

58. *Saturday Evening Post*, March 2, 1912.

59. *Saturday Evening Post*, January 6, 1912.

60. *Overland Monthly*, 60: 1912.

61. *Saturday Evening Post*, January 27, 1912.

62. *Literary Digest*, November 2, 1912.

63. *National Geographic*, January and February, 1913.

64. *National Geographic*, November 1915.

65. *Saturday Evening Post*, January 2, 1915; Wood, *The Story of Advertising*, 309. Wood claimed that McManus wrote the ad on the back of an envelope while riding on a train one day in 1915; however fanciful that might sound it can hardly be true since the ad appeared in the January 2, 1915, issue.

66. Ibid.

67. *Literary Digest*, December 18, 1918; and *Saturday Evening Post*, January 22, 1916.

68. Quoted in John B. Rae, ed., *Henry Ford* (Englewood Cliffs, New Jersey, 1969), 18–19.

69. *Harper's Weekly*, January 1, 1910, quoted in Allan Nevins and Frank E. Hill, *Ford: The Times, the Man, the Company* (New York, 1954), 449.

70. Stuart Ewen, *All Consuming Images: The Politics Style in Contemporary Culture* (New York, 1988), 58.

71. Ibid., 58–59.

72. *Harper's Weekly*, March 4, 1905; and U.S. Department of Commerce, Bureau of the Census, *Historical Statistics of the United States: Colonial Times to 1970*, Part II (Washington, D.C., 1975) 716.

73. Ralph Stern, *The Treasury of the Automobile* (New York, 1961), 167.

74. David Hounshell, *From the American System to Mass Production*, 219.

75. Ibid., 8–10. Hounshell's discussion of the Ford innovations in the technology of production is complete in detail and presented in a clear and lucid fashion. Hounshell's excellent study deserves the attention of business historians as well as students of the history of technology. In particular, the treatment of the implication of mass production seems to me insightful. In addition, Nevins and Hill's *Ford*, composed of *Ford: The Times, the Man, the Company* (New York, 1954); *Ford: Expansion and Challenge, 1915–1933* (New York, 1957); and *Ford: Decline and Rebirth, 1933–1962* (New York, 1962), provide an excellent history of both the man and the company.

76. Ernest S. Turner, *The Shocking History of Advertising* (New York, 1953), 181.

77. Wood, *The Story of Advertising*, 316.

78. Quoted in Ibid., 318.

79. Quoted in Ibid., 316–317.

80. Ibid., 317.

81. Hounshell, *From the American System to Mass Production*, 258–259.

82. Wood, *The Story of Advertising*, 318.

83. *Saturday Evening Post*, March 23, 1912.

84. St. Louis *Post–Dispatch*, February 2, 1913.

85. *Harper's Weekly*, September 18, 1915.

86. Quoted in Hounshell, *From the American System to Mass Production*, 261.

87. Presbrey, *The History and Development of Advertising*, 565–575.

88. Daniel Pope, *The Making of Modern Advertising* (New York, 1983), 229. Most advertising agencies engaged in institutional advertising, and N. W. Ayer & Son may well have been a leader in this regard. For an unabashed example, see Ayer's ad in the *Saturday Evening Post*, October 30, 1920.

89. Bruce Barton, *The Man Nobody Knows: A Discovery of the Real Jesus* (Indianapolis, 1924).

90. Daniel J. Boorstin, "Welcome to the Consumption Community," *Fortune*, September 1, 1967. Copyright 1967 by Daniel J. Boorstin, reprinted in *The Decline of Radicalism* (Random House, 1969).

91. Ibid., 138.

BIBLIOGRAPHY

American Druggist. October 1933.

American Farmer. January 1868–June 1881.

Andreano, Ralph, ed. *The Economic Impact of the Civil War*. Cambridge, Massachusetts, 1962.

Atack, Jeremy. "Firm Size and Industrial Structure in the United States During the Nineteenth Century." *Journal of Economic History* 46:463–475 (June, 1986).

Atherton, Lewis E. *Main Street on the Middle Border*. Bloomington, Indiana, 1954.

———. *The Pioneer Merchant in Mid-America*. Columbia, Missouri, 1939.

———. *The Southern Country Store, 1800–1860*. Baton Rouge, Louisiana, 1949.

Barger, Harold. *Distribution's Place in the American Economy Since 1869*. National Bureau of Economic Research No. 58. New York, 1955.

Barthes, Roland, trans. by Matthew Ward. *The Fashion System*. New York, 1983.

Barton, Bruce. *The Man Nobody Knows: A Discovery of the Real Jesus*. Indianapolis, 1924.

Benson, Susan P. *Counter Cultures: Saleswomen, Managers, and Customers in American Department Stores, 1890–1940*. Urbana, Illinois, 1986.

Billington, Ray A. *Westwood Expansion: A History of the American Frontier*. Fourth Edition. New York, 1974.

Boorstin, Daniel J. "Welcome to the Consumption Community." *Fortune*. September 1, 1967.

Borden, Neil H. *The Economic Effects of Advertising*. Chicago, 1942.

———. "The Role of Advertising in the Various Stages of Corporate and Economic Growth." In *Marketing and Economic Development*. American Marketing Association. Chicago, 1965.

Boyd, Ernest L. "A Critical Study of the Doctrines of Persuasion in Speech and Advertising." Ph.D. dissertation, Northwestern University, 1954.

Bradley, Van Allen. *Music for Millions: The Kimbal Piano and Organ Story*. Chicago, 1957.

Brandon, Ruth. *A Capitalist Romance: Singer and the Sewing Machine*. New York, 1977.

Brough, James. *The Ford Dynasty*. Garden City, New York, 1977.

Bryce, James. *The American Commonwealth*. Volumes I and II. New York, 1888.

Bushman, Richard L. and Bushman, Claudia L. "The Early History of Cleanliness in America." *Journal of American History*. 74:1213–1238 (March, 1988).

Chandler, Alfred D., Jr., comp. and ed. *Giant Enterprise: Ford, General Motors, and the Automobile Industry*. New York, 1964.

————. *The Visible Hand: The Managerial Revolution in American Business*. Cambridge, Massachusetts, 1977.

Christiansen, Richard. "The Commercial View of a Serene America." St. Louis *Post-Dispatch*, July 21, 1972.

Clark, Thomas D. *Petticoats and Plows: The Southern Country Store*. Indianapolis, Indiana, 1944.

Closson, Ernest. *History of the Piano*. New York, 1974 [a Delano Ames translation of the 1947 edition.]

Cochran, Thomas C. *The Pabst Brewing Company*. New York, 1948.

Cowan, Ruth S. "The 'Industrial Revolution' in the Home: Household Technology and Social Change in the 20th Century." *Technology and Culture*, 17:1–23 (January, 1976).

————. *More Work for Mother: The Ironies of Household Technology from the Open Hearth to the Microwave*. New York, 1983.

Cox, Reavis. *Competition in the American Tobacco Industry*. New York, 1933.

Craig, Robert L. "The Changing Communicative Structure of Advertisements, 1850–1930." Ph.D. dissertation, Iowa University, 1985.

Curti, Merle. "The Changing Concept of 'Human Nature' in the Literature of American Advertising." *Business History Review*, 4:335–357 (Winter 1967).

Daves, Jessica. *Ready-made Miracle: The Story of Fashion for the Millions*. New York, 1967.

Davis, Lance E., et al. *American Economic Growth: An Economist's History of the United States*. New York, 1972.

Denison, Merrill. *The Power to Go*. Garden City, New York, 1956.

Depew, Chauncey M., ed. *One Hundred Years of American Commerce, 1795–1895*. Volumes I and II. New York, 1895.

Dodge, Alfred. *Development of the Piano Industry since the Centennial Exhibition at Philadelphia, 1876*. Covina, California, 1980 [a reprint of the 1913 edition].

Dubos, Rene J. *Mirage of Health*. New York, 1959.

Easterlin, Richard A. "International Difference in Per Capita Income, Population and Total Income, 1840–1950." In *Trends in the American Economy in the Nineteenth Century*. Conference on Research in Income and Wealth. Princeton, New Jersey, 1960.

Emmett, Boris and Jeuck, John E. *Catalogues and Counters: A History of Sears, Roebuck and Company*. Chicago, 1950.

Epstein, Ralph Cecil. *The Automobile Industry*. New York, 1972 [reprint of 1928 edition].

Ewen, Stuart. *Captains of Consciousness: Advertising and the Social Roots of the Consumer Culture*. New York, 1976.

————. *All Consuming Images: The Politics of Style in Contemporary Culture.* New York, 1988.

Ewen, Stuart and Ewen, Elizabeth. *Channels of Desire: Mass Images and the Shaping of American Consciousness.* New York, 1982.

Fine, Sidney. *The Automobile Under the Blue Eagle.* Ann Arbor, 1963.

Flink, James J. *America Adopts the Automobile, 1895–1910.* Cambridge, Massachusetts, 1970.

————. *The Automobile Age.* Cambridge, Massachusetts, 1988.

————. *The Car Culture.* Cambridge, Massachusetts, 1975.

Frank Leslie's Illustrated Weekly. January 1890–June 1895.

Fox, Richard W. and Lears, T. J. Jackson, eds. *The Culture of Consumption: Critical Essays in American History, 1880–1980.* New York, 1983.

Fox, Stephen. *The Mirror Makers: A History of American Advertising and Its Creators.* New York, 1984.

Friedan, Betty. *The Feminine Mystique.* New York, 1963.

Galambos, Louis. "The Emerging Organizational Synthesis in Modern American History." *Business History Review* 44:279–290 (Autumn 1970).

Galbraith, John Kenneth. *The Affluent Society.* Boston, 1958.

Glassburg, David. "The Public Bath Movement in America." *American Studies* 20:5–20 (Fall 1970).

Godey's Ladies Book. 1865–1892.

Graves, Benjamin B. "An Inquiry into the Social, Economic, and Business Effects of Financial Advertising." Ph.D. dissertation, Louisiana State University, 1962.

Greer, Douglas F. "Advertising and Competition." Ph.D. dissertation, Cornell University, 1968.

Harper's Bazar (Bazaar). January 1885–December 1920.

Harper's Weekly. September 1866–December 1920.

Higgs, Robert. *The Transformation of the American Economy, 1865–1914: An Essay in Interpretation.* New York, 1971.

Hollitz, John E. "The Challenge of Abundance: Reactions to the Development of a Consumer Economy, 1890–1920." Ph.D. dissertation, University of Wisconsin-Madison, 1981.

Hopkins, Claude C. *My Life in Advertising: Scientific Advertising.* Chicago, 1966.

Horn, Marilyn J. *The Second Skin: An Interdisciplinary Study of Clothing.* Second Edition. Boston, 1975.

Horowitz, Daniel. *The Morality of Spending: Attitudes Toward the Consumer Society in America, 1875–1940.* Baltimore, 1985.

Hounshell, David. *From the American System to Mass Production, 1800–1932: The Development of Manufacturing Technology in the United States.* Baltimore, 1984.

Hower, Ralph M. *The History of an Advertising Agency: N. W. Ayer & Son at Work, 1869–1949.* Cambridge, Massachusetts, 1949.

The Independent. September 1890–September 1919.

Jack, Andrew B. "The Channels of Distribution for an Innovation: The Sewing Machine Industry in America, 1860–1865." *Explorations in Entrepreneurial History* 9:113–141 (February, 1957).

Jenkins, John W. *James B. Duke, Master Builder.* New York, 1927.

Jones, Edgar R. *Those Were the Good Old Days: A Happy Look at American Advertising, 1880–1930*. New York, 1939.

Kahn, E. J. *The Big Drink*. New York, 1960.

Kidwell, Claudia B. and Christman, Margaret C. *Suiting Everyone: The Democratization of Clothing in America*. Washington, D.C., 1974.

Koos, Herman E. *American Economic Development: The Progress of a Business Civilization*. Englewood Cliffs, New Jersey, 1974.

Kuznets, Simon. "Proportion of Capital Formation to National Products." *American Economic Review*, 42:507–526 (May 1952).

Kuznets, Simon and Rubin, Ernest. *Immigration and the Foreign Born*. New York: National Bureau of Economic Research, 1954.

Lacey, Robert. *Ford, the Man and the Machine*. Boston, 1986.

Ladies' Home Journal. December 1883–September 1920.

Lasker, A. D. *The Lasker Story as He Told It*. Chicago, 1953.

Leach, William R. "Transformation in a Culture of Consumption: Women and Department Stores, 1890–1925." *Journal of American History*, 71:319–342 (September, 1984).

Leavitt, Judith W. and Numbers, Ronald, eds. *Sickness and Health in America: Readings in the History of Medicine and Public Health*. Madison, Wisconsin, 1978.

Lebergott, Stanley. *Manpower in Economic Growth: The American Record Since 1800*. New York, 1946.

Lewis, David Lanier. *The Public Image of Henry Ford*. Cambridge, Massachusetts, 1970.

Ley, Sandra. *Fashion for Everyone: The Story of Ready to Wear, 1870's–1970's*. New York, 1975.

Lief, Alfred. *"It Floats," The Story of Procter and Gamble*. New York, 1958.

Literary Digest. April 1905–July 1920.

Marchand, Roland. *Advertising and the American Dream: Making Way for Modernity, 1920–1940*. Berkeley, 1985.

Mayer, Martin P. *Madison Avenue, U.S.A.* New York, 1958.

McClure's Magazine. October 1893–May 1910.

McGovern, James R. "The American Woman's Pre-World War I Freedom in Manners and Morals." *Journal of American History*, 55:315–333 (September, 1968).

McLuhan, Marshall. *The Mechanical Bride: Folklore of Industrial Capitalism*. Boston, 1951.

―――. *Understanding Media: The Extensions of Man*. New York, 1964.

McMahon, A. Michael. "An American Courtship: Psychology and Advertising Theory in the Progressive Era." *American Studies* 13:5–18 (Fall 1972).

Meyer, Stephen, III. *The Five Dollar Day: Labor Management and Social Control*. Albany, 1981.

Mott, Frank L. *History of American Magazines, 1865–1885*. Second Volume. Cambridge, Massachusetts, 1939.

Munsey's Magazine. September 1893–1910.

Murphy, George G. S. and Zellner, Arnold. "Sequential Growth, the Labor-Safety-Valve Doctrine, and the Development of American Unionism." *Journal of Economic History*, 19:402–419 (September, 1959).

National Geographic Magazine. January 1913–November 1915.

Nelson, Saul and Keim, Walter G. *Price Behavior and Business Policy.* Monograph No. 1. Temporary National Economic Committee, 76th Congress, 3rd session, 1939–40.

Nevins, Allen and Hill, Frank E. *Ford.* 3 vols. New York, 1954.

Norris, James D. "Advertising and the Transformation of American Society, 1865–1920." *Year Book of the American Philosophical Society, 1970* 197 (1971).

Nystrom, Paul H. *Economics of Fashion.* New York, 1928.

Outlook. August 1900–May 1910.

Overland Monthly. 1888–1920.

Owen, Charles. "Consumerism and Capitalism: The Politics of Producing Consumption." Ph.D. dissertation, University of Minnesota, 1976.

Paulin, C. O. *Atlas of the Historical Geography of the United States.* Washington: Carnegie Institution, 1932.

Pease, Otis. *The Responsibilities of American Advertising.* New Haven, 1958.

Peterson, Theodore. *Magazines in the Twentieth Century.* Urbana, Illinois, 1964.

Peterson's Ladies' National Magazine. January 1870–December 1882.

Pollay, Richard W., ed. *Information Sources in Advertising History.* Westport, Connecticut, 1979.

Pope, Daniel. *The Making of Modern Advertising.* New York, 1983.

Pope, James P. "His Master's Voice: James Rorty and the Critique of Advertising." *The Maryland Historian* 19:5-15 (Spring/Summer, 1988).

Porter, [Patrick] Glen and Livesay, Harold. *Merchants and Manufacturers: Studies in the Changing Structure of Nineteenth-Century Marketing.* Baltimore, 1971.

———. "Oligopoly in Small Manufacturing Industries." *Expolorations in Economic History* 7:371–379 (Spring 1970).

Porter, Patrick G. "Oligopolists in American Manufacturing and Their Products, 1909–1963." *Business History Review,* 43:282–298 (Autumn 1969).

———. "Origins of the American Tobacco Company." *Business History Review,* 43:59–76 (Spring 1969).

Presbrey, Frank. *The History and Development of Advertising.* Garden City, New York, 1929.

Rae, John B., ed. *Henry Ford.* Englewood Cliffs, New Jersey, 1969.

———. *The Road and the Car in American Life.* Cambridge, Massachusetts, 1971.

Reynolds, Patrick and Shachtman, Tom. *The Gilded Leaf: Triumph, Tragedy, and Tobacco.* Boston, 1989.

Riesman, David; Glazer, Nathen; and Denny, Reuel. *The Lonely Crowd.* New Haven, 1950.

Riley, John J. *A History of the American Soft Drink Industry.* New York, 1972.

Robert, J. C. *The Story of Tobacco in America.* New York, 1949.

Roell, Craig H. *The Piano in America, 1890–1940.* Chapel Hill, N.C., 1989.

St. Louis *Post-Dispatch.* March 1880–November 1920.

Saturday Evening Post. January 1898–December 1920.

Schisgall, Oscar. *Eyes on Tomorrow: The Evolution of Procter and Gamble.* Chicago, 1981.

Seidmen, Joel. *The Needle Trades.* New York, 1942.

Shapiro, Stephen R. "The Big Sell: Attitudes of Advertising Writers and the Trans-
    formation of American Society, 1865–1920." Ph.D. dissertation, University
    of Wisconsin-Madison, 1969.
Sherman, Sidney A. "Advertising in the United States." *Journal of the American
    Statistical Association*, 7:1–44 (December, 1900).
Shroeder, Fred E. H. "Feminine Hygiene, Fashion and the Emancipation of Wom-
    en." *American Studies* 17:101–109 (1976).
Soltow, Lee C. "Evidence on Income Inequality in the United States, 1866–1965."
    Journal of Economic History 19:279–286 (June, 1969).
Southern Planter. February 1855–April 1870.
Spurgeon, Anne M. "Marketing the Unmentionable: Wallace Meyer and the Intro-
    duction of Kotex." *The Maryland Historian* 19:17–30 (Spring/Summer,
    1988).
Steinway, Theodore E. *People and Pianos.* New York, 1953.
Stern, Philip Van Doren. *A Pictorial History of the Automobile as Seen in Motor
    Magazine, 1903–1953.* New York, 1953.
Tilley, Nannie M. *The Bright-Tobacco Industry.* Chapel Hill, N.C., 1948.
———. *The R. J. Reynolds Tobacco Company.* Chapel Hill, N.C., 1985.
Tocqueville, Alexis de. *Democracy in America.* Volumes I and II. London, 1835.
Tull, Donald S. "A Re-examination of the Causes of the Decline in Sales of Sapolio."
    Journal of Business, 28:128–137 (January, 1955).
Turner, Ernest S. *The Shocking History of Advertising.* New York, 1953.
U.S. Department of Commerce, Bureau of the Census. *Historical Statistics of the
    United States: Colonial Times to 1970.* Parts I and II. Washington, D.C.,
    1975.
———. *Thirteenth Census of the United States, Abstract.* Washington, D.C., 1923.
Vatter, Harold G. *The Drive to Industrial Maturity: The U.S. Economy, 1860–1914.*
    Westport, Connecticut, 1975.
Veblen, Thorstein. *Absentee Ownership and Business Enterprise in Recent Times.*
    New York, 1923.
———. *A Theory of the Leisure Class.* New York, 1934.
Walsh, Margaret. "The Democratization of Fashion: The Emergence of the Dress
    Pattern Industry." *Journal of American History* 66:299–313 (September,
    1979).
Watkins, Julian L. *The 100 Greatest Advertisements: Who Wrote Them and What
    They Did.* New York, 1959.
Watters, Pat. *Coca-Cola: An Illustrated Biography.* Garden City, New York, 1978.
Wilcox, Clair. *Competition and Monopoly in American Industry.* Monograph No.
    21. Temporary National Economic Committee, 76th Congress, 3rd session,
    1939–40.
Williams, Marilyn Thorton. "New York's Public Baths: A Case in Urban Progres-
    sive Reform." *Journal of Urban History* 7:49–81 (1980).
Williamson, Jeffrey. *American Growth and the Balance of Payments, 1820–1913:
    A Study of the Long Swing.* Chapel Hill, N.C., 1964.
Winkler, John K. *Tobacco Tycoon, The Story of James Buchanan Duke.* New
    York, 1942.
Wood, James P. *Magazines in the United States: Their Social and Economic Effect.*
    New York, 1949.

————. *The Story of Advertising*. New York, 1958.

Wright, Lawrence. *Clean and Decent: The Fascinating History of the Bathroom and the Water Closet*. New York, 1960.

Yancey, Thomas A. "Some Effects of Selling Effort and Product Quality in a Macroeconomic Dynamic Model." Ph. D. dissertation, University of Illinois, 1957.

Young, Agnes B. *Recurring Cycles of Fashion, 1760–1937*. New York, 1937.

Young, James H. *The Medical Messiahs: A Social History of Health in Twentieth Century America*. Princeton, New Jersey, 1961.

————. *The Toadstool Millionaires: A Social History of Patent Medicines in America Before Federal Regulation*. Princeton, New Jersey, 1962.

INDEX

About the Author

JAMES D. NORRIS is Professor of History and Dean of the College of Liberal Arts and Sciences at Northern Illinois University. His previous books include *Frontier Iron, AZn: A History of the American Zinc Company, Politics and Patronage in the Gilded Age* (With Arthur Shaffer), and *R.G. Dun & Co. 1841-1900: The Development of Credit Reporting in the Nineteenth Century*. Norris is a specialist in business and economic history and is currently working on a study comparing the development of businesses on the American frontier.

ISBN 0-313-26801-0

90000>

EAN

9 780313 268014

HARDCOVER BAR CODE